PROFILES OF THE MANNEQUIN

PROFILES OF THE MANNEQUIN

THE CULTURAL AND HISTORICAL IMPACT OF THE MANNEQUIN

Eric Feigenbaum

BLOOMSBURY VISUAL ARTS
LONDON • NEW YORK • OXFORD • NEW DELHI • SYDNEY

BLOOMSBURY VISUAL ARTS
Bloomsbury Publishing Plc
50 Bedford Square, London, WC1B 3DP, UK
1385 Broadway, New York, NY 10018, USA
29 Earlsfort Terrace, Dublin 2, Ireland

BLOOMSBURY, BLOOMSBURY VISUAL ARTS and the Diana logo are trademarks of Bloomsbury Publishing Plc

First published in Great Britain 2024
Reprinted 2024

Cover design: Paul Smith
Cover image: Ralph Pucci Mannequins, Inflate, 1987, designed by Lowell Nesbitt, photographed by Antoine Bootz

A catalogue record for this book is available from the British Library.

Library of Congress Cataloging-in-Publication Data

Names: Feigenbaum, Eric, author.
Title: Profiles of the mannequin : the cultural and historic impact of the mannequin / Eric Feigenbaum.
Description: London : Bloomsbury Visual Arts, 2024. |
Includes bibliographical references and index.
Identifiers: LCCN 2023053364 (print) | LCCN 2023053365 (ebook) |
ISBN 9781350418110 (paperback) | ISBN 9781350418103 (hardback) | ISBN 9781350418127 (pdf) |
ISBN 9781350418134 (ebook)
Subjects: LCSH: Mannequins (Figures–History.
Classification: LCC NK6214 .F (print) | LCC NK6214 (ebook) | DDC 391—dc23/eng/20240207
LC record available at https://lccn.loc.gov/2023053364
LC ebook record available at https://lccn.loc.gov/2023053365

ISBN: HB: 978-1-3504-1810-3
PB: 978-1-3504-1811-0
ePDF: 978-1-3504-1812-7
eBook: 978-1-3504-1813-4

Typeset by RefineCatch Limited, Bungay, Suffolk
Printed and bound in the United States of America

To find out more about our authors and books visit www.bloomsbury.com and sign up for our newsletters.

Dedicated to the many visionaries whose creativity and passion brought these fabulous forms to life. . .

CONTENTS

ILLUSTRATIONS

Figures

Illustrations

Plates

FOREWORD

Upon my first step inside the windows on Fifth Avenue, little did I know that I was standing on the shoulders of so many artists before me, as they too set sail on their journey. It was here on the stages of the walking streets of high fashion that I learned of the prominent role of the mannequin.

As one who has worked in the windows and interiors of department stores, I went on to create mannequin collections in Paris. This experience introduced me to the sincere intent, discipline, process, and purpose of Rodin's method of creating in clay. Today, I continue to stand in amazement at all of my design colleagues, predecessors, and talent of today, who bring artistry to life through our diverse cultures and rituals on the fashion stages of our time. The mannequin acts as a mirror to our inner self, it celebrates the human condition, launching time capsules of society's vision of beauty. These iconic figures live not only in the windows but have a permanent residency at the Metropolitan Museum of Art, the Brooklyn Museum, Cooper Hewitt, the classrooms at Parsons, and my alma mater, the Fashion Institute of Technology, where I studied display and exhibition design. Since then I have learned of its higher purpose through various manifestations. The mannequin has become the global ambassador of taste and style.

The following pages are the backstage stories of this theatrical production. Through this historical journey, Eric Feigenbaum has captured the accounts of those responsible for the continuing quest for modern beauty. He also pays homage to all of us who have been stopped in our stride by these street theater compositions, igniting our imagination and luring us inside the store. Therefore, the mannequin acts as a provocateur of commerce. *Profiles of the Mannequin* provides a history lesson filled with the deep insights of those who brought the mannequin to life at the intersection of art, fashion, and business.

Through curiosity, inquiry, and dedication, Eric has awakened our voices and tapped the memory banks of our collective journey. He lifts the veil through his carefully crafted narrative, celebrating the role of the mannequin as the silent salesperson. These iconic figures were the image makers of our lost emporiums and continue to stand as our reliable source on the runway of today. Preserving history is noble and we must insist that these stories be told and retold, inspiring new generations to pick up the baton.

Thank you for this invitation to step foot once again into the windows and know it as if it were the first time.

Welcome to *Profiles of the Mannequin.*

James Damian
Brand Integration Services, LLC

ACKNOWLEDGEMENTS

Mannequins have been elevated to an art form by the many visionaries whose passion and creative sensibilities brought this medium to life. It was their unbridled dedication and artistic sensibilities that led to the writing of this book. I would like to give special acknowledgement and thanks to Marcos Andrade, Ralph Pucci, and Marjorie Lee Woo, all of whom inspired and supported this endeavor from the beginning. I also wish to express my gratitude to Georgia Kennedy, publisher of fashion and textiles, Bloomsbury Visual Arts, for her invaluable guidance and direction.

In addition, I want to recognize and thank the following friends, colleagues, and creative professionals who made a significant contribution to the writing of *Profiles of the Mannequin*: Rachael Arnold, Kerry Barry, Tom Beebe, Carol Barnhart, James Chiao, Harry Cunningham, James Damian, Shane DeRolf, Joe Feczko, Barbara Gifford, Frank Glover, Mark Goldsmith, Ignaz Gorischek, Ron Gosses, Sharon Govern, Carly Hagedon, Amanda Hallay, Jack Hruska, Phyllis Magidson, George Martin, James Mansour, Paul Olszewski, Roe Palermo, Candy Pratts Price, Brian Preussker, Rob Smith, Michael Southgate, James Talaric, Leigh Ann Tischler, David Wolfe, Paul Wolff and Matthew Yokobosky.

INTRODUCTION
FANTASY OR REALITY

They're visions of style and grace, standing tall in the show windows of the most exclusive shopping avenues around the world, from Avenue des Champs-Élysées, Paris to Via Montenapoleone, Milan; Fifth Avenue, New York; New Bond Street, London; Causeway Bay, Hong Kong; Pitt Street Mall, Sydney; and Ginza, Tokyo. They also grace the aisles of the largest regional malls from Garden State Plaza in Paramus, New Jersey to Parque Arauco in Santiago, Chile; and of course on main streets everywhere.

Their wardrobes are extensive and all-inclusive; they only wear the best, and they only wear an outfit once. Their lives seem to be a fantasy woven by the hand of an artist or the pen of a poet. We live vicariously through them as they dress for the grand opening, the opera, the theater, or merely a day at the beach or an afternoon in the park. They're always beautifully accessorized, wearing designer handbags and elegant shoes. They're aspirational, they always seem to wear what we would love to own.

Unlike the rest of us, they don't appear to have a care in the world; life is bliss. While we mere mortals worry about the rent and the mortgage, and the bills and the taxes, they don't give money a second thought. While we worry about our families; their health, education, and welfare, and what Aunt Mary may have said to upset Cousin George; their only family stands next to them frozen in statuesque indifference. While we worry about the ravages of foreign wars and the indignity of social injustice, on the surface at least, they don't seem to exhibit the slightest trace of political leanings.

Outwardly, they seem to be the epitome of perfection; but they never attend the ball or go to the opera. They never have a walk in the park or a day at the beach. There aren't theaters or restaurants, ballgames or rides in the country on their agendas. They don't indulge in fine wine or chateaubriand, not even a slice of pizza and a soda. They're beautiful and handsome, and yet they never have a date, a lover, or a confidant. They may dress for the interview, but they never get the job.

Mannequins don't define our culture, but rather herald it and celebrate it. They reflect our values, traditions, and conventions. And while they never raise families of their own, and appear to be socially disconnected, they in fact make a significant contribution to the social fabric and societal constructs of the times. Case in point, as societal awareness evolves, more attention is being given to issues of body diversity, race, and gender, rather than presenting idealized images of what has been perceived in the past to be the perfect body type. Moreover, as some may think of mannequins as symbols of dehumanization, it is quite the opposite. No, they are not a panacea for all that ails us, but rather a snapshot in time, providing a moment of relief and or fantasy. And while conventional wisdom teaches us to seek authenticity over flights of fancy, mannequins in all of their inanimate splendor provide a temporary lull, a respite from the challenges of daily life. They give us hope, they allow us to dream, they permit us our aspirations.

Mannequins are an art form. And just as in great works of art, be it from the hand of Michelangelo holding chisel to stone, or the hand of Shakespeare holding quill to parchment, they convey reality through beautiful visions of fantasy.

Joe Feczko, with a varied and distinguished career path that led him to positions as vice president of visual presentation at Bloomingdale's, senior vice president of creative services at Neiman Marcus, and vice president of integrated marketing at Macy's, among other positions along the way, recalls his mannequin epiphany:

> I remember the first time I realized the power of mannequins. It was in the early 1980s and I was in San Francisco for the annual display show. All of the retailers were looking their best knowing that visual merchandisers from all over the world would be walking through their stores, both to learn and to judge. Macy's on Union Square in downtown San Francisco was always a must-see. Bill Withers was the vice president director of visual merchandising for the store at that time. He was a true master of illusion with a great sense of flair and sophistication. Upon arriving on the main floor I was greeted by over 100 mannequins on the store's center core ledge tops. All were staged in a dynamic diving pose. Walking through this amazing arcade of bodies reminded me of a 1940s Busby Berkeley movie.

Feczko recalls that up until that time, mannequins were made to be as life-like as possible.

> Female forms donned wigs, red lips, and eyelashes. One of the window dressers that taught me early on would actually apply make-up to his mannequins because it made the light reflect differently on them. In contrast, the mannequins in Macy's San Francisco were abstract in form and painted bright red. Walking through this canopy of figures allowed me and all the other customers to interact with the display. This was a valuable lesson I've never forgotten and in fact, used myself over the years. There's an old retail adage "Customers may not remember what they bought, but they will always remember how you made them feel." I still remember how I felt walking out of Macy's that day and it still makes me smile.

They've been referred to as the quintessential silent sales force. And yet mannequins have assumed a greater role with a more enduring effect. Certainly, they have fulfilled an important utilitarian function in terms of showing and ultimately selling apparel. But they are so much more than fancy clothes hangers. They cross the line from being a strictly functional selling tool, to a breath of life, emotion, and animation in retail environments across the world. They are works of art that tap into the emotions and aspirations of all who engage them. While stoically standing in place, they move the viewer through spirit and imagination to another place, another time, and another state of mind. While seemingly locked in place and time, they take us vicariously to a life that we would like to live. What follows is an exposé not only about these fabulous forms but also about the creative visionaries who brought these seemingly inanimate objects to life, and who have made significant contributions to the art of the mannequin.

In documenting the vision and artistry of the many personalities featured in *Profiles of the Mannequin*, I called upon long-time colleagues, friends, and industry associates to recant some of their experiences, philosophies, and stories relative to the evolution of the mannequin and its impact on our culture. Additionally, extensive qualitative historical research, including primary and secondary sources, has been conducted to bring into focus and to interpret, how past events, concepts, and philosophies have affected the role and development of the mannequin, both as a utilitarian object and as an artistic statement.

As a long-time design and visual merchandising professional, I have worked in several sectors of the industry including visual merchandising, store design, editorial, and education. Like so many of my colleagues, I have been fascinated by the allure and power of the mannequin. As such, this account also includes many of my own experiences with these beguiling sculptural figures.

Profiles of the Mannequin looks back at history, with eyes focused on the future. In addition to inspiring established professionals by documenting and celebrating those who have come before, the book is intended to encourage those who will define the retail and fashion industries in the years to come. For students of visual merchandising, fashion design, fashion history, fashion merchandising, and marketing, the text offers several specific learning objectives based on the philosophies, techniques, and real-world experiences of some of the industry's most iconic leaders.

After completing each chapter, and understanding the specific learning objectives, the reader should be able to do the following:

Chapter 1

- Recognize the mannequin as an art form and as an integral touchstone of the brand.
- Identify the first commercial use of the mannequin.
- Discuss the historical beginnings of the department store.
- Explain how early 20th-century technologies led to the advent of the modern mannequin.
- Describe the materials used in the early renditions of the mannequin in the late 1880s.

Chapter 2

- Develop an understanding of various mannequin profiles and body types.
- Develop an appreciation for diversity and inclusion in mannequin design.
- Recognize that mannequin design responds to the prevailing wants, needs, and concerns of the consumer.
- Understand the development of gender-neutral mannequins.

Chapter 3

- Discuss how technology, architecture, and the harnessing of electricity led to a new profession, visual merchandising.
- Discuss how mannequins became a staple tool of retailers everywhere.
- Explain how the evolution of the fashion industry, the growth of the department store, and political and cultural events impacted the development of the mannequin.

Chapter 4

- Recognize the impact of Art Deco on fashion, architecture, art, illustration, and mannequins.
- Discuss the influence of surrealism on mannequin design and presentation.
- Discuss the power of the mannequin as a marketing tool.

Chapter 5

- Understand how global events such as The Great Depression and World War II impacted the fashion industry and mannequin design.

Chapter 6

- Recognize the impact of innovative mid-century technologies and merchandising philosophies on both retail and mannequin design.
- Recognize the impact of cinema, photography, and television on show window design and mannequin presentation.

Chapter 7

- Recognize the impact the counter-culture of the 1960s had on fashion and mannequin design.
- Discuss how mannequins became focal points in new approaches to department store layouts.
- Discuss how Adel Rootstein elevated the mannequin to a fashion statement and an art form.

Chapter 8

- Understand how mannequin designers responded to new levels of social awareness with a heightened degree of realism.
- Recognize a new show window design concept referred to as "street theater," and how mannequin designers responded with groupings of mannequins.

Chapter 9

- Understand the role of the mannequin in establishing and projecting a store identity.
- Recognize the sculptural and artistic aspects of mannequins.
- Understand the adaptability of mannequins in meeting the ever-evolving needs of the retailer.
- Discuss how mannequin design is an interdisciplinary art.

Chapter 10

- Understand mannequin groupings and mathematical progressions.

Chapter 11

- Understand how mannequins elevate merchandise presentation while adding style to the projected brand experience.
- Develop skills in composition and positioning.
- Understand the power of repetition and simplicity.

Chapter 12

- Recognize the importance of mannequins in non-retail environments.
- Understand the challenges, techniques, and philosophies of museum curators when working with mannequins.

Chapter 13

- Discuss the evolution of mannequins in terms of advancing technologies and materials.
- Discuss initiatives toward sustainable, environmentally friendly mannequin production.

Chapter 14

- Recognize the difference between abstract, partly abstract, and realistic mannequins.
- Discuss realistic representations of the human form versus abstractions of the human form.
- Discuss customization of mannequins.

Chapter 15

- Understand the expanding role of the visual merchandiser in the age of connectivity.
- Recognize the impact of technology on mannequin design.
- Understand the digital manifestation of the mannequin.

Chapter 16

- Understand the importance of selecting the appropriate mannequin to project a branded image.
- Understand the role of the mannequin as a tool of engagement.
- Recognize the need to reach out to other industries for inspiration, technology, and technique.

CHAPTER 1
ACTORS ON THE STAGE

They're part of our lives and part of our culture. Often taken for granted, they touch us every time we walk down a major urban retail corridor or visit our favorite neighborhood store. They adorn the show windows of specialty stores and department stores alike; standing stoically with a seemingly unbridled sense of self-confidence. Thespian-like, they pose as actors on stage, interacting, if only silently, with all who pass. Inside the stores, they're magnets, drawing visitors toward them and through the selling zone. Some think of them merely as fancy clothes hangers whose only purpose is to give garments greater hanger appeal in the hope of tweaking the consumer's aspirational desires. In some cases, they even have the power to change desired luxuries into absolute necessities, as they convincingly populate the selling floors in the role of the archetypal silent sales force. Others see beyond the surface, considering them sculptures, or pieces of art. And so the question must be asked; when does any object, craft, or an artistic endeavor, enter into the realm of art? The answer: when it moves the emotion or elicits a response. And after all, isn't that what retailers, across different segments of society, and in varying cultures across the globe, strive to do; strike a responsive chord in all who visit their stores? While some mannequins remain pedestrian, merely positioned to wear a garment, most go beyond the simple and obvious functionality of displaying clothes. Arguably, art serves two main purposes: it documents any point in time, serving as a bookmark and commentary on history and culture, and it enriches our lives. The well-designed and strategically positioned mannequin does both.

Moreover, while their primary purpose of showing and displaying merchandise remains vital, they touch us on a subliminal level. Through careful selection, design, and placement they function as critical touchstones of a retailer's brand. The discerning retail designer knows that not just any mannequin will suffice; but rather the appropriate mannequin is necessary to project a store's individual and carefully crafted image. Image is one of the determining factors in why a customer shops one store rather than another. Every gesture that a retailer makes must be in sync with the message and the image they are hoping to project. From the sign above their door to the mat below; from the stationery they use to the nature of their sales associates who represent them; and from the interior design to the logo; everything must be intrinsically connected. Everything must convey the same message: this is who we are, this is what we have to say, and this is how we say it. The right mannequin is a vital component of that conversation; it's a critical part of the retailer-to-customer dialogue.

The first known mannequin dates back to circa 1323 BC in the time of Egypt's King Tutankhamun. When the Boy King's tomb was discovered in 1922 by English Egyptologist Howard Carter, the archeologist found a carved wooden form in the likeness and size of the young king. It's believed that the mannequin was used each day to prepare

Tutankhamun's wardrobe. The subsequent evolution of the fabulous forms has taken a fascinating course. The intriguing history of the mannequin is a reflection of society and a timeline of our culture.

The commercial use of mannequins found its beginnings soon after the Industrial Revolution in the United States and Western Europe. The machine age brought mass production of ready-to-wear fashion into the newly born department stores. For the most part, the early department stores came into being in England, France, and the northeastern portion of the United States. These large-scale buildings, constructed in the late 1800s and early 1900s, established themselves in large urban centers such as New York, Chicago, Philadelphia, Paris, and London. While these new buildings were filled with merchandise, no one quite knew how to present, organize, and show the goods. The American writer, L. Frank Baum, author of *The Wonderful Wizard of Oz*, published the first periodical that detailed techniques and philosophies for what was then referred to as the display (now visual merchandising) industry. Two years before writing *The Wonderful Wizard of Oz*, Baum used his creativity to write and publish *The Show Window*. And so, the display (visual merchandising) profession was born. *The Show Window* became the bible for retailers hoping to present their goods in a meaningful manner. Two years after the first issue of *The Show Window*, he published a book titled *The Art of Decorating Dry Goods Windows and Interiors*. In it, he spoke about the importance of mannequins.

Marshall Field's, the influential and groundbreaking Chicago department store founded in 1881, was one of the first supporters of Baum and his creative merchandising

Figure 1.1 The first edition of L. Frank Baum's periodical, *The Show Window*. Courtesy VMSD Magazine.

techniques. With a background in theater, Baum recognized the store as a selling stage. In agreement with that notion, Harry Gordon Selfridge, who began his retail career at Marshall Field's before becoming the founder of London's famed Selfridge Department Store, said, "Everyday is show day in this establishment." So the stage was set in the world of retail, and the mannequin was to become the star player on that stage.

Since its inception, modern retail has always been quick to embrace the new technologies of the day. As the 19th century was giving way to the 20th century, two of the defining technologies at the time, as it relates to the advent of the modern mannequin, were cast-iron architecture and plate glass. Prior to the 18th century, cast-iron was in short supply, and extremely expensive. In 1709, innovations in England led to the beginnings of mass production and easy access to this important building material. Soon, the discovery of vast iron and coal resources, particularly in the northeastern section of the United States, increased the production of cast-iron.[1] As the Industrial Revolution gained momentum, new types of commercial buildings featuring wide expanses were being built in mid- to late 19th-century America, England, France, and even Mexico. In 1891, a group of French entrepreneurs brought luxury goods from Europe into Mexico City and built Palacio de Hierro, the Iron Palace, one of the first iron-framed buildings in Mexico.

At the same time, plate glass became more readily available at cheaper prices and with enhanced quality. Previously, American businessmen had little option but to import good quality plate glass from France. By the late 1800s, domestic American factories produced tremendous amounts of high-quality plate glass. Within fifteen years, Americans were consuming about half of all the plate glass produced worldwide.[2] The combination of cast-iron architecture, which allowed for large expanses; and plate glass, which allowed for the enclosing of the expanses to create windows, set the stage for a new type of theater in which mannequins would become the star players.

Innovation typically brings about cultural change and even shifts in values. Prior to the advent of retail's new show windows, mid-19th-century values deemed it indiscreet and distasteful to stare into windows.[3] Retail not only reflects our culture but at times even drives it. By the beginning of the 20th century, passersby on busy streets were invited and encouraged to look into store windows and marvel at the beautiful scenes before their eyes.

When discussing the development of retail's new theatrical window sets, L. Frank Baum's most important message involved the merchandise itself. "Use the best of art to arouse in the observers the cupidity and longing to possess the goods. As long as the goods are properly displayed, the show window will sell them like hot cakes, even though the goods are old enough to have gray whiskers."[4] Baum called on the merchants to bring the goods to life. He cautioned them not to crowd the windows with merchandise, but rather to highlight single pieces. "Don't let the lamps and tin pots sit there. Make them come alive as if they were figures on the stage." He went on to say, "Look for the possibilities laying dormant in the beautiful goods. Suggest possibilities of color and sumptuous display that would delight the heart. Bring the goods out in a blaze of glory. Make them look like jewels."[5]

In 1895, while still associated with Marshal Field's, Selfridge hired a young man named Arthur Fraser for display work. A true visionary in his own right, Fraser introduced windows that were brimming with color and life. And then after becoming the head of display in the early 1900s, in keeping with the directives of Baum, he significantly reduced the clutter in the windows by limiting the amount of goods on display. In 1913, he forged a new direction by introducing full-bodied realistic papier-mâché mannequins into Field's windows.[6] Purportedly, Fraser was the first to accessorize mannequins. He recalled, "I tried to get the mannikins (another accepted English spelling) so real that the woman would feel it was she wearing it."[7] Fraser was also enamored with the theater. "I went to New York to the theater a lot. I derived more from the theater than anything else."[8] Fraser's love of the theater coupled with his use of mannequins, created a new genre for retailers to present their goods and to communicate with their customers.

Fraser became the most prominent display director of the decade. Totally theatrical in his approach, he added drama, artistry, and excitement to the retail stage. In 1913, presenting a line of merchandise inspired by Japanese tradition, he enhanced his windows with large Japanese landscapes to celebrate the theme. *The Merchants Record and Show Window* wrote, "The soft, hazy tones and vague lines, with the faint, snow-capped Fujiyama in the distance, gave wonderful perspective to the whole setting."

In 1922, *The Show Window* called Fraser America's foremost artist in window display. When Fraser started at Field's, the display department employed seven people. By 1916, he had a staff of fifty.[9] As retailers across the country started to emulate Fraser's approach, mannequins increasingly found their way to the center of the show window.

A window display designed by Arthur Fraser at Marshall Field's, November, 1925. *Photo in the public domain*

Figure 1.2 A window display designed by Arthur Fraser at Marshall Field's, November 1925, Public Domain.

Influenced by Fraser and Baum, mannequins were gaining great popularity and acceptance among retailers. Baum was as certain as he was convincing, telling merchants that mannequins were important tools to attract customers into the stores and to the goods. He said, "Without such displays, the merchant sinks into oblivion. The busy world forgets him and he is left to himself, to rust, vegetate or fail ignominiously."[10] Was this merely the ranting of a creative genius who gave the world the Tin Man, the Scarecrow, and the Cowardly Lion, or a visionary who recognized the value of storytelling, whether in a retail venue or the pages of one of the world's most beloved literary tomes?

The presentation of goods in the newfound department stores was becoming theatrical. The curtain was about to be raised on new retail stages in major cities across the world. Mannequins would be the star players, but the name of the show was "consumerism," and the dialogue was centered around the merchandise. Show windows began to appear everywhere. New York's Ladies Mile became a crystal palace of glittering glass. While most still shopped in traditional open-air markets, glass was defining a new way of looking at merchandise. A new class culture was being formed. From the late 1890s, the affluent shopper looked to the new uptown show windows, while those in the working class still shopped in the familiar outdoor marketplaces.[11] But this was just the beginning; show windows would soon proliferate, and mannequins would become one of the most important tools in the retailer's repertoire. What follows is a detailed look at the evolution of the fabulous forms; their function, their structure, and their impact on retail and on society.

THE FACE IN THE MIRROR

If one were to hold a mirror to the face of fashion, the reflected image would be us. Fashion, like art, is a bookmark of our times. A long debate has been waged over the relationship between fashion and art. Miuccia Prada said, "Whether fashion design is art, or even if art is art, doesn't really interest me. Maybe nothing is art." If nothing is art, as Prada contends, then what is art? Elsa Schiaparelli said, "It's the way we live."[12] Clearly, fashion has the ability to move emotion, another requisite quality of any art form. As Schiaparelli implied, fashion is an art, and as such a reflection of the way we live. It can also be said that mannequins are not merely fancy clothes hangers, but rather three-dimensional representations of the way we live. Accordingly, if a mirror were held to the face of retail and the mannequins it employs in any given corner of the world, the reflected image would be the society and culture of that place. Moreover, the mannequin is not only a reflection of society but also the embodiment of its culture.

The word mannequin (English and French), manequim (Portuguese), maniqui (Spanish), is derived from the Dutch word maneken meaning little man. The Merriam-Webster Dictionary (English) defines the word mannequin as "an artist's, tailor's, or dressmaker's lay figure"; also: "a form representing the human figure used especially for displaying clothes." Historically, it is widely believed that the original commercial use of mannequins can be traced back to the 1600s when miniature mannequins were used to show the latest fashions. Of course, it is well known that artists have traditionally used articulated wooden mannequins as models for drawing the clothed human figure. This allowed for a more studied composition of draped clothing rather than drawing from a live model who may not remain perfectly still.

Whatever the origins, it is clear that throughout history, people have always been fascinated by idealized representations of the human form, whether found in the annals of art, the workshops of craftsmen, or the minds of cunning marketers and advertising agencies. From Michelangelo's *Last Testament* and awe-inspiring *Pieta*; to a 16th-century German tin soldier and a European bisque doll from the 1870s, we have long been captivated by creatively rendered versions of the human body. In the late 1800s and early 1900s, an overabundance of goods in the marketplace led to the rise of consumerism and desire, which directly led to the birth of the department store. As this new commercial institution gained momentum, the art of the mannequin gained popularity among the early merchants. Not only did these romanticized forms appeal to the universal fascination with the representation of the human figure, but they also served as idealized human surrogates appealing to the aspirations and desires of all who encountered them.

Retail stores became theatrical selling stages that appealed to the hopes, dreams, and fantasies of all who entered their domain. Enclosed windows created a new street theater. Elaborate sets were created with brightly colored glass and lavishly draped fabrics of velour and silk. The next advancement of the day was electrical lighting. Now the stage was truly set for drama and pizazz. As window theater on city streets and boulevards began to flourish, window shopping became a preoccupation among city dwellers. It was a form of entertainment that enthralled whole communities. The mannequin was an instant star.

The early rendition of mannequins in the late 1800s was simplistic and mundane. Most were headless bodies made from a variety of materials including wood, leather, wire, and wicker. The next iteration was papier-mâché, an art form that is still used today in the manufacture of bust forms and torso forms. The first papier-mâché mannequins were made in France. A major advancement occurred when several companies, most notably La Vigne, a Parisienne company, started creating mannequins with faces. Artisans skilled in mask-making were used to create papier-mâché heads to be attached to existing headless mannequins. Companies competed with one another to create the most realistic-looking mannequins. Papier-mâché was mixed with other materials such as wax and plaster. Some began to use wigs made from human hair, while others inserted glass eyes.

The darlings of window theater were clearly in their infancy. More and more, as mannequin manufacturers strove for realism, the waxen and papier-mâché starlets began to be reflective of cultural attitudes and fashion directions. Experimentation brought innovation, as the mannequin marched to the beat of evolving societies and new technologies.

THE COMMUNICATOR OF THE BRAND

Some won't recognize the name, but to be sure, he has touched the lives of millions. Raymond Loewy was an important industrial designer of the early to mid-20th century.

Even if you've never heard of him, it's probable that you have used or at least seen an item or a product that he has created. He designed everything from lipstick to locomotives. His impressive design portfolio includes the Coca Cola bottle inspired by the female form, the Studebaker automobile, streamline locomotives for the Pennsylvania Railroad, the Greyhound bus and logo, NASA interiors for Skylab and Apollo programs, logos for Shell, Exxon, TWA, Nabisco, and the US Postal Service.

In his earlier years, he was injured as he fought valiantly for the French in World War I. In the aftermath of the war, he moved to New York City and found work as a window designer for such notable department stores as Macy's, Wanamaker's, and Saks Fifth Avenue. With multiple talents, he also worked as a fashion illustrator for *Vogue* and *Harper's Bazaar*. Sometime before his illustrious career as a world-renowned industrial designer, toward the end of his time with Macy's, he took one mannequin, dressed her in an evening gown, positioned her in the show window, and focused two spotlights on her. The window was stunning in its simplicity and made a striking statement to all who viewed it. Loewy, although quite pleased with his window design, quit the next day before Macy's could fire him. In those days, retailers put all that they had into the show windows. They were unduly populated with everything from dinnerware to evening wear. Loewy knew, however, that his window creation wasn't there necessarily to sell the beautiful evening gown the mannequin was wearing, but rather to project the nuances of the Macy's brand onto the street. Loewy understood that the window was a portal to the soul of the company, and the mannequin was a standard bearer of the brand. Yes, a mannequin will sell an evening gown any day, but it will also embed a visual brand image into the customer's mind. In the words of Loewy, "I'm looking for a very high index of visual retention." The mannequin in the show window should be memorable and recognizable, it should be the visual embodiment of the brand. Keeping the mannequin display in the show window simple was central to Loewy's design philosophy. Toward that end, the famed designer said, "Simplicity is the deciding factor in the aesthetic equation." As mannequins adorn store windows across the world, it's the successful visual merchandiser who understands Loewy's vision. Famed artists and architects have mirrored Loewy's thoughts in their own words. The influential German–American architect, Ludwig Mies van der Rohe said, "Less is more," while the iconic early 20th-century sculptor Constantin Brancusi said, "Simplicity is complexity resolved."

When employed strategically and thoughtfully with strong aesthetic sensibilities, mannequins have the ability to make quality statements to those whose gaze meets theirs. Loewy's philosophy speaks to the magic of mannequins in two ways. First, mannequins are not merely fancy clothes hangers, they are important touchstones of the brand. They provide retailers with the opportunity to engage customers by letting them know, this is who we are, this is what we have to say, and this is how we say it. It's not only about the merchandise the mannequin is presenting, although that is clearly important, it's also about the brand statement. Second, Loewy would applaud the contemporary mannequin makers who have elevated the craft to an art form. To those demanding more realism, consider that craft becomes art when it moves emotions. Art moves emotion when it is evocative, not overt; when it is suggestive of an idea. In his iconic sculpture "Bird in

Space," Brancusi reduced the winged, beaked, feathered creature to a precious few gestures; this is art! Through simple lines, perhaps elongated, curvilinear or abstract, mannequin designers have provided retailers with the opportunity to elevate the in-store shopping experience for customers by integrating art into the selling environment.

In 1960, the American writer Gay Talese wrote the following about mannequins, in an article for the *New York Times*:

> At 4 A.M. Fifth Avenue is deserted by all but a few strolling insomniacs, some cruising cab drivers, and a group of sophisticated females who stand in store windows all night (and day), wearing cold, perfect smiles—smiles formed by lips of clay, eyes of glass, and cheeks that will glow until the paint wears off.[13]

The famed and often controversial journalist knew that the elegant and seemingly lifeless women who graced myriad show windows along fashionable Fifth Avenue did indeed challenge the boundaries of the inanimate, and therefore had a life of their own. Talese recognized that these were not merely fancy clothes hangers, but rather representations of who we are as a society. Certainly of equal importance, they are brand medallions with distinct personalities that move the emotions of all who engage while defining the personality of the stores they represent.

> And not only are mannequins natural, but they have different human personalities. For example, the mannequins sold to Peck & Peck should have a youthful and demure air, while in Lord & Taylor they should be more mundane and ventilated. In Saks they are dignified and refined, while at Bergdorf they have the aggressive elegance of self-assured wealth.[14]

In the same article, Talese quoted New York mannequin maker Mary Brosnan, speaking at her Long Island factory. "We would prefer, however, that all the mannequins we now have in the New York department store give the impression of being good girls. We do not care about their morals, but we do want them to look well educated."[15]

Talese's mannequin expose was an eye-opener into the world of these sultry but silent seductresses. With an uncanny knack for delving behind the scenes, he spoke with Tom Ellery, an English window aficionado who trimmed the windows at Saks Fifth Avenue at the time. Ellery said,

> Mannequins in Italy must be sullen and disheveled, and in France they look like prostitutes. In England they have thick bodies and lack refinement. But since I've been in the United States, I've finally learned to consider mannequins something more than clothes hangers. Here they put realism. They even scared me. At certain times of the night, when I am in the window and a bit tired, maybe I touch them by accident or they touch me and I think they are real. Sometimes I talk to them. When dressing one of them I might say, "You look wonderful today," or, "Sorry, I'll have to use someone else today."[16]

With an understanding of regional variables and the power of the mannequin to connect to a particular area or demographic, Brosnan went on to say,

> The mannequins that we send to Miami Beach or to Las Vegas have a glamorous air and a little too much make-up, and the mannequins that we send to California are always blond and deeply tanned. We also sell a few in England and in Europe, but not many. Most of the stores there do not like the American look. They prefer that their mannequins look like strippers.[17]

In the days of the grand old department stores, mannequins silently sold the retailer's goods. Whatever was put on them flew out the door. Going forward in a modern economy and for a different consumer, mannequins are entrusted with selling something else: the retailer's brand. The mannequin is a vital tool of communication. It may not sell that evening gown on that particular day, but it will leave a memorable and recognizable impression in the mind's eye of the consumer.

Differentiation is critical in the competitive marketplace, with each retailer required to develop an image that sets it apart. Mannequins are key touch points of the brand image. Selecting the right one is essential, as the right mannequin is an integral component of a company's DNA.

DEFINING AN IMAGE

Fifth Avenue has always been a window to the world; a place for retailers to plant their branded flag and be seen by the millions of tourists and locals alike who are drawn like magnets to the renowned retail corridor. The visual merchandising team at Saks Fifth Avenue's flagship in New York has always been true to the understanding that the mannequins they position in the windows and in the store interior are true ambassadors of the Saks Fifth Avenue brand. They developed a mannequin style and approach over the years that is totally representative of who they are. To put it simply, their mannequins speak their language and the language of all who enter the store. Harry Cunningham, SVP Store Planning, Design, and Visual Merchandising from 2010 to 2014 said, "My approach for Saks was that the mannequins we use should be recognizable Saks Fifth Avenue, part of our DNA." Toward that end, Cunningham and his staff worked with a number of mannequin houses to develop programs that were identifiable and distinctive.

In 2012, Saks was developing a new women's floor concept. As in other areas, they wanted to develop a mannequin program that was unique to them while supportive of the brand image and the new women's environment. Cunningham recalls, "We decided to sculpt our own mannequins that would be ours and ours alone. Toward that end we worked with two famous models, Pat Cleveland and her daughter, Anna Cleveland, to become the 'faces' of the floor. Their likenesses were sculpted and used throughout, and at the opening party, we had both of them join us to celebrate." Along with the environmental decor and the merchandise offerings, the two new mannequins became representative of the Saks Fifth Avenue brand image.

Cunningham also believed that mannequins positioned directly on the floor versus on platforms tend to be much more interesting. In seeking more compelling mannequin placements, the Saks Fifth Avenue approach under Cunningham was to break aisle lines, pull tables halfway into aisles, and stand mannequins around them. At times the visual team would even sit them on the tables in a life-style position; the way real people would actually sit in their own homes or when out on the town.

To further project and emphasize the Saks Fifth Avenue culture and mystique, Cunningham believed in celebrating the history and heritage that Saks has enjoyed in the fashion world.

> Some of the best windows ever installed at Saks were using realistic mannequins. So as I began shifting our approach in our windows, we did a big purchase of realistic mannequins to support that vision. We didn't do it randomly though, we went into the basement (three floors below ground) where the window team worked, and where the mannequins were stored. We looked through all the old collections we had used. We chose a number of those collections from Rootstein, and then we worked with the mannequin house to reinvent the collection. We updated their hair and makeup, and made them look fresh again. There's a whole new generation that hasn't been exposed to realistic mannequins, whether to dress and rig them, or to see fashion on them. As important as it is today to celebrate so many different cultures, people, and images, it's the perfect time to embrace realistic mannequins again.

(As a point of reference, rigging is an industry term used for dressing and trimming a form or mannequin).

In celebrating Saks Fifth Avenue's illustrious history, Cunningham certainly had a long list of visual merchandising notables to reference who have made significant contributions to the industry. The first and foremost name that comes to mind is Henry Callahan, the legendary visual merchandiser from Saks Fifth Avenue who once said, "We make magic, and we create it with nothing."

Callahan, who was born in Oakland, California, and grew up in Philadelphia, joined Saks Fifth Avenue in 1957 as vice president and corporate director of visual merchandising. He held that lofty position for twenty years, creating memorable window and interior presentations that clearly separated Saks from its competition. His work at the venerable high-end retailer propelled him to the top of the visual merchandising industry. He fondly recalled that his favorite windows featured a group of Southern belles napping in hammocks and wearing lace pastel-colored dresses. He went on to describe a hidden mechanism under the dresses that made their chests gently rise and fall as they slept; a scene seemingly drawn from the big screen production of *Gone With the Wind*.[18]

The leading display directors of that time helped usher in a new approach to mannequin design. Many of the more notable retailers cultivated a mannequin style that was unique to them—a style that supported their individual brand image. The one consistency as stores strategized to differentiate their brand, was all were using faces on mannequins that were imminently recognizable to all who passed by their windows or walked through their stores.

In 1964, Callahan used the iconic visage of Audrey Hepburn on mannequins for a Fall launch. Callahan recanted, "The mannequin looked pretty much as Hepburn looked in the movie *Charade*."[19] A few blocks away, Lord & Taylor's display director Paul Vogler was drawn to Katherine, the other famous Hepburn. What was notable to Vogler, and anyone else who was captivated by the young star, was her striking and innate ability to wear clothes. Enamored by Hepburn's style and grace, Vogler had a grouping of mannequins fashioned after her. The posture, movement, and attitude of the Hepburn-inspired figures were based on a series of photographs taken when she was in her twenties.[20]

In earlier times, mannequins in the likeness of revered movie stars graced the windows of venerable stores, not only on Fifth Avenue but also across the entire retail scene. From Bergdorf Goodman's and Saks Fifth Avenue to Lord & Taylor and Bonwit Teller, the likeness of stars including Grace Kelly, Betty Grable, Greta Garbo, Jean Harlow, Rosalind Russell, and Vivien Leigh, stood as silent actors on retail's greatest selling stages. In the early 1960s, however, display directors only looked to the two Hepburns for mannequin inspiration. The two movie icons were the only stars of the day whose recognizable faces and association with style, fashion, and grace were deemed appropriate for the fast-moving mannequin world.[21]

Callahan, who enjoyed a long and storied career in display, was quite respected and influential within the industry. In addition to his Audrey Hepburn look-alike mannequins, he had a penchant for figures modeled after the young socialites of the day. He said, "I find this group of sophisticated young New Yorkers, with their expensive wardrobes, a lot more exciting and interesting than movie people."[22] He was convinced that this group exhibited more excitement than even the most beloved actresses. In addition to Callahan's use of imagery gleaned from young socialites, display directors also began to employ photographers' models for inspiration.[23]

Callahan also became a proponent of using male mannequins in both window and interior store presentations. Male mannequins have long been an enigma for visual merchandisers across the industry; they never quite seemed right. In the early 1970s however, Callahan began to include more male mannequins in Saks Fifth Avenue's presentations. He said, "It comes from real life. More and more couples are shopping with each other these days."[24]

As the 1960s eased into the '70s, fashion and culture evolved, and so did the mannequin. A new movement in visual merchandising was being driven by the changing times and by a group of daring New York City visual merchandisers. The show windows in New York were garnering a great deal of interest and excitement as Candy Pratts Price at Bloomingdale's, Robert Currie at Bendel's, Victor Hugo at Halston, and Saks Fifth Avenue's Robert Benzio threw away the rule book and started to redefine the aesthetic of the show window. It was no longer pretty red roses and yellow daffodils, but rather thematic presentations that commented on the issues of the day.

A new mannequin type was an important tool for visual merchandisers in these changing and sometimes turbulent times. "We've been oversaturated with realism," said Robert Benzio, vice president and director of visual merchandising at Saks Fifth Avenue from 1976 to 1987. "With the return of more glamorous clothes, we're reflecting the glamour of the 1950s and the early 1960s. The new mannequins have a lot of presence; there's a soft watercolor technique that looks very much like a fashion drawing. Some are in ballet positions and generally they're much more sophisticated than they've been in the last decade or two."[25]

Benzio enjoyed a retinue of 300 mannequins that were at his disposal, serving as actors on stage, silently reciting the doctrines of the brand. While there was great drama in the windows of New York, Benzio wasn't necessarily a believer in "street theater." While his windows were socially relevant, projecting the brand image and selling merchandise remained paramount. He said, "I'm a visual merchant. People are supposed to want the clothes in the window."[26]

Cunningham understands that it's not only the style, type, or mannequin maker that will best project the brand image, but also the usage and the level of standards applied. As such, he developed a mannequin philosophy that was synonymous with the Saks Fifth Avenue image and aesthetic. Mixing groupings and styles is a personal thing for him from two different vantage points.

> A large group of mannequins can be a much stronger statement. I remember an installation we did on the second floor of Saks that incorporated 12 mannequins; three lines of four clustered together in a space that typically would have just housed three to five mannequins. It became a much bolder story; it was much more disruptive, and the sheer impact forced you to stop and look.

In terms of mixing styles, Cunningham believes that a realistic mannequin positioned together with a dressmaker form, or with an unfinished egghead, tells a totally different story; a much more diverse story.

> We aren't all the same, so it's logical that mannequins don't need to all be the same. I remember well when there was a trend to use two or three of the same mannequin in the same finish, and in the same pose, clustered together or in a straight line. I guess the purpose was that it would make the customer look more closely at the clothes. For me, however, I always got distracted by the fact that the mannequins were all standing in the exact same unnatural pose.

Cunningham relates his mannequin philosophy on mixing to his role as a father of twins, "I always think it's important for my twins to be able to embrace and celebrate their individual style. Why should mannequins be different?"

In terms of establishing and maintaining a proprietary approach to mannequin usage, Cunningham has long been an advocate of maintaining high standards in the windows and on the selling floor. Cunningham said,

> It's my opinion that high standards are the price of entry. My standards don't change based on window, shop floor, prop, or mannequin. Each element you touch reflects your brand. A simple scratch on a mannequin quickly becomes a gouge to the eye. It jumps out at me the same way a left behind t-pin might, or a drop of paint on a piece of glass, or a letter installed backward of its parent font. It's not so much that perfection is demanded, there's a place for imperfection, and a big, valid one. However, if a gloss white mannequin has a scuff from being moved into the window, it either needs to be fixed, replaced, or removed.

In 2014, Cunningham moved on to become the VP / Retail Brand Experience for Vera Bradley, where the same high standards are maintained to project the company's brand image.

References

1. *The Encyclopedia of Greater Philadelphia* available online: https://philadelphiaencyclopedia.org.
2. William Leach, *Land of Desire* (Vintage Books, 1993).
3. Leach, *Land of Desire.*
4. Leach, *Land of Desire.*
5. L. Frank Baum, *The Show Window* (Vintage Books, 1899. Illustrated edition, September 6, 1994).
6. Leach, *Land of Desire.*
7. Earl Dash, "Fraser was the Greatest Displayman of Them All," *Women's Wear Daily* (July 8, 1947).
8. Arthur Fraser, Lloyd Lewis Interviews.
9. *Art & Design in Chicago* (WTTW Chicago TV series, 2018).
10. L. Frank Baum, *The Art of Decorating Dry Goods Windows* (Lulu.com, 2021).
11. Leach, *Land of Desire.*
12. Eric Feigenbaum, "The Art of Design," *Visual Merchandising and Store Design Magazine* (November 26, 2012).
13. Gay Talese, *New York Times* (February 7, 1960).
14. Talese.
15. Talese.
16. Talese.
17. Talese.
18. Obituary "Henry Callahan," *New York Times* (July 23, 1985).
19. Virginia Lee Warren, "Beauty of Mannequins in Store Window Often Draws Its Pattern From Real Life," *New York Times* (September 16, 1964).
20. Lee Warren, "Beauty of Mannequins."
21. Lee Warren, "Beauty of Mannequins."

22. Lee Warren, "Beauty of Mannequins."
23. Lee Warren, "Beauty of Mannequins," 34.
24. Obituary "Henry Callahan."
25. Enid Nemy, "A New Breed of Mannequins," *New York Times* (July 22, 1983), section A, page 12).
26. Angela Taylor, *New York Times* (November 28, 1977).

CHAPTER 2
PROFILES, BODY TYPE, AND GENDER

They come in a variety of shapes, forms, sizes, and poses. They're large, they're small, demure, and bold. Some are nondescript, featureless, and unmemorable, while others are spirited, confident, and self-assured. They're black, white, green, yellow, red and blue. Some are even colorless, transparent, rough, and raw. Then there are the realistic mannequins; but are they truly real? Does anyone really look like that? Are they trying to be literal, or just suggestive of a theme or concept? Some prefer abstract mannequins; forms that merely reference reality, and perhaps differentiate one brand or point of view from another. Outwardly, their purpose is to show and sell merchandise. But the question must be asked, are they simply utilitarian or are they works of art that enhance the customer experience?

Throughout history, there have been wide-ranging interpretations of the female form. The passage of time, multicultural constructs, and geographic variables have all contributed to the many visions of perceived beauty. From the Venus of Willendorf, dating back over 25,000 years, to the 700-year-old statue of the Hindu goddess Parvati; and from the caryatides of ancient Greece to the idealized figures of the Renaissance, the female form has been represented with realism, idealism, and abstraction through the hands of the craftsman and the heart of the artist.

It's quite clear that mannequin designers have also been inspired by perceived visions of beauty, whether driven by the values and mores of the times, or the wants, needs, and aspirations of the consumer. In the early days of the 20th century, Lena Bryant opened the first store ever designed to cater exclusively to women considered to be of "above average size." The visionary entrepreneur founded Lane Bryant in 1904, and in an advertisement in the late 1920s coined the term "plus-size." Over the course of time, there were many terms, now recognized to be pejorative and hurtful, used to describe this classification, such as gracious, regal, above average, half-size, full-figured, and even chubby.

In the late 1970s, model agencies began to use plus-size models, and soon after, they were featured in many ad campaigns. Plus-size mannequins followed. In addition, there was a call for petite mannequins, needed by retailers to display and promote apparel for women five foot four or under. Before long, department stores from New York to London, began featuring plus-size and petite mannequins in what was fast becoming a very lucrative classification.

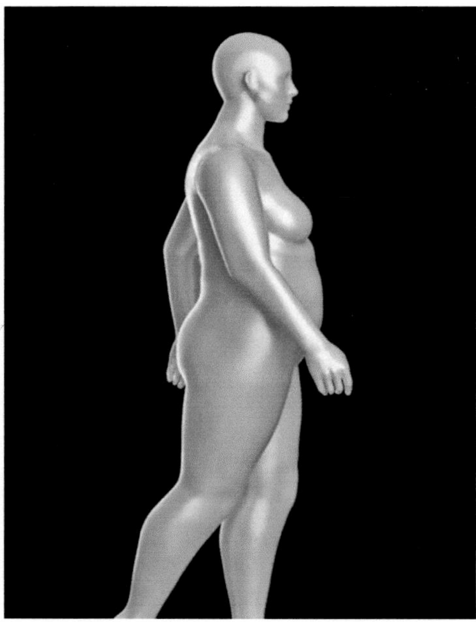

Figure 2.1 Plus Size by Expor Mannequins. Courtesy of Expor Mannequins.

POSITIVE BODY IMAGE

Even with shifting values at the turn of the 21st century, and the introduction of plus-size models and mannequins, the fashion industry continued to promote and glamorize a rail-like, slender, and even diaphanous look. As the primary tools of choice for displaying the latest fashions, styles, and trends, mannequins continued to support fashion's concept of ultra-thin beauty while tapping into the aspirations and desires of the targeted customer.

As the decade progressed, a stroll down any urban retail corridor, or through any suburban mall, revealed legions of tall, thin, featureless, white, and willowy mannequins. Increasingly, however, retailers are striving to project environments that are inclusive and welcoming to all. When engaging a grouping of mannequins, the enlightened retailer hopes that the customer, regardless of background, will see themselves in the presentation.

While the primary reason for using nondescript abstract mannequins is based on aesthetics and cost, they also allow the retailer to avoid issues of age, ethnicity, and body type. Mannequin makers, however, must continue to respond to the wants, needs, and desires of the well-informed, and socially concerned consumer. And while mannequin designers get many of their cues from the runway, they too are instigators of change, responding to the prevailing conditions of the day. Their creative vision sees beauty in the overlooked, the unexpected, and the unappreciated. In lock-step with the fashion runways, whose models have become more reflective of a diverse population, with body-positive profiles, shapes, and attitudes, mannequins are also celebrating the richness of diversity. Many stores no longer sidestep ethnic differences, characteristics, and attitudes, but rather they are now projecting images of inclusivity and diversity with multi-ethnic mannequins, body types, and features.

Moving deeper into the 21st century, amid the relentless march of technology, increased connectivity, and uncertainty brought on by a worldwide pandemic, consumers began pushing back against outmoded, idealized, and unhealthy representations of beauty and the female form. Heightened levels of social awareness, empathy, and understanding raised many questions and inspired a deep dive and introspection among retailers and consumers alike. Focus groups and social media platforms openly criticized retailers for mannequins that project unrealistic images of the female form. In a 2017 study published in the *Journal of Eating Disorders*, Eric Robinson and Paul Aveyard stated, "The average female mannequin body size was representative of a very underweight woman and 100% of female mannequins represented an underweight body size." The study concluded, "The body size of mannequins used to advertise female fashion is unrealistic and would be considered medically unhealthy in humans."[1]

In 2019, Nike garnered a great deal of attention with the introduction of plus-size mannequins in their stores, beginning in the London flagship and then rolling out to locations across the world. Although met with some controversy and even criticism from some quarters, Nike's goal was to recognize the diversity and inclusivity of sport while also displaying their plus-size product offerings. Other brands and mannequin makers soon followed suit.

GENDERLESS MANNEQUIN

Rob Smith's first job while still in college at Michigan State University was as a waiter in the "Miss J" food section of Jacobson's, Michigan's iconic specialty department store. Located in East Lansing, Jacobson's was a go-to place in the Midwest college town serving faculty and students alike as well as the town residents who affectionately referred to the local emporium as "Jakes." Little did Smith realize at the time that this was the beginning of an exciting retail career as he would go on to do groundbreaking work in the ever-changing retail industry.

Today, as the founder and CEO of the Phluid Project, Smith considers himself to be a futurist, activist, educator, retailer, entrepreneur, and community builder. Over the course of his retail career, he has proven to be just that and so much more. Smith credits his heritage as a third-generation Native American from the Ojibwa tribe for instilling in him what he considers his greatest passion, advancing humanity.

A true visionary, Smith's professional life has taken him on a journey not merely defined by entrepreneurship but rather laced with empathy and a deep sense of caring. In 2018, Smith founded the Phluid Project, the first gender-free retail store, as a way to honor the "Two Spirit" indigenous leaders of the past and present. "I created a place where I could leverage 30 years of fashion, leading multi-billion dollar brands from

Macy's, Levi's, Nike, and Victoria's Secret, coupled with decades of work fighting for human rights and social equality," said Smith. "I am a futurist who thrives working at the intersections of free enterprise and humanity. Several years ago, I began a journey to live a more honest, authentic, altruistic life." This epiphany led Smith to merge his professional career with his desire to do good; to build a company around a purpose.

At the height of his retail career, Smith found himself living in two different worlds. During the day, he lived, worked, and dressed the part of a corporate executive. At night he worked for nonprofit organizations raising money. Searching for a better way, and perhaps a more balanced way, Smith quit his job and began traveling around the world. During his multicultural journey, the concept of the Phluid Project came to him. The idea was built upon the notion that fluid is having the freedom to not be stuck in just one space. He thought about gender fluidity, gender identity, and being one's true authentic self. He explained, "The reason I decided to spell Phluid with PH is because PH represents balance."

The creation of the Phluid Project opened Smith up to new vistas and a new way of looking at the world. "By creating The Phluid Project, I've immersed myself in an adventure of creating and exploring unchartered territories," said Smith. "I've chosen to unlearn in order to relearn. I went off into this wilderness with curiosity, parked both judgment and ego, and rooted myself in honest connection, social justice, and a deep interest in the desires of our youth." It was Smith's vision and commitment that created the Phluid Project, a gender-free fashion brand grounded in activism and community. "Through The Phluid Project, I've had the great fortune of getting to know humans of every generation, gender, race, religion, and socioeconomic status; better understanding the reality of the limiting labels society prescribes to us," said Smith. "Creating the space between the binaries allows each of us the curiosity and freedom to truly be our authentic selves."

The first phase of Smith's vision was a 3,000-square-foot space in the NoHo section of New York City. The Phluid Project was reportedly the first gender-neutral retail space in the world, making a significant statement with its large welcoming windows, a soothing white color palette, a coffee bar, and a relaxing community area offering a convivial environment for gender-fluid consumers. "People felt comfortable in the store," said Smith. "We created a space where people felt warm and without concern of judgement. Some had a hard time understanding the dresses and make-up, so we eased the journey into the store with more conservative presentations. As the customer continued to move through the space, we engaged them with more progressive and even outrageous concepts." Smith created a space where people of all backgrounds felt safe and even at home.

While the pandemic wreaked havoc across the retail spectrum, the Phluid Project was already in the process of closing its Manhattan-based retail store as it transitioned to an e-commerce platform. Smith considered the physical retail space as a starting point for a larger online business. And while Smith left the physical store behind, the Phluid Project gained a significant presence with 7,000 doors across the country from Sam's Club to Nordstrom.

As the concept continues to evolve in an ever-changing world, Smith sees the Phluid Project as a memorable and recognizable brand, fueled and inspired by the outlook and philosophy of younger generations. "We are a label with brand extension through licensing, wholesale, pop-up shops, partnerships, and collaborations," said Smith. "We are also an education and training vehicle, helping to facilitate learning about the new generation and the non-binary mindset through Gender Expansive Training."

When Smith first opened the Phluid Project, he searched for the appropriate mannequin, not merely to display merchandise but also to project a lifestyle and positive vibe for the community he was serving. He realized they wanted to dress and express themselves in a way that heightens self-empowerment and demand for equality. "We settled on an existing mannequin and modified it by removing any element that bore an indication of gender," said Smith. "The store and the mannequin, with modifications, were featured on the cover of WWD."

As Smith extended the brand beyond the confines of a single store in the NoHo section of Manhattan, to 7,000 doors across the retail spectrum, he felt it was time to develop the industry's first-ever genderless mannequin.

Figure 2.2 Non-Gender Conforming Mannequins designed by Rob Smith of The Phluid Project. Courtesy Fusion Mannequins.

Smith partnered with Fusion Mannequins, a large maker of custom-designed mannequins, for the project. The process began with a series of focus groups to discuss body shape, form, the line of the hip, and hand size. Next, Smith directed a photo shoot to capture the nuances of the mannequin they wanted to create. After a vision for the new mannequin emerged, Smith and the team worked with a digital designer to develop a three-dimensional reality based on photo imagery and feedback from the focus groups. From that point, the designer began to digitally construct the new mannequin by trimming or adding to the body where appropriate to a place that would show clothes without screaming gender. There was no visible crotch or breasts. Four body types were developed; body-positive, trans fem, trans masculine, and gender neutral.

From Smith's perspective, mannequins were more extreme. "Men's were broad with broad shoulders and chest. Females had large breasts and very small waist. Who looks like that?" He wanted to design with inclusion and consideration for all different body types, round or square. Through all four of the body types developed, Smith expresses concern for the emotional well-being of young people, regardless of their body type or background. The body-positive mannequin moves beyond unrealistic female shapes and presents a body that is inclusive for all. He also wanted to move beyond aggressive male stances and more passive female stances or poses.

Equally important to Smith were the mannerisms and attitudes of the mannequins. In addition to the appropriate form, they had to exhibit a positive attitude and an air of confidence and pride. The merchant in Smith also wanted a head that could wear sunglasses and was accessories friendly. In addition to multiple sales, this would also help to project an attitude, a lifestyle, and a point of view in a positive and uplifting way.

"Half of Generation Z doesn't identify as heterosexual," said Smith. "Rather, they are looking at binary constraints and saying this doesn't make sense. This is not a trend, but a movement. Clothing reflects who we are. We want to allow everyone to be their authentic self."

The entrepreneur, futurist, and activist in Smith considers it to be his greatest honor to be a part of this moment in history. "I recognize my privilege to be a part of this cultural zeitgeist as we all learn to free ourselves of the past and move toward the future . . . free to be."

Reference

1. Eric Robinson and Paul Aveyard, "Emaciated Mannequins: A Study of Mannequin Body Size in High Street Fashion Stores," *Journal of Eating Disorders* (May 2017).

CHAPTER 3
IN THE BEGINNING: 1900–1930

The early promise and excitement of the blossoming 20th century marked the beginning of the mannequin as we know it, and its role as a bookmark of contemporary culture and modern society. The advent of the Industrial Revolution brought about the birth of the department store, an institution that we seem to take for granted; it hasn't always been here. Major cities from the east coast of the United States to the boulevards and avenues of Paris and London were the spawning grounds for grand commercial buildings that housed everything from pots and pans to glamorous evening gowns. The factories of industrialized countries were churning out goods so rapidly that there was soon a glut of merchandise available to the general public. Factories in America's industrial north became self-feeding machines. The factories produced goods, factory workers had jobs and made money and bought goods, and so factories produced even more goods. Soon, people wanted more and more. They wanted more today than yesterday and more tomorrow than today. Emily Fogg Meade wrote, "A magnitude of goods were produced to satisfy the needs that no one knew they had. Consumers wanted berry spoons, mustard spoons, sugar spoons, and soup spoons in ever-increasing variety."[1]

Ready-to-wear was the order of the day as sewing machines buzzed with activity across the world, producing the latest styles and fashions. In New York, a small but vital area of Manhattan was dubbed "Ladies Mile," a section that ran from Twenty Third Street to the north, Fourteenth Street to the south, and Broadway and Eight Avenue to the east and west. Appropriately named, the streets of this section were lined with the first department stores carrying all of the new fashions of the day. Two architectural innovations at the time became the catalyst for a new retail and a new profession. Cast-iron architecture allowed for great expanses, and readily available plate glass allowed for the transparent closing or covering of those expanses. And so, the show window came into being, and with it a new profession, display (later to be called visual merchandising). This new craft became an art and a science as clever retailers found new ways to show and present their wares. The next important component of retail's newfound magic was the easy availability of electricity. When all of these ingredients were stirred together the result was retail theater. Sixth Avenue in New York's Ladies Mile became the epicenter of retail showmanship. A walk down this retail thoroughfare and bustling new shopping district was like a walk through a glittering crystal palace as the newfound show windows graced every single storefront; there was glass everywhere.

And if that wasn't enough, great architectural edifices from the Siegel and Cooper Building with its Beaux-Arts facade, to the Hugh O'Neill Building with its two shining gold cupolas, framed the sparkling show windows, thereby increasing the drama, pizazz, and theater that spilled onto the street. Customers came from far and wide, many arriving in horse-drawn carriages, to experience the theatrics and glamor of the windows, and the wonders of the stores.

As the Industrial Revolution expanded and goods became more plentiful and readily available, stores took on greater importance. Dress forms, once exclusively the domain of tailors and dressmakers, became important tools used by shopkeepers to show their goods and create interest and excitement in their new storefronts. The late Victorian dress forms were highly idealized versions of the female body. These early forms, often made of wood or solid wax, were big busted with surprisingly thin waistlines known as "wasp waists."

The ever-changing calendar coupled with new technologies and new fashions brought the Western world to a new place and a new sensibility. The easing of the 19th century into the 20th century saw the ending of the Victorian period and the birth of modernism. The values and moralities of the day started to change. While accepted Victorian mores demanded a code of modesty for women, the new fashions of the young century rejected the censorship of the female form. Dressmaker forms and mannequins changed with the changing fashions and styles. This newfound sensibility allowed shopkeepers to display their wares in a more attractive and compelling way while allowing customers a better rendition of the garments they wanted to buy. Prior to the turn of the twentieth century, full-bodied mannequins were only seen in obscure dime museums, places popularized for their display of oddities and curiosities, presentations of rare animals and historical figures such as kings, queens, and infamous criminals. Toward the later part of the 19th century, more sophisticated mannequins were seen grouped together in anthropological exhibitions at the world fairs in Philadelphia and Chicago.[2] In sharp contrast, retail stores at the time typically featured headless dress forms without arms or feet. After 1912, as the large retailers continued to roll out ready-to-wear garments, complete full-bodied mannequins became increasingly popular. As dressmaker forms and the early mannequins became more representative of the female form, they were more in demand by both shopkeepers and customers alike. The mannequin was well on its way to becoming a staple tool of retailers and their display departments in both large department stores and small neighborhood shops. From that point in time, mannequins became an iconic component of the retail industry.

Made of wax, the mannequins in the early years of the 20th century were primitive at best. Mostly female, they had curious, unseemly, and unnatural doll-like features. Going forward, photography had a great impact on the development of the modern mannequin. With the advent and subsequent rise in the use of photography, which influenced all forms of representative image production, retailers wanted more realism, with authentic-looking hair, adjustable limbs, natural facial features, and animated attitudes.[3] Fashion photography at the turn of the century, through composition and the creative manipulation and use of light, emulated the great portrait paintings of the masters. A quiet and austere pose, coupled with a self-absorbed attitude and the luxurious elegance of the highlighted garments, suggested a fine but palpable line between the image and the viewer. The next phase of mannequin design was clearly challenged by the new wave of photographic expression.[4]

Prior to the crowning of Louis XIV in 1643, France's longest-reigning monarch, the seat of high fashion wasn't in Paris, but rather in Madrid. As Spain flexed its muscle and dominance, particularly in the New World, it also spread its fashion sensibilities throughout the old world, most notably Europe. France at the time was merely an importer of fashion and style, mostly from Spain, Venice, and Milan. During his 72 years on the throne, Louis XIV changed everything. Under his rule, France became the world's leading style influencer in everything from furniture and textiles to apparel and jewelry. This marked the beginning of France's longstanding position as the world's foremost leader in fashion and style.

The prominence of French fashion was further bolstered mid-way through the reign of Louis XIV with the creation of the fashion press in the early 1670s. This helped to revolutionize the fashion industry by promoting French fashion to a broad international market outside of France, and by promoting new concepts such as the fashion season and changing styles.[5]

As the 17th century progressed, the fashion industry in France grew exponentially in international prominence. Fashion became so vital to the French economy and Western culture that it prompted the Royal Minister of Finances, Jean-Baptiste Colbert to say, "Fashion is to France what the gold mines of Peru are to Spain."[6] The French preeminence in haute couture continued well into the late 19th and mid-20th centuries with the establishment of the renowned couturier ateliers, from the house of Jacques Doucet and Jeanne Paquin in the late 1800s, to Paul Poiret and Madeleine Vionnet in the early 1900s, and later the house of Elsa Schiaparelli and Chanel.

With the preeminence of French fashion design, it was inevitable that two of the first mannequin companies at the turn of the century were based in Paris. Pierre Imans and Siégel (still in existence today under the name of Siégel and Stockman) were the foremost mannequin companies serving the retail industry in the early years of the 20th century.

As retail continued to evolve, particularly with the growth of the department store in the first two decades of the young century, a new class of mannequins was in great demand. Stores wanted the latest creations from Pierre Imans and Siégel. The two Parisienne firms were primarily working with wax due to its malleability and its capacity to replicate the feel and look of human skin. Imans in particular perfected sophisticated techniques, making his mannequins as life-like as possible. He considered himself not as a wax modeler but as a "sculptor and ceroplastician" (statuaire céroplasticien), purging the very word "mannequin" from his promotional vocabulary and describing his figures simply as "Les Cires de Pierre Imans" ("The waxes of Pierre Imans").[7]

Imans began producing wax mannequins in 1896. His new creations were a great departure from the common nondescript forms and dolls that were seen in store windows up until then. Imans' waxen figures were an art form. In fact, when considering the work of Imans, there is a fine line between high art and commercialism. In 2018, one of his historic mannequin busts travelled to New York, on loan to the Metropolitan Museum of Art from the Fashion Museum Bath, in England. The catalogue description of the form read as follows:

The mannequin bust by French mannequin manufacturer Pierre Imans dates to around 1910-1920 and is made of painted wax. Unlike the generic, faceless fashion dolls that decorated shop windows across Europe at this time, Imans produced unconventional, naturalistic mannequins in wax complete with face paint, resin eyes, eyelashes, and wigs of human hair. Each figure had her own personality and Imans gave them all names such as Elaine, Roberta, and Nadine. We wonder who this lovely lady is!

In Chicago, Marshall Field wouldn't permit the use of wax mannequins in his show windows due to an obvious problem, they melted in the heat of the sun. He wasn't going to allow Marshall Field & Co. to suffer the same indignity experienced by some of the less than elegant show window displays that he had encountered. As legend has it, while visiting New York, Field came across a window with a mannequin whose head had ignominiously slumped downward to its bosom because the heat of the sun melted its neck.[8]

A major leap forward occurred in the 1920s when Imans developed a new material called "carnasine." A plaster-based composite, the new medium was significantly lighter in weight than his earlier wax creations, and it was heat resistant, so it did not melt in the heat of the window. Additionally, it was easier to work with so it speeded up the manufacturing process allowing for mass production.

The artist's mannequin has been used by painters and sculptors since the Renaissance to accurately examine principles of perspective, foreshortening, light, shadowing, and the draping of fabric and articles of clothing on the human figure. In 2014, the Fitzwilliam Museum in Cambridge, England staged an exhibition titled "Silent Partners: Artists and Mannequin from Function to Fetish." In its catalogue, the University of Cambridge reported:

> As the demand for the artist's lay figure fell away at the beginning of the 20th century, it was replaced in the creative imagination by the shop-window dummy. Trade catalogues by leading French mannequin manufacturers and vintage wax display mannequins show how, in less than a generation these figures evolved from a cumbersome approximation of the human form to become sleek, abstract, and self-styled "artistic creations."

FROM EXTRAVAGANCE TO DISCRETION

As the 20th century moved into its second decade, political upheaval was running rampant across the world. It was a time of hope and a time of despair. A century of peace succumbed to worldwide war, and extravagance yielded to discretion. The ravages of the Great War spawned movements in art and literature. Wassily Kandinsky, Franz Marc, and the other German Expressionists portrayed the human condition. John McCrae wrote eloquently of the ravages of the great war, "In Flanders fields the poppies blow between the crosses, row on row . . ."

Undeterred, however, by global theater and international events, commercialism persevered in the large cities across the Western world, especially in the United States as it flourished and continued to grow.

As the 1910s began, a theatrical approach to retailing was beginning to evolve. Goods were imbued with associative qualities, equating them to people, places, and events. The show window was fast becoming an important tool in the retailer's repertoire. "Displaymen" used fantasy and theater to link merchandise to perceived and desired lifestyles. The great and elaborate show windows, most notably in Chicago and New York, would transport viewers to another place, another time, another point of view. Macy's 1914 spring window extravaganza allowed customers to stroll down a promenade on the French Riviera. Mannequins were the stars of the intricate window drama as they were staged in an opulent ballroom and cloaked in luxurious evening gowns.

In Chicago, Arthur Fraser, of the world-renowned Marshall Field's department store, became the most prominent display director of the decade. Totally theatrical in his approach, he added drama, artistry, and excitement to the retail stage. An example of his theatrical genius was his presentation of a merchandise collection inspired by Japanese culture and tradition. In this 1913 presentation, Fraser enhanced his windows with large Japanese landscapes to highlight the thematic scene. *The Merchants Record and Show Window* wrote, "The soft, hazy tones and vague lines, with the faint, snow-capped Fujiyama in the distance, gave wonderful perspective to the whole setting."[9]

Marshall Field's habitually covered its show windows on Sundays, inadvertently escalating the anticipation. Thousands lined up for the unveiling of Fraser's weekly creations. As Field's entered the fall selling season of 1916, gold curtains were installed on the windows to properly introduce the latest production.[10]

William Leach noted in *Land of Desire* that the show window had become so important by 1910 that retailers vied with one another for valuable window exposure, both above and below ground. Retailers negotiated with local municipal authorities for the rights to below-ground subway station windows, invaluable marketing tools directed toward the captive daily commuter. From Filene's subway windows on Washington Street in Boston to Philadelphia's Market Street (where Wanamakers, Snellenberg's, Lit's, and Strawbridge & Clothier all enjoyed prime station exposure), retailers were taking advantage of this new marketing venue. In Chicago, Field's and Carson Pirie Scott built underground windows. The trend also caught on in New York's new Interborough Rapid Transit (IRT) subway stops.

Retailers came to appreciate the inherent value in the "art of display" and the power of the show window. Independent manufacturers began providing them with equipment and supplies—pedestals, fabrics, decorative backgrounds, and the increasingly popular mannequin. In 1911, the first abstract mannequin was presented at the *Salon d'Automne*. Inspired by the early stages of cubism, it was covered with shards of broken mirror.

The "Belle Epoque" was over. A new ethic defined the face of Western society. Europe was at war and America eventually joined the fray. As women became integral parts of the war effort, constricting wardrobes and bruising whalebones gave way to more utilitarian dress, and the idea of women as independent workers, voters, thinkers, and executives, began to take hold.

In large numbers, European and American women were entering a workforce previously dominated by men. The practical attire of the new woman had a tremendous effect on fashion. In Helen Brockman's *The Theory of Fashion Design*, she quotes from a 1918 issue of Vogue: "Now that women work, working clothes have acquired a new social status and chic." Soon after the war, Coco Chanel popularized the Garçon style, with sweaters, jersey dresses, and high-fashion pants for women.

New trends in fashion and the growing acceptance of "ready-to-wear" created incredible popularity for the complete mannequin, which now graced the show windows of most major retailers in America. Through whims of fancy and artistic inspiration, these almost animate forms focused the viewer's eyes on individual items, sparking interest, desire, and enthusiasm. With elegance, attitude, and emotion, mannequins soon became the star performers on retail's great stage.

SELL THEM THEIR DREAMS

The Great War was over and young men returned home in droves from the battlefields of France. And while politics, reparations, and demilitarization dominated the headlines, another powerful army of energized and emboldened major American corporations mobilized and began a hard march across the landscape. The economy started to churn like the gears of a powerful engine in a new era of big business. Mergers, conglomerations, and large capital investments were the order of the day. With the scarcities of a wartime economy relegated to a distant memory, a new age of desire and demand started to take hold. This new and pervasive ethos was driven by the insatiable demand of big business. A relentless call for increased production led to an abundance of merchandise which in turn led to the new art form of enticement. People, particularly in the northern industrial states, had jobs and as such, had money. Media moguls, in concert with the great merchants of the day, recognized the vast opportunities in the offing. All aspects of the media, from popular magazines to motion pictures and radio drove a new desire to emulate and imitate those who led lives that the masses could only dream of. A popular advertisement of the day read, "Rudolph Valentino wears an Arrow collar – so should you."[11]

It didn't take long before the great merchants of the day seized the opportunity to capitalize on the dreams and aspirations of the multitudes glamouring to live vicariously through their product offerings. Helen Landon Cass, a popular radio personality, told a display convention in 1923: "Sell them their dreams. Sell them what they longed for and hoped for. Sell them this hope and you won't have to worry about selling the goods."[12]

The strategic seduction of the masses was fueled by the four A's: advertising, art, architecture, and air conditioning. In 1925, Secretary of Commerce Herbert Hoover said, "The Midas of advertising has given artists freedom and independence." Sherwood Anderson, John P. Marquand, and F. Scott Fitzgerald were writing ad copy. The paintings of Georgia O'Keeffe were seen in the windows at B. Altman's and Marshall Field's; the murals of Boardman Robinson graced the walls of Kaufmann's. The promise of advertising and the enhancement of fine art were bolstered by a commitment to customer comfort. Retailers now prolonged the selling season into the dog days of summer thanks to the magic of air conditioning. Additionally, imposing retail edifices were being constructed in major urban downtown centers. These elaborate architectural statements represented power, fashion, and aspirational lifestyles.

As demand multiplied exponentially, it became clear that bigger was better, and more, better still. As real estate increased in value, store construction was not only linear but vertical as well. Urban centers began to feature new retail skylines. In 1926, Gimbels unveiled a 12-story megastore on Philadelphia's Market Street. The following year, L. Hudson's opened a 21-story behemoth in Detroit. But Macy's ruled supreme. With an influx of investment capital, Macy's increased its Herald Square store to a staggering 1.5 million square feet.

The new Golden Era of Enticement continued to flourish as the department store flexed its newfound muscle. Fine art and the art of display developed an iron-clad bond. Increasingly, displaymen turned to the allure of fine art as a form of enticement, and artists turned to retail venues as a form of inspiration. It was the artist Fernand Léger who equated the art of window display to his own search for a new approach to realism: "Mundane objects could be shown with a gravity and weight previously denied them."[13]

There was a new commingling of fashion and art as images of European royalty with nipped and tucked bodices and intricate lacings became a memory of a bygone era. The stylized Art Deco illustrations of Erté were emblazoned on the covers of all the influential fashion magazines from *Harper's Bazaar* to *Vogue*. With the war's end, many of the artists, writers, musicians, and philosophers gathered in Paris, spawning the beginnings of the Bauhaus and Art Deco. The world was turning on its axis. Women were working and voting. Mannequins, no longer purely utilitarian, evolved beyond realism to become the stylized embodiment of a new femininity. In August 1925, *Vogue* proclaimed, "A new art form has been born, evoking the complex personality of the modern, well-dressed woman." Perhaps inspired by Modigliani as well as the Art Deco movement, there was an elongation of gesture and figure alike, and the hint of a modern attitude.

In 1928, Frederick Kiesler of Saks Fifth Avenue created what he proclaimed to be America's "First representative exposition of modern show windows." The integration of modernism into the retail venue brought with it a sense of simplicity, allowing the viewer to focus on the goods. Kiesler spoke of his "spotlighted" windows: "Accent one chair – one white fur. One sees only a chair – a white fur collar."[14]

With show windows now recognized as an art form, lighting became paramount. New techniques were explored. Herpolsheimer in Grand Rapids, Michigan, installed spotlights into its storefront architecture. During a brief stint as Macy's display director, Raymond Loewy used light in a more profound manner. "I left the window in semi-darkness," he said in *The American Show Window*. "The only illumination came from three powerful spotlights focused on the figure. It was dramatic, simple, and potent. It sang."[15]

With its simplicity of form, modernism forever altered the course of display. In the *Journal of The American Institute of Architects* in 1927, Lee Simonson, a stage designer and consultant to Macy's, elaborated on a new approach to retail design: "We must break up vistas, isolate objects, use every constructional means to focus vision instead of dissipating it."[16]

References

1. William Leach, *Land of Desire* (Vintage Books, 1993).
2. Ira Jacknis, *Franz Boas and Exhibits* (Harvard University Press, Peabody Museum of Archeology and Ethnology. Video: All the World Is Here: Anthropology on Display at the 1893 Chicago World's Fair, December 6, 2017).
3. Leach, *Land of Desire.*
4. Sara K. Schneider, *Vital Mummies / Performance Design for the Show-Window Mannequin* (Yale University Press, 1995).
5. Amanda Vickery, "18th-century Paris: the capital of luxury," thegaurdian.com/artanddesign (July 2011).
6. Vickery, "18th-century Paris."
7. Jane Munro, *Silent Partners* (Yale University Press, 2014).
8. Marlise Schoeny, *The Art of Selling: A History of Visual Merchandising, Historic Costume and Textiles Collection* (The Ohio State University, 1999).
9. Leach, *Land of Desire.*
10. Leach, *Land of Desire.*
11. "Sell Them Their Dreams," *Visual Merchandising and Store Design Magazine*, May 3, 2001.
12. "Sell Them Their Dreams."
13. "Sell Them Their Dreams."
14. Leach, *Land of Desire.*
15. Leach, *Land of Desire.*
16. Leach, *Land of Desire.*

CHAPTER 4
FASHION, ART, AND HOLLYWOOD: 1930–1940

As the Roaring Twenties were coming to a close, the stock market crashed, and America fell into a deep decade-long economic crisis. The ravaging effects of the Great Depression were felt all over the world. As people struggled on a daily basis just to get by, they turned to the movies as a form of escapism from the challenges of everyday life.

Outside, people were consumed with breadlines and bankruptcies. Once inside the darkened movie houses, they were exposed to wealth and glamour. Hollywood had a tremendous influence on fashion and style. And while the depression continued to shatter hopes and dreams, young men and women were captivated by the lifestyles and personalities that appeared on movie screens across the country. People lived vicariously through the images they saw in the movies. They aspired to the looks and style of Fred Astaire, Betty Grable, Greta Garbo, and Jean Harlow. In sharp contrast to the harsh realities of the Depression, the 1930s was the most elegant period in Hollywood's history. And retail took its cues from the movies.

ELEGANCE AND ESCAPISM

In 1935, Cora Scovil, a renowned American mannequin sculptor and window-dresser, captured the attitude of Hollywood's elite in a series of mannequins bearing the likenesses of Joan Crawford, Greta Garbo, and Joan Bennett. At the time, most high-end New York dress shops and department stores favored the use of headless forms in their windows. The concern among most of the chic Fifth Avenue retailers was that detailed heads would become the star of the window presentation, thereby serving as a distraction from the merchandise on the mannequins. Scovil, a talented young designer, seeing the value in emulating the faces of well-known celebrities, developed a lighter, more malleable plaster composition to create the likeness of the most recognizable Hollywood heartthrobs. Bonwit Teller, a high-end New York store, ordered several of Scovil's creations, thus beginning the trend away from headless forms to the new and exciting movie star mannequins.

Two years later, Lester Gaba, another American mannequin designer, produced a series of papier-mâché mannequins modeled after Garbo, Marlene Dietrich, and Carole Lombard. Through the influence of Scovil and Gaba, mannequins assumed a new posture in American retail, as these mannequin "actors" became the stars of the show window and retail stages across the country.

Fashion has always been a reflection of the times, and mannequins have always been a reflection of fashion. The aesthetic sensibilities of the times were driven by Art Deco, a dynamic movement that dominated the design world during the period of time between

World War I and World War II. After World War I, artists, writers, philosophers, and designers all congregated in Paris. The movement started to develop as Paris ventured to rebound after the ravages of war. This group of intellectuals and creatives provided the seed for a design movement that influenced art, architecture, fashion, jewelry, automobiles, trains, ocean liners, textiles, and industrial design.

This important period of design began to gather momentum after the *Exposition Internationale des Arts Decoratifs Industriels et Modernes*, held in Paris in 1925. The term Art Deco is derived from the exposition. The dominant geometries of Art Deco were influenced by Cubism, the machine age, and the distinctive design sensibilities of ancient Egyptian and Aztec art. Its bright colors were extracts from the Fauves and the *Ballets Russes*. From this conglomeration of influences came Art Deco's distinctive smooth lines, geometric machine-like forms, streamlined profiles, and bright colors.

The fashion world was also directly influenced by Art Deco. Russian illustrator and designer Romain de Tirtoff, better known as Erté (1892–1990), had a major impact on fashion with his highly stylized Art Deco fashion illustrations. In addition to his illustrations, Erté designed sets and costumes for the Paris Opera, the *Folies Bergère* in Paris, the *Ziegfeld Follies* on Broadway, and many silent films. His distinctive illustrations of highly fashionable women were featured on magazine covers, with more than 200 for *Harper's Bazaar* alone. In his long and distinguished career, Erté made Art Deco costumes famous around the world.[1]

In the 1930s Jeanne Lanvin created evening gowns that reflected the very essence of the Art Deco movement. Bold geometries and long fluid shapes were the hallmarks of her designs.[2]

Jewelry designers of the period also gravitated to the geometries of Art Deco. In 1930, the Parisian jeweler Raymond Templier (1891–1968), commented in the *Goldsmiths' Journal*, "As I walk in the streets I see ideas for jewelry everywhere, the wheels, the cars, the machinery of today." His bold, abstract designs evoked the dynamism of modern urban culture, earning him the reputation of "architect of the jewel."[3]

"Art has influenced fashion in many ways," said renowned millinery and fashion designer, Marjorie Lee Woo.

> If you think about each fashion season, there is a period of art that has played a significant role in its inception and development. Specific decades have been influenced by particular periods of art, thereby influencing what is seen in stores. Art Deco designs remain one of my favorite periods because of the architectural references; the geometries, lines, and shapes. I'm also drawn to the colors; black, gold, silver, blue, and yellow. I love the drapes of fabric, the elegance, and the sensual fluidity of Art Deco fashion as the garments skim the body.

Fashion visionaries in the late twenties and thirties inspired and motivated the retail world. One fashion merchandiser said, "There is not a commodity today that escapes fashion; there is fashion in furniture, cars, washing machines, and tires." Design elements such as color, line, and form assumed an integral role in the manufacture of consumer goods. A new contour characterized industrial design, defined by the word "streamline." This compelling aerodynamic profile influenced the design of everything from locomotives to lipstick. On the all-important railroads of the day, the new diesel-electric locomotive was called, simply, a streamliner. Streamline sensibilities were married to the nuances of Art Deco, inscribing a distinctive line upon store interiors and across the face of the ever-evolving mannequin.[4]

As Art Deco expanded into the ateliers of the world's most influential fashion designers, retailers took note. Soon, mannequins were being designed with clear references to this important period of art and architecture. In 1925, a hand-painted plaster mannequin head with elongated features and blue-tinted skin referenced the works of artists Amedeo Modigliani (1884–1920) and Henri Matisse (1869–1954). This mannequin was a clear representation of a new generation of avant-garde mannequins displayed at the 1925 Paris Exhibition and used to showcase high-end fashion in exclusive Parisienne boutiques.[5]

In 1931, the famed mannequin designer Pierre Imans modeled a mannequin after French jazz legend Josephine Baker. Imans' creation was the epitome of Art Deco design with its elongated hands and facial features, in addition to the subtle bend of the neck. The mannequin's head was inspired by the imagery of an Erté illustration titled "Queen of Sheba."

In 1926 the *Exposition des Arts Decoratifs* traveled to the United States for a three-city tour of New York, Chicago, and Boston. As America looked to Europe for fashion and creative inspiration, the American tour and the original Parisienne Exhibition came at the perfect time to energize the North American fashion industry and to encourage a new direction in mannequin design. In addition to Imans, Siégel & Stockman made a significant leap forward toward the development of the modern mannequin. When Victor-Napoleon Siégel, a Canadian entrepreneur and mannequin maker combined forces with Fred Stockman, it marked a critical moment in the business and design of mannequins. Together, they turned heads at the Parisienne Exhibition when they presented a highly stylized mannequin collection the likes of which had never been seen before. Elongated features and sculpted hair raised the utilitarian doll-like mannequins of the past into sculpture-like performers demanding the attention of all who gazed upon them. And to make the Siégel & Stockman statement more stunning and compelling, the mannequins were proudly wearing and presenting the fashions of the leading designers of the day in Paris, from Chanel to Vionnet. Siégel said,

> The old mannequin, too realistic to respond to the abstract form assumed the architecture and decoration, could no longer fit into the window display with its effective and sober luxury as it is now conceived. This basic conviction prompted me to make an appeal to a new form of expression in order to bring about a timely rejuvenation and modernization.[6]

By 1927 Siégel & Stockman had 67 factories in major cities across the world including New York, Stockholm, Amsterdam, and Sydney. With the vision and determination of

Imans, and Siégel & Stockman, the mannequin was quickly becoming a vital component of retail strategies across the globe.

The availability of electricity was also an important factor in the dramatics of window art, and the enhancement of mannequins. Lighting became the icing on the cake, adding magic to the static theater of display. Under the guidance of display director Irving Eldredge, Macy's rewired its show windows, installed adjustable spotlights, and initiated the use of multi-colored filters. For the first time, display windows and their associated mannequins not only highlighted specific merchandise but also promoted and enhanced the store's image. Environmental branding was born, and the spotlighted mannequin led the way.[7]

As retail moved deeper into the 1930s, it became the showplace for new ideas, new concepts, and new products. The store environment became the selling stage and theater for the offerings of the day. Following the examples of Woodward & Lathrop, and Marshall Field's, merchants began to accessorize goods and to group kindred merchandise together to facilitate ease of shopping and encourage multiple sales. Mannequins were accessorized to show complete outfits. As a precursor to this practice, Field's Clara Wilson positioned the first "spotlighted" color-accessorized mannequins throughout the store's fashion departments. She later remarked, "Spotlighting made it possible to create a dramatic ensemble of goods." As the decade progressed, the drama and theater associated with elaborate show windows were imitated on the selling floors.

SURREALISM

Mannequin design, as well as store and display design, have all been significantly influenced by movements in art, most notably Art Deco, Cubism, and Surrealism. Fashion magazines, in underscoring the intrinsic relationship between art and fashion, have long heralded new genres in art. Through their pages and the use of illustration and photography, they have been conduits for the dissemination of new aesthetic directions and sensibilities.[8]

The 1925 *Exposition des Arts Décoratifs* ushered in a dramatic new approach to the presentation of merchandise. Prior to the Exposition (which originated in Paris, but then traveled in subsequent years to New York, Chicago, and Boston), the overarching technique among retailers and their displaymen was to clutter the window with everything they had to offer. Art was scarcely a consideration in the aesthetic approach to window design. The Exposition in Paris changed everything. *Vogue* announced, after viewing the artistically rendered mannequins exhibited by Siégel & Stockman, "the art of the mannequin, which did not previously exist, has now been perfected."[9] As the mannequin evolved, moving from a mere utilitarian tool to an artistically rendered, three-dimensional reflection of the times, many of the more avant-garde artists of the day became enamored with this new medium, and then further with the show window.

Mannequins have been used by painters and sculptors as study tools for generations. However in the 1930s, in addition to being vital components in the repertoire of window trimmers across the retail world, they once again were being used by artists. The allure for artists in the 1930s was not as an aid in studying perspective and draping but rather as subjects and components of their works, be it sculpture, painting, or photography. The surrealist movement led by such artistic icons as André Breton, Marcel Duchamp, Paul Éluard, Man Ray, Max Ernst, and Salvador Dalí, eagerly adopted the mannequin as a form of symbolism and as an object to project avant-garde images of an otherworldly and unusual state of mind. Often dealing with themes of polarity, the surrealists gravitated toward the mannequin as a symbol of the dichotomy between the animate and inanimate, or the real and the unreal.

The surrealist movement came into full blossom in January of 1938 with the somewhat scandalous *Exposition Internationale du Surrealism* held at the Galérie Beaux-Arts in Paris. Divided into three distinct sections, one of the features of the exhibition consisted of redesigned and reimagined mannequins. In March of 1995, the Ubu Gallery in New York paid homage to the surrealist movement in a retrospective titled *Exposition Internationale du Surrealisme, Galerie Beaux-Arts, Paris, 1938, 'An Homage'.*

The importance of the 1938 exposition cannot be underestimated. It was a groundbreaking surrealist exhibition celebrating avant-garde art in Europe just before the devastation of World War II. It is presumed to be among the first events that centered around installation art. Salvador Dali set the mood of the exposition with a composition in the lobby titled *Taxi Pluvieux* (Rainy Taxi). Typical of his style, the famed surrealist positioned two mannequins in an aging automobile that was enveloped in vines of ivy. The mannequins were covered with crawling snails and soaked in dripping rain falling from the ceiling above.[10]

Another composition was titled, *Plus belles rues de Paris* (The most beautiful streets of Paris). It featured a series of sixteen surrealist mannequins rented from a Parisienne manufacturer. The mannequins were arranged to project subject matter most closely associated with Surrealism: lust, unconscious desire, and the breaking of taboos.[11]

Art continued its profound influence on display. In 1942, André Breton published his third surrealist manifesto. Seeking inspiration, display artists turned to both cultural and current events. In 1945, a Saks Fifth Avenue window featured a mannequin lying on a psychiatrist's couch while a "dream-dress" appeared through a transparent wall. Thought-provoking images abounded in show windows across the country. In 1948, a young Gene Moore used surrealism as a selling tool in Bonwit Teller's window: a grid of boxes, each displaying a fashionable hat. The center grid featured an elegantly dressed mannequin sporting two heads. Moore reflected, "I wanted to show a woman who loved hats so much she grew an extra head to wear them."[12]

Man Ray, another leading contributor to the surrealist movement, worked with mannequins as subjects of intrigue. Growing up in New York in the early part of the 20th century, Ray had a natural exposure to mannequins through his father who worked in the garment industry as a tailor, and his mother as a seamstress.[13]

Born Emmanuel Radnitzky in 1890 to Russian émigrés, Ray rebelled against the family's wishes and desires for his future. Hoping their eldest son would pursue a career in architecture, he instead changed his name and decided to become an artist. While his chosen direction in life differed greatly from what his parents envisioned, their influence remained, as one of his earliest works, *Tapestry*, featured scraps of fabric from his father's tailor shop. Additionally, mannequins and dress forms frequently appeared in some of his future works.[14]

As the decade progressed, the lords of merchandising introduced shoppers to high art, co-joining two unlikely entities—fine art and mass culture. Museums and great retail emporiums began selling dreams in the guise of culture. And as merchants appealed to the consumer's lust for status, display artists turned to the influence of fine art. In 1939, that conspiracy went over the top as the temperamental Dali took New York's Fifth Avenue by storm. In 1939 he was hired by the upscale department store Bonwit Teller to create two window presentations, one symbolizing Day and the other Night. The Day window was titled Narcissus White. In true surrealist fashion, Dali placed an old-fashioned claw foot bathtub, lined with black Persian lamb skin, in the window. The bathtub was then filled with dark swamp-like water. Stepping into the tub was a mysterious mannequin scantily dressed in a revealing see-through negligée made of long green feathers. To complete the scene, several hands emerged from the murky water, each holding a mirror focused on the mannequin's anguished face, with a tear of blood running down her cheek and swarms of beetles crawling through her long blond hair.

Upon completion of the window, Dali, who once proclaimed, "I myself am surrealism," stepped back and looked with satisfaction at his creation. Unfortunately, passersby the next morning didn't share the enthusiasm of the Catalonian surrealist as they viewed the window. To put it mildly, they were horrified at what they saw. Some took their complaints to store management. When Bonwit Teller executives viewed Dali's window creation, they too were horrified. They immediately called on store personnel to change Salvador Dali's artistic creation. A few hours later Dali stepped out of a taxicab to see his masterpiece. And that's when the drama began. When seeing that Bonwit Teller dared to alter his installation, he angrily protested, wildly gesticulating and howling in both Spanish and French. The scene deteriorated further as an infuriated Dali ran into the store and headed directly to the door leading to the show window. Once inside the window, the enraged artist stomped about cursing those who dared question his vision. Then after attracting a large group of onlookers, he picked up the bathtub and tossed it through the window. People on the sidewalk scattered as the bathtub, water and all, hurtled through the window. The sound of a big crash punctuated the air as shards of shattered glass flew onto the city sidewalk like tiny missiles. As a large crowd gathered and people drew closer to see what the drama was about, store management called the police.

Dali paid a price for his theatrics, but he had the last laugh. While nobody was injured, the artist was arrested on a charge of malicious mischief and fined $500, the exact amount of his commission for creating the window. The charge was later changed to disorderly conduct, and a judge issued a suspended sentence, saying of Dali's actions, "These are some of the privileges that an artist with temperament seems to enjoy."[15]

When the dust settled Dali famously said, "If I ate all of Fifth Avenue, I would not have gotten as much publicity as I got now."

CYNTHIA: A MARKETING MARVEL

Some laughed, others thought him mad. Mad? Hardly. A great designer and a brilliant marketer? For sure. Lester Gaba, a notable mannequin designer of the 1930s had one true love; her name was Cynthia. Her skin wasn't soft, supple, or smooth; Cynthia was made of plaster. Cynthia was Lester's creation, a mannequin. Although not flesh and blood, she was stunning. Sitting elegantly in a striking and seductive pose, she caught the eye of all who looked her way. And wherever Lester went, Cynthia was by his side.

There are many different accounts of the Gaba story and the legend of his famous companion, Cynthia. The son of a shopkeeper in the Midwestern town of Hannibal, Missouri, young Gaba envisioned a life of excitement and glamour in a big city such as Chicago or New York. He was ultimately able to realize his dream through a unique talent he exhibited for soap carving. While thousands struggling through the challenges of the Great Depression turned to this fad and preoccupation as a form of escapism, Gaba excelled at this art form. As he developed his skill, he made his mark professionally with beautifully articulated miniature soap sculptures that he produced for companies such as Procter and Gamble.

While creating these delicate pieces of soap art, his fortunes changed dramatically when he met Mary Lewis at a cocktail party in Chicago. Lewis, the president of Best Department Stores, known to the shopping public as Best & Company, was drawn to the young sculptor after reading an article he published about the lack of style in the show windows of the day. Having seen his tiny sculptures, Lewis asked if he would design mannequins for Best and Company's show windows. Since his sculptural accomplishments were based on small soap carvings, Gaba was somewhat taken aback by the request. Lewis assured him that if he could achieve the quality in life-size mannequins that he had in his small soap carvings, they would be fantastic, and she would buy them for her company's windows. With encouragement from Lewis and a new challenge at hand, he set off for New York to design and produce Gaba Girls, a line of life-sized soap sculptures inspired by the likeness of well-known New York debutants, celebrities, and socialites. Next, Gaba transposed his visions carved in soap to a more durable plaster of Paris. Before long, the Gaba Girls were all the talk in New York and all the rage in the window trimming industry.

Gaba's brilliance as a marketing guru became evident with his next creation, Cynthia. Modeled after the likeness of the wife of a well-known American industrialist, she struck a self-assured pose, sitting with an elbow confidently positioned on one hip and a cigarette in her hand. She became the designer's constant companion. As Gaba rode down the avenue on the upper level of an open-air bus, Cynthia was in the seat beside him. Whenever he went to the opera he bought two box seats, and of course dear Cynthia was by his side. Dinner at the chicest restaurant or the hottest bar? He would always demand a table for two.

His genius wasn't merely her comely looks; rather that and the brilliant pose that allowed her to accompany him as he wined and dined, traveled, listened, and looked. Before long, Lester's Cynthia was in high demand. Whether it was the launch of a new clothing line or the latest fragrance, Cynthia was the spokesperson they all clamored for.

The 5'6" stunner soon became the darling of New York's fashion and social scene. And if that wasn't enough, the vivacious Cynthia hosted her very own radio show. As she made her way about town, the famed gossip columnists of the day began to write about her exploits as though she were a real flesh and blood woman of the world. Gaba infused life, spirit, and soul into his plaster muse. He molded raw plaster into a goddess, and this was nothing to laugh at.

So popular was she, that she adorned the cover of *Life Magazine*. As her popularity and charming allure began to grow, *Life* hired Alfred Eisenstaedt to do a photo essay of the rising starlet. The Eisenstaedt photo documentation that appeared in the December 13, 1937, issue of the highly respected periodical was accompanied by the following text:

> New York's café society includes actors and interior designers and gossip writers and bogus noblemen and reporters and torch singers and international bankers and Romanoffs and former waiters and tailors and milliners and retired pugilists and at least one laundryman. But not until very recently did it include anyone like Cynthia. A tall statuesque blond, Cynthia lives in a Gramercy Park apartment with Lester Gaba, a Manhattan artist whom she has to thank for everything in her life.
>
> Because of her brittle charm and Mr. Gaba's sponsorship, Cynthia is getting to be a familiar figure at chic parties and at smart night clubs like El Morocco and the Stork Club. Mornings, Cynthia haunts the better department stores, such as Saks Fifth Avenue, where she is a welcome visitor. Afternoons she usually goes to some such swank fashion show as Milliner Lily Daché's. Evenings she dines in good restaurants with Mr. Gaba, goes to the theatre. On these pages you will see Cynthia gadding about on a typical round of café society activities. Her remarkable constitution enables her to stand up under an evening's hard fun better than many a social veteran.[16]

Yes, the plaster mannequin became a cultural icon, more famous and in demand than the seemingly eccentric Gaba. Cartier and Tiffany adorned her with luxurious jewelry, while Lily Daché designed hats specifically for the larger-than-life Cynthia. Couturiers sent her their latest fashion creations and Saks Fifth Avenue issued her a credit card. She accompanied Gaba to every highbrow social event imaginable from dinner at The Stork Club to The Marquert. She was even invited to the wedding of the Duke of Windsor (formerly King Edward VIII) and Wallis Simpson. Whenever party hoppers, revelers, or fashionistas tried to strike up a conversation with Cynthia, the protective Gaba insisted that she had to save her voice as she was stricken with a touch of laryngitis. While an Academy Award wasn't quite in the offing, the silent starlet of New York did make it to the silver screen as she appeared with Jack Benny in the Hollywood movie *Artists and Models Abroad.*

With Cynthia and the rest of the Gaba Girls, Lester redefined the mannequin and its use and importance in the retail environment. Previously, mannequins were cumbersome, heavy, and somewhat unrealistic. Gaba led the charge of a new breed of mannequin designers and visionaries. Not one to shy from the dramatic, Gaba added style, grace, and realism to his fabulous forms. Gaba boasted that his mannequins were nearly indistinguishable from well-dressed human women, and pointed out that his creations had charming imperfections just as real women did, such as freckles and different-sized feet.[17]

At the height of her fame, the unthinkable happened. It was at a beauty salon; the room was crowded. Cynthia sat in regal beauty, resplendent in the finest couture dress. Champagne flowed as cigarette smoke filled the air. There was a crash, an excuse me, and then a shriek. One of the patrons, perhaps an admirer or fashion reveler with possibly a bit too much to drink, awkwardly bumped into Gaba's queen. Not flesh and blood was she, but merely a plaster girl. She slipped from her chair, and with a thud and a boom hit the ground; and as she did, the plaster beauty exploded into a thousand pieces. While there was only one Cynthia, heartbroken though he was, some claim that Lester never made another. Other accounts, however, confirm that another was made to return to the fashion scene until Lester was inducted into the army in 1942 as WWII raged on. At war's end, Gaba returned with the hope of bringing Cynthia back into the limelight. But much like the caprice of fashion, times changed, and Cynthia's fickle admirers turned their attentions elsewhere. And so is the story of the plaster goddess who rocked the fashion world for oh too short a time.

References

1. *Sidewalls Magazine* (November 14, 2015).
2. Victoria and Albert Museum, London, England.
3. Victoria and Albert Museum, London, England.
4. Eric Feigenbaum, "Fashion, Art and Hollywood," *Visual Merchandising and Store Design Magazine* (May 3, 2001).
5. Victoria and Albert Museum, London, England.
6. Tove Hermanson, "The Politics of Mannequins," *Huffpost* (April 26, 2010).
7. Feigenbaum, "Fashion, Art and Hollywood."
8. Sara K. Schneider, *Vital Mummies / Performance Design for the Show-Window Mannequin* (Yale University Press, 1995).
9. Schneider, *Vital Mummies.*
10. Balasz Tabac, "Behind the Scenes of the Legendary International Surrealist Exhibition," *Widewalls* (December 16, 2018).
11. Balasz Tabac, "Behind the Scenes."
12. Eric Feigenbaum, "Guadalcanal to Levittown," *Visual Merchandising and Store Design Magazine* (July 11, 2001).
13. Hermanson, "The Politics of Mannequins."
14. Karen Rosenberg, "Mercurial Jester, Revealing and Concealing," *New York Times* (November 19, 2009).
15. Michael Pollak, "Dali on the Warpath," *New York Times* (November 5, 2006).
16. Alfred Eisenstaedt, *Life Magazine* (December 13, 1937).
17. Ben Cosgrove, *Time Life* (August 4, 2013).

CHAPTER 5
TO WAR AND BACK: 1940–1950

If fashion is change, few decades reshaped style and trend more than the 1940s. War dominated the first half of the decade, with a madman rumbling in a troubled world. Murdered millions were discovered in Europe, innocent victims of an insane holocaust. Across the globe, one four-ton bomb dropped on Hiroshima killed 140,000 people almost on impact. (Another bomb on Nagasaki added 70,000 fatalities.) Clouds of death hovered over the earth for decades, claiming an untold number of further victims.

A shaky Cold War peace dominated the second half of the decade. Nazis disappeared, but Communists replaced them. Prosperity returned to America. War veterans returned to jobs and earned money. The birth rate escalated. Families outgrew their crowded urban apartments and fled to the countryside. A new term was coined for the residential communities circling the cities. These nearby counties, communities, hamlets, and towns were called the "suburbs."

As the conflict ravaged Europe, America became isolated from the influence of Parisian fashion and searched for its own signature. A new generation of American designers emerged. Claire McCardell originated the "American Look" inspired by the working attire of the nation's farmers, railroad engineers, soldiers, and sportsmen. McCardell and her contemporaries defined a more casual attitude. The basic construction of American sportswear was compatible with mass production, greatly influencing international fashion, store design, and even visual merchandising. The war years also led to the prominence of American mannequins. As the war began, America no longer had access to European mannequins. American manufacturers quickly filled the void.[1]

In the years immediately before the war, the depression hit hard with devastating consequences around the globe. Worldwide economies were in shambles as people in big cities and in rural areas struggled to get by. With training from the National Academy of Design in New York as a portrait painter, a young Mary Brosnan needed work in those most difficult of times. Realizing that she would be at best no more than a mediocre portrait painter, she sought a career related to the arts. She found what seemed an interesting job in window display as an assistant to the accomplished and well-recognized Cora Scovil. New horizons and new opportunities were opened for Brosnan as Scovil firmly believed that window dressing was an art form. As Brosnan learned the trade, she quickly developed a love of mannequins. While positioning mannequins in her windows, she realized that the industry needed more glamorous and stylish poses. She and Scovil decided that the pedestrian-looking mannequins had to go. Brosnan helped to imagine and design a new type of mannequin. She created stuffed bodies with arms, legs, and hands with glued-on artificial fingernails. She worked closely with the sculptors in the display shop to produce a charming doll-like figure, complete with long eyelashes.[2]

With the outbreak of World War II, it was nearly impossible to import mannequins from Europe. In 1941, Brosnan teamed up with sculptor Kay Sullivan to create Mary Brosnan Inc., a new mannequin company that went on to provide American retailers with domestically produced mannequins. Later that year, the two creative entrepreneurs designed and launched their first collection. Everything was new and fresh including the spelling of "manikins," to differentiate themselves from the live French models who were called mannequins, and from all the other mannequin makers. The new Brosnan manikins had the perfect form and attitude for the year's new look of broad shoulders for padded suits, and long legs for short skirts. Brosnan's new manikin line was hailed by all as a great success.[3]

All of the high-end stores on Fifth Avenue took notice of the new Brosnan girls. Soon, the orders rolled in and Brosnan and Sullivan became the talk of the industry. As their success continued, D.G. Williams, Inc., the biggest supplier of store display equipment in the United States, bought into the business and managed the distribution of manikins all over the country. Mary Brosnan was now a force to be reckoned with in the fast-paced retail industry.

RATIONING, CONSERVATION, AND THE MAGIC OF DISPLAY

Rationing became an unmistakable part of life. Wartime regulations restricted the use of fabric and trimmings. As true ambassadors of their times, mannequins were not immune to the stringent regulations—they became noticeably shorter, saving materials by reducing the length of a mannequin's legs.

Ironically, however, the constraints of the war years actually boosted business for Brosnan, while increasing the value and effectiveness of display. With manufacturing geared toward the war effort, and stringent rationing regulations, merchandise offering in stores became increasingly inferior. Retailers quickly realized that the best way to sell and promote merchandise that was not quite up to the standards of the past was through the science, art, and magic of presentation and display. The Brosnan manikins were so well conceived and designed that they were perfect for the fashions of the day. They naturally wore their clothes well in a relaxed manner and attitude, in whatever pose or position they were placed in.[4]

The up-start manikin company was buzzing with activity as new orders continued to stream in. Brosnan and Sullivan realized they had outgrown their facility in Manhattan. In 1947 they moved the operation across the East River to Long Island City. Once they settled in, they quickly retooled and hired sculptors, hairstylists, and makeup artists. So emboldened were they with their fast-paced rise to success that they expanded the line to include men's and children's manikins.

In speaking of her success, Brosnan always credited her ability to keep ahead of the fashions of the day; to always know what was coming next. In an interview with journalist Betty Reef of The St. Louis Globe-Democrat, Brosnan said, "This constant change, this keeping up with and ahead of fashion, is what keeps us in business. I keep in touch with dress designers, milliners, and beauticians, who dictate each year's special look. Our manikins have to epitomize the trend, and even anticipate it."[5]

As battle-weary men returned home after the war, women re-embraced traditional roles, leaving the workforce for the household. Fashion responded with longer, fuller, more feminine skirts with thin, fitted waists. Mayorga Mannequins introduced a line of "Welcome Home Mannequins" featuring the outstretched arms of a young couple and the longing gaze of their little girl. It was a quest for tranquility. Young families searched for a new life, a new start, and an escape to a new world.[6]

The fashion industry was a dynamic cultural and economic powerhouse in Paris before the onset of World War II. There were upwards of 70 recognized couture houses in the City of Light at the time, and scores of smaller designers working in the industry. The turmoil and destruction of the war years severely impacted the French fashion industry as couturiers and designers fled occupied France, and shops and boutiques closed their doors. The few shops that remained open struggled with extreme shortages of fabrics, thread, and other basic sewing supplies. Part of the long-term German "master plan" was to replace Paris with Berlin as the generator of European fashion design. The Nazi blueprint for this transformation was to establish Berlin and Vienna as the centers of European couture by forcing leaders in the French fashion industry to go to Germany to establish a dressmaking school there.[7]

Fashion, however, was more than just an economic driver in France, it was part of the heart and soul of France; it was a defining factor of their national identity. As such, French designers resisted the devious Nazi plans. Lucien Lelong, president of the *Chambre Syndicale de la Couture Parisienne*, proclaimed, "It is in Paris or it is nowhere."[8]

The ravages of war left Paris and the fashion industry in shambles. As the world embarked on the long road to recovery, Paris was resolute in its efforts to pull itself up from the ashes. Robert Ricci, the son of the well-established couturier Nina Ricci, came up with the idea of a miniature theater of fashion, *Théâtre de la Mode*. Recognizing the scarcity of materials after the war, Ricci proposed using miniature mannequins in an effort to conserve textiles and other materials such as leather and fur.[9]

What resulted in 1945 through 1946 was a touring exhibition of miniature fashion mannequins that were approximately a third of the size of the average human scale. They measured 27.5 inches (700 mm) tall and were primarily fabricated of wire. More than 50 Paris couturiers including Nina Ricci, Jeanne Lanvin, Balenciaga, and Madeleine Vramant participated in *Théâtre de la Mode*. Contributions came from all sectors of the fashion industry. Couturiers offered scrap materials and labor to create the latest styles and fashions in miniature form to fit the diminutive mannequins, while milliners designed and created miniature hats, and jewelers supplied small necklaces and other accessories. Every detail was considered, as hairstylists even coiffed each mannequin's hair.[10]

The *Théâtre de la Mode* was conceived and developed to raise money in support of the survivors of the war, and in part to help resuscitate the French fashion industry. The exhibition opened at the Louvre in Paris on March 28, 1945, with 237 mini-mannequins. Wildly successful, the exhibition drew 100,000 visitors and raised a million francs for war relief. Soon after, the *Théâtre de la Mode* went on to tour major European cities, including London, Leeds, Barcelona, Stockholm, Copenhagen, and Vienna.[11] After the European tour, the *Théâtre de la Mode* was brought to the United States. Today it is part of the permanent collections of the Maryhill Museum of Art in Washington State.

As the war ended, society yearned for a return to normalcy. With the rationing and austerity of the war effort a thing of the past, display departments across America became vital tools to encourage consumer interest and confidence. Display budgets were increased with the strategic plan to tap into the aspirations and desires of the shopping public. The increased allocations for display brought a sudden surge in the purchase of mannequins. Stores across the industry were purchasing mannequins for windows and store interiors. As always, fashion and retail mirrored the mindset and mood of society in the postwar era of the late 1940s. The war was over and people looked toward a brighter future. An air of optimism abounded as the soldiers returned and people were eager to start a new life. Accordingly, the mannequins of the day sported a different and more optimistic attitude. The somber look of the war years was gone, replaced by smiling, upbeat poses and faces. The future looked bright for retail and for display.

PROSPERITY AND MOBILITY

The end of World War II prompted a dramatic economic upturn and population explosion. As the baby boomer generation was born, sales at Sears exceeded $1 billion. With the struggles of the war years behind them, young families were on a quest for tranquility as they searched for a new life, a new start, and an escape to a new world.

By 1946, a frenetic postwar building boom had a great impact on downtown stores. By 1947, more than half of America's households had automobiles. Affordable housing, wash-and-wear fabrics, and suburban shopping centers were becoming exceedingly common. With an uptick in automobile traffic, a trip downtown became less desirable. Suburban stores began to blossom with broad merchandise offerings as downtown merchants struggled to maintain their client base.[12]

An advertisement for D.G. Williams, Inc. in the August 1948 edition of *Display World* read, "A Macy's Grows In Brooklyn. Opening of the new Brooklyn Macy's poses the familiar question: Whose mannequins will model the Macy merchandise? Answer: Mary Brosnan's. And why has Macy's chosen Mary Brosnan mannequins despite the blandishments and special inducements of other makers? Answer: Because Mary Brosnan mannequins are the dominant, sales-making beauties of the Visual Merchandising world."

References

1. Eric Feigenbaum, "Guadalcanal to Levittown," *Visual Merchandising and Store Design Magazine* (July 11, 2001).
2. Betty Reef, "Manikins Made a Mint for Her," *St. Louis Globe-Democrat* (February 17, 1958), 11.
3. Reef, "Manikins Made a Mint for Her."
4. Reef, "Manikins Made a Mint for Her."
5. Reef, "Manikins Made a Mint for Her."
6. Feigenbaum, "Guadalcanal to Levittown."
7. Yuniya Kawamura, *The Japanese Revolution in Paris Fashion* (Berg, 2004), 45.
8. "Post-War & the Théâtre de la Mode," Victoria and Albert Museum.
9. Kawamura, *The Japanese Revolution in Paris Fashion*, 4.
10. Denise Brian, "Théâtre de la Mode, part IV: The Fashion Designers," Maryhill Museum of Art in Washington State.
11. Kawamura, *The Japanese Revolution in Paris Fashion*, 47.
12. Feigenbaum, "Guadalcanal to Levittown."

CHAPTER 6
MID-CENTURY, AN AGE OF AWAKENING: 1950–1960

Culturally, the 1950s was the decade of Mies van der Rohe and Ozzie & Harriet, Hollywood Cinemascope and Hollywood blacklists, Frank Lloyd Wright and Elvis Presley, gray flannel conformity and cuffed jeans irreverence. It was the decade of McCarthyism, nuclear fears, beatnik poetry, and the hula hoop. It was also the decade of suburban sprawl. Economic expansion was fueled by a new affluence. Post-war America's patchwork of suburban communities—single-family homes sprouting quickly like mushrooms across the landscape—were connected by highways of enthusiasm.

In 1951, Victor Gruen, an Austrian-born architect, philosophized that if suburban communities were to survive they must provide places for people to interact. Gruen presented a progressive vision to Minneapolis-based Dayton's department store: two competing department stores in the same center. Since Minneapolis was subject to extreme weather conditions in both winter and summer, Gruen proposed a completely enclosed mall. His vision featured an interior vertical space with a central "Garden Court" reaching upward to a grand ceiling. The resplendent court would provide a balanced focal point between Minneapolis's two largest retailers, Dayton's and Donaldson's. Gruen also commissioned a sculpture for the court. For the first time, art was specifically conceived for an American shopping center. Before long, the footprint of the great American shopping mall would leave its mark across the fabric of a growing nation. That same year, Stanley Marcus started the Neiman Marcus art collection, the largest of any retailer in America. In the ensuing years, Neiman Marcus continued collecting, considering art an important part of their store environments.

As the decade progressed, newly established suburban branch stores featured open, rectilinear plans, allowing for maximum flexibility and interchangeability. They also provided continuity of flooring, ceiling, and lighting. Larry Israel, formerly the chairman of Copeland, Novak & Israel, and WalkerGroup/CNI, recalls how Gimbels in Upper Darby, Pa., incorporated "screen-like" elements to define and subdivide departmental spaces, allowing visibility while still providing a structured, uniform space. Mannequin platforms were positioned perpendicular to the screens, with a background panel to support a motif. The placement of mannequins helped to identify each area and create a transition point from one department to the next.

NEW TECHNOLOGIES, ART, AND TELEVISION

New technologies abounded. Maury Wolf, an enterprising young storeowner, was so enamored with mannequins that he positioned as many as 40 in a single shop window.

Searching for new materials, he and partner David Vine introduced the first reinforced fiberglass mannequin. At first, the new material took on a greenish appearance as its glycerin component reacted to the spotlights. Undaunted, Wolf perfected the fiberglass mannequin. The new material brought a fresh fluidity and flexibility. Mannequins seemed to possess a sense of movement that did not exist before. These lightweight figures began to run, sit and walk.

The 1950s mannequin profile was an exaggerated embodiment of femininity. Sculptors idealized features to satisfy the day's notions of beauty: an hourglass waist, rounded hips, and a voluptuous bust. (It was, after all, the Marilyn Monroe decade.) Increasingly, celebrities were used as mannequin models. In 1953, under the direction of legendary window designer Gene Moore, Bonwit Teller staged a promotional event featuring Rosalind Russell as the inspiration for a new mannequin. After her Broadway appearance in *Wonderful Town*, Russell was asked to perform as a live mannequin in Bonwit Teller's windows. She agreed with one stipulation: Moore had to appear with her. An unassuming man, Moore posed as a photographer in each window, capturing Russell as she mirrored the mannequin's sensual poses.

Photography greatly impacted the artistic evolution of the show window. Moore was particularly influenced by Richard Avedon's technique of leading the viewer from one image to the next. Moore's translation was a pagination, leading the viewer in a sequential path from one window to the next. The narrative approach led visual merchandising to a sparkling new age.

Serafino Silvestri recognized the potential of Hollywood's emerging movie industry in the early 1930s. Seizing the opportunity, he founded Silvestri Studios in 1934 as a resource for props for moviemakers. The company's portfolio included props and sets for blockbuster movies such as Ben Hur and Cleopatra. Silvestri's equally talented brothers also displayed their design sensibilities; one started the Silvestri decor line in Chicago and another started a fountain manufacturing company in San Francisco.

Serafino's son Roland eventually took the helm of the company soon after his return from the Army in the early 1950s. Sharon Govern, long-time account executive for Silvestri California, as the company is now called, fondly remembered Roland Silvestri as one of the finest men she had ever met.

> When I joined Silvestri in 1980, Roland and his wife Luenda embraced my daughter Kelly and I as family. Kelly was six years old, and they loved having her play in the Los Angeles showroom full of oversized, hanging Christmas ornaments. Roland and Luenda would be thrilled to know that Kelly is maintaining his legacy. She grew up in the company and began working at Silvestri a week after graduating from college. We are all family.

In the mid-1950s, Roland recognized the opportunities in retail and the expanded entertainment industries. During this period, he and the elder Silvestri started producing mannequins for stores across the country. It was also at this time that the television industry recognized Silvestri Studios as a reliable source of well-made props.

In 1957, the Desilu prop department commissioned Silvestri Studios to create a statue of an American Minuteman to be used as the central theme in the 179th episode of the *I Love Lucy Show*. The episode titled "The Ricardos Dedicate a Statue" was the 26th episode of Season 6, the final season of the beloved television series starring the effervescent comedic genius, Lucille Ball. It was also the finale episode, aired on May 6, 1957, before the popular sitcom was changed to a new one-hour series.

The storyline revolved around Yankee Doodle Day in Westport, Connecticut. Lucy was appointed chairman of the event. In that capacity, she was responsible for all aspects of the festivities to honor the anniversary of the 1777 Battle of Compo Hill in what was then the small village of Westport. Enthusiastic about her assignment, Lucy commissioned a statue to be made of one of the Revolutionary War heroes who fought in the battle. The plan was to position the statue in the Town Square in homage to Westport's proud patriotic history.

As the story unfolded, the loyal townspeople of the small New England suburb were eagerly awaiting the unveiling of the monument Lucy commissioned in celebration of their forefathers. Lucy's husband Ricky, played by her real-life husband Desi Arnaz, was given the honor of presenting the dedication speech at the long-anticipated unveiling of the statue. Lucy, of course in her inimitable way, was over the moon with excitement about the coming event. Ricky, however, made the unfortunate mistake of entrusting Lucy with the task of getting the statue to the dedication site.

While Lucy was gushing about the upcoming event, she was seen on set showing the statue, complete with muskets and tricorn hat, to her best friend Ethel. Suddenly her son Little Ricky appeared wailing over the fact that his dog Fred had run away. Quick to action, Lucy jumped into the family station wagon totally forgetting that the statue was in a trailer hitched to the rear of the car. As she sped off, the audience heard a bone-rattling crash and the horrific sound of the statue being smashed to pieces.

Panic-stricken, Lucy was in a frenzy, not knowing what to do. After buzzing about frantically, it suddenly occurred to her, why not call Mr. Silvestri, the sculptor who made the statue. Surely he must have another. What follows is Lucy speaking into the phone to the unseen sculptor, the senior Mr. Silvestri:

"Mr. Silvestri, this is Mrs. Ricardo."

Lucy listens . . .

"Ya."

Lucy listens . . .

"You know the statue you made for us?"

Lucy listens . . .

"Well, by any chance do you happen to have a spare?"

Lucy listens . . .

"Oh you don't huh."

Lucy listens . . .

"Could you make another one?"

Lucy listens . . .

"Oh good. How long would it take?"

Lucy listens . . .

"Two weeks!!!

Oh dear, could you make it sooner?"

Lucy listens . . .

"Well I was thinking in about an hour maybe."

Lucy takes the phone away from her ear as Mr. Silvestri responds.

Lucy listens . . .

"Well alright, alright Mr. Silvestri. Well just that and the other one.

Thanks very much."

It's quite apparent from the skit that everyone loves Lucy, even Mr. Silvestri.

CHAPTER 7
COUNTER-CULTURE AND THE AGE OF AQUARIUS: 1960–1970

The baby boomers were coming of age, and college campuses were evolving from fraternity keg parties and goldfish swallowing contests to more serious concerns and a heightened sense of awareness. It was a tumultuous decade that began with the assassination of a young president who offered visions of style and grace in a newfound Camelot. The nation's youth grew increasingly restless as an unpopular war raged on, and issues such as civil rights came into question. An entire generation questioned authority and a blind faith in antiquated traditions. Staring into the face of growing civil unrest and the outrage over a foreign war, young people across the country began to ask the question, why?

Music, drugs, and a heightened awareness fostered a newfound spirit of self-expression, humanism, and social revolution. As young people in America were turning away from a culture of apathy and ambivalence, their counterparts in Britain were rejecting centuries of an outwardly prim and proper and unchanged order. James Bond captured their hearts, the Beatles captured their souls, and Mary Quant and Vidal Sassoon captured their fashion sensibilities. It was the dawning of the Age of Aquarius. Values were changing rapidly as rebellion and irreverence pushed ambivalence aside.

In London, small independent shops sprouted up like magic mushrooms on Carnaby Street and Kings Road. A new "mod" unisex look became the fashion statement of the day for London's youth while in America this newfound idyllic decadence began to appear on the racks in Macy's, Sears, and JC Penney as well as on main streets across the country.

The haute couture hold on fashion loosened. Style no longer revolved around a single trend. Instead, fashion in the decade became a kaleidoscope of inspiration, mirroring myriad experiences in all aspects of life. For the first time, youthful fashion did not follow pre-existing values dictated by an older generation.[1]

As fashion evolved in the turbulent and unpredictable '60s, there was a definitive line between the indifference and irreverence of the British youth culture and the ever-present craving for French style. "Youth fashion of the Sixties was defined by a global discussion on the notion of 'cool,'" said Amanda Hallay, fashion historian, author, and professor. "The immediate Postwar Period saw the Rive Gauche in Paris dovetail into the sensibilities of disenfranchised American youth and their rejection of long-accepted societal mores. The beat movement was born with the clichéd sartorial appropriation of French fashion." Hallay further explained that the "Beatniks" of the day creatively adopted the nuances and elements of French fashion such as Breton shirts, berets, and neatly cropped goatee beards. In a continuance of the Nouvelle Vague movement of the late 1950s, the newfound "Beatnik" style greatly influenced the fashion direction among America's youth.

It must be noted that the winds of change didn't merely sweep across the Atlantic and gust over the Channel, but rather they blew across the entire continent. As the fashion sensibilities in London and Paris were impacting both Haute Couture and Prêt-à-Porter, Italy was enjoying a second cultural Renaissance. Hallay reminds us that Fellini films during this period featured heroes wearing slim-cut suits and women wearing bouffant hairstyles which transcended far beyond the cafes of Rome. This imagery created a smooth and slick style that was quickly embraced by British youth, fostering the beginnings of the Mod movement that defined the early days of the decade.

As the '60s shifted into high gear, Britain spread its wings shedding its Postwar challenges, obstacles, and problems. A newfound economic prosperity swept across the working class like a windstorm that the previous generation never could have imagined. "While the young men of the Mod movement may have held the traditional working-class jobs of their fathers, they did so to far greater financial success," said Hallay. "With more disposable income than ever before, Britain's youth began to spend on bespoke 'tonic' suits worn with slim ties and Chelsea boots in imitation of Marcello Mastroianni." As large numbers of Italian immigrants flooded into Britain in the Postwar era, they brought with them many of the latest cultural nuances that defined a new Rome. From Italian espresso bars to Vespers and Lambrettas, England of the early '60s looked remarkably similar to the streets and byways of Rome.

Fashion follows the times, and mannequins follow fashion. As such, mannequin icon Adel Rootstein introduced an inventive and original realistic mannequin that truly captured the nuances of the times. In 1966 Rootstein premiered a slimmer-than-slim Twiggy mannequin, a stringy and sinewy Sandie Shaw, and an exotic Luna, the first black mannequin. The highly influential mannequin maker's vision sparked a new direction and attitude in mannequin design.

American merchants were greatly influenced by both defining fashion trends coming out of London and Paris. As small Yves St. Laurent Rive Gauche shops were opening across the globe, from the Champs Élysées in Paris to Fifth Avenue in New York, American retailers became enamored with the word boutique. According to Hallay,

> The idea of the boutique as a youthful and deliciously trendy retail concept took hold in London in the late 1950s and early 1960s with Carnaby Street gaining prominence and attention as an interwoven tapestry of exciting small and colorful shops that served as a magnet for the youth culture of the day.

As the term "boutique" became synonymous with young, cool, hip, and sexy, American retailers were lining up to be part of this fast-moving European phenomenon.

In a stunning strategy, Henri Bendel opened the "Street of Shops" in their Fifth Avenue flagship store. It didn't take long before these ubiquitous boutiques became the order of the day in major cities across America. Catching the attention of retailers around the country, this was the first assemblage of boutiques within an individual department store footprint. This bold and creative initiative sparked an industry-wide revolution. Store designers took on the challenge of promoting customer traffic flow through and around this new format. Highly defined racetrack aisles carried customers around the newly discovered center core. Focal points were designed to compel customers to bounce from one visual merchandising moment to the next.

Mannequins became front and forward as the new racetrack floor plan maximized merchandise exposure and departmental frontage. Mannequins were no longer relegated to the deep reaches of the department but rather became "windows on the aisle" announcing each classification and welcoming customers into the area. They became the department sentinels and the standard bearers of style, fashion, and trend. Standing tall at focal points, hot spots, and keyhole presentations, they became the stars much like Hollywood actresses under the lights. Their presence and attitude were brighter than ever before.

SWINGING LONDON AND THE ROOTSTEIN REVOLUTION

It was the art of a Rootstein Mannequin that elevated it to another realm. It was the subtle bend of the neck, the penetrating gaze, and the hand position that no others could seem to replicate. It was the distinctive subtleties that labeled Rootstein the "Rolls Royce" of mannequins. According to Michael Southgate, the creative director of Adel Rootstein Mannequins for twenty years, the art of a Rootstein mannequin begins with the sculpting.

> Adel would go to great lengths to make sure the sculpting was just right. When told that you can't get that hand position out of the mold, Adel would figure out a way. And then she added vertebrae, something no one had ever done before. It was these fine details or touches that differentiated the Rootstein line. The other distinguishing factor was the makeup and styling. Our makeup was more artistic than others. There were many layers, a first layer, a second, and then the finishing coat.

Adel Rootstein was a trailblazer in the evolution and development of the modern mannequin. All too often taken for granted, she pushed this vital component of the retail industry to another realm. She elevated the utilitarian display mannequin to a fashion statement, and further to an art form. Through her unique vision, mannequins became standard bearers of the times, and reflections of our culture. Adel Rootstein was more in the moment than anyone else who has ever produced mannequins. She understood the world around her, and she had a keen sense of any direction in which it might turn. She had the rare ability to recognize fashion trends before they became trends.

Born in Warmbaths, South Africa in 1930, Rootstein immigrated to the United Kingdom in the 1950s. It was there that she changed the world of retail display for ever. In 1956, she and her husband, Rick Hopkins, opened her own mannequin company. In the ensuing years, she created a new path for mannequins that had never been traveled before.

When Rootstein arrived in London, she got a job at Aquascutum on Oxford Street. "Rick was the display manager at Aquascutum and Adel was the window dresser," recalled Southgate.

> Rick was tall and strapping at 6'3" with an all-American-Boy look, although he was Canadian. Adel was quite different, standing at 5'2" in her stocking feet, she was very artsy. Everyone was amazed when they got married. Aquascutum informed them, however, that they couldn't employ them both since they were married. So Adel had to find a job. She hated the idea of going on interviews, so she decided to start her own business.

And so the fledgling mannequin company got its start. Rootstein began by creating millenary heads and small prestige figures used to display small items such as pens and earrings, and then theater props and display props for large prominent fashion stores such as Harrods and Dickens & Jones. She knew she needed help to grow the company.

> Hopkins told her to form a proper company. When she said that she would, Hopkins asked her what she would call it? When Adel said she would use her name, Adel Hopkins, Rick said, 'no way.' He told her in no uncertain terms that if she was going to fall on her ass, she was going to fall on her own.

When Rootstein first decided to make mannequins, she was approached by a woman named Pam Gems who married into a family that produced wax mannequins and museum figures. Gems Wax Models, founded by Julius Frederick Gems, first started producing dressmaker forms in the late 1800s. When the business started to struggle in the early 1940s, Leopold Gems, one of the founder's two sons, found a new market that included making wax figures for Madame Tussaud. In the early 1950s, the business began to flounder again until Leopold's son, Keith Gems, revitalized the company with a focus on fashion mannequins. He brought in a successful French mannequin designer named Jacques Bodart. The young designer had visions of a worldwide mannequin business that also included theatrical props and sets. When he tragically died at a young age, Keith's wife, Pam Gems, took charge of mannequin design with two successful mannequin ranges. Her design acumen and efforts were a key factor in saving the display component of the family business.

Pam Gems, who later went on to become a successful playwright best known for her 1978 musical play *Piaf* about French singer Édith Piaf, asked Rootstein to produce wigs for Gems mannequins. Southgate explained, "Adel was making quality wigs out of nylon from Switzerland." Soon after her work with Gems, Rootstein started to make her own mannequins. For the next three or four years, she collaborated with a Polish sculptor by the name of George Staftski. "Rootstein never sculpted," said Southgate. "Her talent was visualizing the style and presence needed to sell clothes."

It all took off from there; this marked the beginning of the Rootstein revolution. First there were two or three realistic figures. "Mannequins, however, were typically taller sizes with exaggerated waist and bosom like a fashion sketch," said Southgate. "Adel tried to be more realistic, but they weren't totally realistic." After the third group, Rootstein enlisted the talents of John Taylor, a classically trained freelance sculptor, to express her vision of the ideal mannequin. Together, they created a reclining mannequin after the model Imogen. This was the beginning of her first full mannequin line called "Model Girl." Rootstein and Taylor worked together for the next twenty-eight years. Rootstein began with one small showing of her mannequins, and then another. Then in 1956, according to Southgate, "She turned the basement of a small newspaper shop in Earl's Court into a workshop and began making mannequins. Next, she established a small studio and brought in people to help. She and those she hired all trained and learned together."

Everything fell into place for Rootstein in the late 1950s when the American press coined the phrase Swinging London. "The Londoners didn't know that they were swinging," laughed Southgate. Before World War II, Regent Street was a sophisticated high-end retail corridor. A small street behind the fashionable Regent Street serviced the high-end thoroughfare with small tailor shops, cleaners, and restaurants. After the war, things were quite austere in England until the early 1950s. When Britain's economic outlook began to improve, Regent Street started to bounce back. The small street behind Regent Street, however, was filled with empty storefronts. The stores that remained on the little back street couldn't attract the well-known designers. At the same time, the art colleges were producing talented young people. The teachers and professors returned from the war and began to teach a new way of free thinking. With this fresh outlook and newfound thought process, the art colleges began to produce a new generation of forward-thinking creatives. This progressive cohort of nineteen and twenty-year-old students became the visionaries and new designers of the day. Southgate explained, "Before this time it was all about Paris, everything was Paris. All the fashion inspiration came from Paris. It was Paris this and Paris that. It was Paris says ... And everyone listened. Big posters were sent out to all the department stores and all the mannequins were dressed accordingly."

This new group of fresh faces that took the fashion scene by storm included Mary Quant, Gina Fratini, Marion Foale, and Sally Tuffin among others. They changed everything at a time that was ripe for change. As Britain shook off the horrors and resultant doldrums of the war, young people began to enjoy higher incomes and increased economic means. They were also in search of a new identity and a new form of self expression. The fashion of the prewar period was no longer fashionable. Young people were hungry for new designs that were expressive of their lifestyles. The new upstart designers were the answer to their quests for a new direction.

The young designers took their creations to London's Fashion Week. Then they took over the empty shops with affordable rents on the small street behind Regent Street. That little back street began to blossom and come alive along with London's new style and new fashion. The street became Carnaby Street, the engine behind London's emerging fashion scene. However, Regent Street wasn't buying it at all. "The mainstream English retailers wouldn't even look at the kaftans and mini skirts the young English designers were producing," remembered Southgate.

> It was the Americans who would stop off in London after visiting Paris that recognized the trend. Soon Bergdorf's and Saks started to show the new English fashions. And as they showed them, they couldn't cope with the demand. The English soon realized that they missed the boat, and they started to want it too because the Americans were buying it. Suddenly it was at Selfridge's, Harrods, and Dickens & Jones.

Rootstein was quick to recognize that while the existing mannequins and dressmaker forms worked well for the classic fashions of the '50s that were popularized by Hollywood stars such as Grace Kelly, Marilyn Monroe, and Audrey Hepburn, they weren't quite right for Swinging London. "The liberation of fashion called for a new mannequin, one with more movement, freedom, and a decidedly youthful attitude," said millinery designer Marjorie Lee Woo. "The '60s were the beginning of an era that allowed the individual to decide what's in fashion."

"Stylized looked ridiculous on dignified upmarket ladies. The mannequins were all wrong," said Southgate. "Designers such as Ossie Clark and Mary Quant reached out to Adel, telling her that their designs looked ludicrous on the current mannequins. They asked her to make mannequins that worked for the clothes they were designing."

Southgate was freelancing for Rootstein in London at the time. He was not employed full-time by the visionary mannequin designer until he moved to New York. "Adel was one of my first customers. I did a small show with her. I installed the show, dressed the mannequins, and styled the show. It wasn't a real job; I did it on a friendship basis because of our relationship and my admiration of Adel." An artist in his own right, Southgate was an actor by trade with a fairly accomplished career in theater. As a child, his mother taught dancing, so he had good references when he wanted to get a job on stage. He told his mother that he wanted to go to London to work in theater. Once there he and a fellow thespian performed as Rogers and Stan (Michael Rogers). The two traveled about doing late-night satirical cabaret shows, often performed in drag. They were eventually booked at the Criterion Theater on Piccadilly, and the Victoria Palace.

With his background in theater and his inherent artistic sensibilities, Southgate brought a great deal of creative inspiration to Rootstein. The company hierarchy had Adel at the helm as creative director, supervising all sculpting and model selection. She felt out the trends and ultimately made all of the creative decisions. Hopkins was an excellent businessman with sharp instincts to grow the company. Rootstein was quite content to keep the company as it was, small and manageable. Hopkins insisted that if they were to survive, they had to grow the business. In his capacity as the second in command, Hopkins also ran all of the back-of-the-house functions, including the running of the factory. In his years as a freelancer for the company, Southgate staged exhibitions and did visual work as well as working on ads and layouts. He also worked closely with Hopkins who was a qualified designer in his own right. Southgate would present his ideas for exhibitions, and Hopkins would create detailed working drawings for each project.

In his capacity as a freelancer designer, Southgate vividly recalls Rootstein saying, "If London is swinging, we should do a mannequin modeled on the people who are making it swing." This new revelation sparked Rootstein's ascent to the top of the mannequin world with the sculpting of fashion notables Patti Boyd and Twiggy. From that point on, it was full speed ahead for Rootstein and her innovative company. Southgate explained, "We tried to model someone who would get publicity. We wanted to make mannequins after people who were making fashion. We wanted to capture their body shapes and attitudes and the nuances of the day or the political and social essence of the times. We wanted broad shoulders and clenched fists."

"Adel thought to do a realistic mannequin because the concept was so strong," said Southgate. "She wanted it to be more realistic, but she didn't want it to be mannequin-like, or just another mannequin. Up until that point, mannequins were inspired by the looks and physical attributes of people like Marilyn Monroe—curvy, busty, and big hips." Rootstein looked beyond to a new attitude and a new persona. Twiggy, originally known as Lesley Lawson, née Hornby, emerged from her job as a shampooist in a hair salon, to become a trend-setting teenage model and cultural British icon. Rootstein zeroed in on the rising star with her androgynous look, almost clown-like big eyes, long lashes, a boyish short bob, long legs, and turned-in toes.

Southgate had his doubts about selling the 5'2" pigeon-toed mannequin. A few were sold in Europe. Then D. H. Holmes, a New Orleans-based department store, became the first American retailer to buy a set of Twiggy mannequins. Shortly after, Henry Callahan of Saks Fifth Avenue in New York purchased a set of both Twiggy and Donyale Luna mannequins for their Fifth Avenue windows. Saks soon became known as the company that did Twiggy. Rootstein also bent the norm by sculpting Luna, the first African American to have a mannequin created in her image.

At the same time, Barbara Hulanicki started the cult-like fashion brand Biba with the launch of *Biba's Postal Boutique*. Strictly mail order at the time, Biba offered a simpler fashion with cheaper make-your-own dresses. *Biba's Postal Boutique* then evolved into a department store in London's Abingdon Road in Kensington. Biba soon became the epicenter of London's swinging '60s scene with exotic ostrich feathers, 200 pairs of shoes piled on the floor, fantastic styling, and droopy poses, with no busts, purple lips, and pansy-like faces much in the style of Twiggy. Women, whether beautiful or not beautiful before, all had style and a new look. Southgate remembers Rootstein hated pretty. "Although the Americans insisted on pretty, Adel always avoided pretty girls. Instead, she looked for style. She looked for unusual and unconventional beauty. Perhaps it was a sharply angled nose or cheekbones. She was drawn to the atypical beauty of Sara Kapp. Henri Bendel championed Kapp one year in a classic collection featuring Rootstein mannequins."

Rootstein always thought ahead of the game. If there wasn't a trend she would invent one. Whenever she introduced a new line of mannequins, she referred to them as a collection. Using the word collection was very important to her. Every collection represented a new look that she would always release on fashion week. Through her vision and creative marketing skills, she pushed mannequins into a fashion image on the international stage.

Southgate, Rootstein, and Hopkins would brainstorm when they started selling in America. Southgate traveled to New York twice a year on a freelance basis in the early

Figure 7.1 Twiggy mannequin by Adel Rootstein. PictureLux / The Hollywood Archive.

days. Rootstein only ventured to New York once a year. Rootstein and Hopkins then decided to open a showroom in America. They said to Southgate, "You've been to America more than any of us, and you know it and you know the customers. Will you open the New York showroom?"

Southgate said yes he would, but he would like a two-year contract. Rootstein said of course. Rick said no. "Why should I give you a fucking contract, just do the job." Southgate went to New York without a contract and set up the showroom. Rootstein and Hopkins were so pleased with the results that they offered him a ten-year contract. Southgate declined the offer but agreed to become a full-time employee with the position of creative director. In that capacity he would go back and forth from New York to London, spending three months in each city meeting with clients and setting up the showroom.

As the '60s rolled into the '70s, Rootstein was again ahead of the capricious winds of an ever-changing culture, and the ephemeral and fickle ways of fashion. With her radar turned on, she was quick to pick up on the driving beats of the flourishing music industry and the corresponding rhythms of the thriving club scene. She also built upon her early success in featuring highly recognizable fashion models who dared to be different such as Luna and Twiggy. She sculpted mannequins after a wide variety of striking, colorful, and in some cases exotic-looking fashion models such as Marie Helvin, Tina Chow, Pat Cleveland, and Sayoko Yamaguchi. Cleveland famously said, "If you become an Adel Rootstein mannequin, you're lucky. People will know who you are." Rootstein of course, while looking for the right models to best represent the brand and capture the moment, also altruistically hoped to help the careers of the fashion runway's rising stars.

Figure 7.2 Adel Rootstein illustrated advertisement. Courtesy VMSD Magazine

With her thumb firmly positioned on the pulse of popular culture, Rootstein's vision took a turn toward the more realistic. As the decade moved into full swing she introduced the next significant change of shape, with wide poses, spread legs, and big arms. Social values, customs, and mores were changing and becoming more unconventional. The civil rights movement was expanding, and the sexual revolution was exploding. As sexual freedom and women's liberation became the order of the day, Rootstein sculpted the first mannequin with nipples. While controversial at the time, Rootstein continued to respond to the ever-evolving culture of the day.

According to Marsha Bentley Hale, "A fashion revolution was set into motion by such futurist designers as Rudi Gernreich (known for his topless swimsuit) who brought a whole new freedom to a woman's body. Mannequin manufacturers followed suit."[2]

Toward the end of the 1970s, Rootstein once again demonstrated that she was always one step ahead of the trends. Her radar landed on Joan Collins prior to the actress's big splash into the hearts of popular culture. Long before being cast in her iconic role as Alexis Colby-Carrington in the hit soap opera *Dynasty*, Rootstein introduced a new collection of mannequins called *Body Gossip*. First shown at Euroshop, the collection was modeled after the likeness of the soon-to-be megastar.

Collins had recently returned to the UK from Hollywood, hoping to relaunch her career. She signed a contract to do a series of ads for a martini brand. She was ravishing in the ads, and Rootstein noticed. Suddenly she was in the news, recognized as the most beautiful fifty-year-old in the world. Rootstein, recognizing that retailers were trying to

Figure 7.3 Adel Rootstein photographic advertisement. Courtesy VMSD Magazine.

appeal to fifty-year-old women because they had money, thought Collins would be the perfect subject for a collection of mannequins. *Body Gossip* was a huge success.

The body shape of the '80s moved away from extreme realism to a more idealized perfection. Muscle tones were pronounced and defined with a more sculpted athletic look, ideal for presenting workout apparel. Another shape was also offered to wear luxurious party dresses being featured in a revival of the late 1950s style of couture clothes. As the decade moved along, stores wanted a tall, elegant, and glamorous attitude. Rootstein was always there to fill the need.

Shapes seemed to change with every changing decade. This was in large part due to changing fashion photography, an art form in its own right that always progressed in stages. In the late 1980s and early 1990s, fashion photographers moved away from the big wide look to a more fashion-oriented profile. Retail wanted a healthier and fleshier look. Once again Rootstein flexed her artistic instincts in selecting Dianne Brill as her model of choice for the new decade. While many questioned her decision, the selection of Brill proved to be brilliant. "Adel always seemed to know when someone was about to shine," said Southgate. Brill became "the face of the '90s," photographed by every photographer of note from Annie Leibovitz and Robert Mapplethorpe to Mario Testino, Patrick McMullan, Greg Gorman, and Bill King. She emerged as the queen of the New York night scene. So much so that Andy Warhol was heard to say, "If you were at a party and Dianne Brill was there, you knew you were at the right party!" Once again, Rootstein struck gold.

The fashion world and the mannequin world always looked to Rootstein to see what Adel would do next. With her radar always on, she attended a fashion photography shoot and was struck by the way the photographer grouped the models. This triggered an idea and began a new trend in mannequin design. Going forward, Rootstein always created groupings of three figures, left, center, and right. She envisioned customers arriving at an escalator landing greeted by a dynamic grouping of fashion mannequins. It also helped visual merchandisers in the mannequin selection process when deciding which mannequins worked well together. Southgate explained, "Everything was done for a reason or to satisfy a need."

Every Rootstein collection consisted of six to ten figures. There was always one key figure that the whole group was based on. Each figure in the collection took its cue from the attitude, feeling, and height of that key girl. A perfect example of the power and effect of a collection was when Armani introduced the "power suit." Feminism continued as an important social movement well into the 1980s. Like Rootstein, Mr. Armani always recognized a need. Women were increasingly working in executive positions and had the need and the desire to dress appropriately in their professional lives. To best present this important fashion statement, a Rootstein collection was used, all with the same power attitude, height, and shoulder position. Of additional note, every head was different. Rootstein never made a standard head, she insisted that the sculpting should always capture each individual model's head. For that reason, Rootstein never offered interchangeable heads on any of her figures.

In keeping with the essence of the mannequins and the defined Adel Rootstein brand image, the showrooms were always spectacular productions. When stepping across the threshold of Rootstein's front door, visitors were always transported to another reality far from their usual daily retail experiences. "We designed and installed the showrooms to entertain and try to have some element of current fashion," explained Southgate.

> We wanted to entertain people who typically spend their time looking at racks of clothes. We didn't want to be straightforward but rather somewhat intellectual. We would always be thematic, basing the showroom on a current art show or movie or what's happening in the news. That's how we designed. Adel hated the word vendor; Rootstein was so much more than that. . . . Adel always wanted to be an artist.
>
> At fifty she wanted to retire, but Rick and I wouldn't let her. At sixty she finally retired. She always had a keen interest in art. She always felt uneducated and was eager to learn new things. She loved English literature and was mad about theater. When people met her, whether they were reporters or interviewers, they were always surprised; she was not what they expected. She was this little demure woman who didn't necessarily dress as though she was driven by fashion. When asked what she thought fashion should be, her reply was simple, 'It should be comfortable.' But for TV, she could really pull it off with something from Chanel.

With all of their success, Rootstein and Hopkins never changed their lifestyle. Although their highly successful and lucrative mannequin company provided them with the means to live anywhere they chose, they lived in the same modest house that they always loved and enjoyed. After finally retiring, to the dismay of Southgate and Hopkins, she decided to go to art school. Upon reviewing her portfolio, her school of choice turned her down. They said her work was not good enough. "Adel may have been small and quiet, but she had a very strong will," recalled Southgate. "You could never say no to her." Undeterred, she convinced the admissions officer at the art school to let her attend for a year, and then review her qualifications. After a year she gained full entry. Then, unfortunately, she became ill, and the doctors wanted to give her a test. She said she would take the test, but it would have to wait until after her final exams at school. She insisted that she had to take her finals. She passed her exams with flying colors. Two or three weeks before she passed away, she received her bachelor's degree in art after all those years. She was delighted, she was an artist.

FROM OHIO TO THE BRITISH INVASION

David Wolfe's love of mannequins began as a young boy growing up in rural postwar Ohio. His family lived in a small house next to a cornfield, not too far from Cleveland. Things were changing rapidly as the Midwest was experiencing a tremendous postwar industrial boom. As a child, he and his sister would excitedly jump on a Greyhound bus to travel to the big city to see what was happening. Their destination once they arrived in Cleveland was Sterling Lindner Davis, a well-known local department store located in the city's theater district. He recalled, "There was a seated mannequin in the window wearing a red wig. Every time we visited Cleveland we would run from the bus station to the store with great anticipation to see what she was wearing." After many exciting trips to the big city, his sister eventually became a teenage model in Cleveland. Her budding modeling career together with the enchanting red-haired mannequin in the store window, were the seeds that grew into an amazing career in the fashion industry. It was then that he discovered his love of fashion and of mannequins. While other boys were passing a football around, Wolfe was voraciously devouring the pages of *Vogue Magazine* and copying all of the fashion illustrations in each issue. He was the only ten-year-old boy in Ohio who had a subscription to *Vogue*. Diana Vreeland was the editor-in-chief at the time. As the driving force at the helm of the prominent fashion publication, she greatly influenced everyone involved with the world of fashion, from designers to the visual merchandisers who showcased the latest creations on store mannequins. Vreeland famously said, "The only real elegance is in the mind; if you've got that, the rest really comes from it." Wolfe, a great admirer of Vreeland said, "I loved what she did to *Vogue*. She was my mentor in a way as I developed my love of fashion." From those early days, Wolfe dreamed of becoming an illustrator. "Back then, every store had an illustrator on staff, and I just wanted to be one of them."

Totally self-taught, Wolfe would copy every fashion illustration he could get his hands on. In his words, "It was monkey see, monkey do. I would copy everything that was being done by the important illustrators of the day." Before long, he developed a style that was uniquely his own. Illustration was beginning to fade out as an important advertising tool at the time, giving way to the power and appeal of photography. Illustrators desperately wanted visual signals that would set them apart. Wolfe's recognizable signature centered around his dramatic highly stylized long-legged girls. "I loved illustration," said Wolfe. "The designers loved my work because I would put the seams of the garments into the drawings. I learned all about pattern making, which helped to define my illustrations. I brought the structure I learned in pattern making into my illustrations. Then I elongated everything." Wolfe loved clothes and he loved mannequins. He would use mannequins for his illustrations where others would hire a model.

As Wolfe's love of fashion grew, he got a job in the fashion industry in Ashtabula, Ohio. At 19 years old, he was the visual merchandising director of a small family-owned chain of department stores in northern Ohio called Carlisles. Among the young creative's many responsibilities was designing and installing window and in-store displays. The love affair deepened as he actually got to work with mannequins, dressing them in a way that brought them to life. In addition, young Mr. Wolfe also illustrated advertisements and supervised the visual merchandising throughout all of the Carlisles stores.

One summer his sister came to visit. While in Ashtabula, she befriended a woman who worked in the cosmetics department at Carlisles. The young woman was British and traveled to the United States to work in the circus. She was enjoying a fun, exciting, and rather offbeat career as a circus performer until she fell off an elephant. While she was convalescing from her injuries, the circus moved on without her. Alone in Ashtabula, she married an older man so she could stay in the country. When the marriage ended she got a job at Carlisles. It was then that Wolfe's sister introduced her to him, and the rest was history. "It was very romantic," said Wolfe. "We became known as the

Richard and Liz (Richard Burton and Elizabeth Taylor) from Ashtabula, Ohio." The happy couple soon married.

He loved what he was doing in Ohio as a visual merchandiser. However, anyone in fashion at the time knew that London was where it was at. "I would still be in Ohio today if it wasn't for my wife," claimed Wolfe. "She was like Mama Rose, the stage mother in Gypsy. She believed in me. She said I turned Ohio into a hotbed of fashion with my visual displays. She said I was too good and deserved more money and pushed me to ask for a raise." In 1967, the young visual merchandiser together with his British wife and three-year-old daughter, left Ashtabula, Ohio behind and headed to London, England.

Eager to leave Ohio for the excitement and stimulation of London, the young family boarded a plane for the journey to Great Britain. At the time, London was the epicenter of a Pop Culture and youth movement that was spreading across the world. The swinging scene of the 1960s was fueling a new and exciting "British Invasion" in America. The Beatles and The Rolling Stones, along with many other British bands were rocking the world. Young people in America and across Europe looked to Carnaby Street in London for fashion inspiration. In Wolfe's own words,

> The swinging '60s was futuristic. It was a natural reaction to the war; if you were attracted to fashion it was a quantum leap from World War II. The world was

Figure 7.4 Art Deco fashion drawing for Adel Rootstein by David Wolfe. Courtesy David Wolfe.

> reinventing itself after recovering from the devastation of the war. Much like the end of World War I and the Art Deco movement, creativity was blossoming. It was coming out of the closet so to speak.

As Wolfe's understanding of the world deepened, he realized that fashion is not cyclical, but it's easy to track.

Once settled in London, Wolfe began a very successful career as a freelance fashion illustrator. His style was unlike any illustrations being done at the time. His figures were elongated, long-legged, and often in dramatic poses and dynamic motion. He often sketched recognizable models, actresses, and socialites. His very first freelance job in London was for the *Daily Express* national newspaper. It was a sketch of the fashionable French socialite, the Vicomtesse Jacqueline de Ribes wearing a Christian Dior gown. Among his more important clients was Fortnum & Mason, one of the finest and most exclusive stores in London. He did their advertisements that appeared monthly in *British Vogue* and *Harper's Bazaar*. In addition, Wolfe's work appeared in the London *Sunday Times*, *Women's Wear Daily*, *Drapery & Fashion Weekly*, the *Telegraph*, *International Textiles*, and in advertising campaigns including Aquascutum, Liberty of London, and Selfridge's.

His work came to the attention of Adel Rootstein who had recently started what was to become one of the foremost mannequin companies in the industry. He was contacted by Rootstein and her husband and business partner, Rick Hopkins. What ensued was a long introductory interview with Rootstein and Hopkins. From that moment, it was obvious to Wolfe that the three were destined to work together. "I was surprised that they wanted artwork instead of photographs of their famous celebrity mannequins," said Wolfe. "Rick, a brilliant marketer, explained to me that every photo looks the same, but artwork is unique, one-of-a-kind."

Wolfe thought it was very brave on the part of Rootstein and Hopkins to embrace illustrations rather than photography in their marketing campaigns. "It was a tribute to their love of creativity. Rick understood artistic concepts; he saw the illustrations as figments of erotic phantasies."

It was quite clear to Rootstein and Hopkins that Wolfe loved mannequins and he loved to sketch them. In fact, Wolfe thought "mannequins were an improvement from the human race." As an artist, he was thrilled to have three-dimensional models to sketch. Whereas he usually sketched a live model who didn't hold still while he drew, the Rootstein girls never moved a muscle. He much preferred realistic mannequins because he wanted to see how fashion looks in real life on real people. "Of course, the 'real people' can be really beautiful," he added.

Rootstein and Hopkins marveled as he filled notebook after notebook with sketches of the fabulous forms. They were so touched by the exuberant young artist's passion, that they gave him a mannequin sculpted in the likeness of Twiggy. One of Rootstein's early claims to mannequin fame was the sculpting of celebrities. Twiggy's claim to fame was as a waif-like supermodel whose image graced the cover of every notable fashion magazine. Her name and her image were sweeping across Europe; through London, Paris, and

Milan. And as the British Invasion reached America's shores, she became a household name in the United States.

Wolfe loved the Twiggy mannequin. He said the undernourished Twiggy and the tall and graceful Donyale Luna are extreme examples of Rootstein's fashion awareness and sensitivity to the rapidly shifting trend scene. Having the much-sought-after Twiggy in his possession was a great source of pride, inspiration, and fun for the Ohio-born illustrator and lover of fashion's silent partner, the mannequin. Living in a two-story walk-up in London, Wolfe cleverly and mischievously positioned her on the staircase landing leading up to his flat. He would change her outfit every week and then take delight at the surprise of his visitors when they encountered Twiggy on his staircase.

Looking back, Wolfe recalled that Rootstein and Hopkins were true visionaries, exceptional at trend spotting.

> They realized that visual merchandising would need to keep up with the accelerated pace of changing trends and they seized the opportunity. They were open-minded, always knowing where the next creative influence was coming from. So many people are territorial about creativity. Adel and Rick, on the other hand, would share and inspire. I was a novelty act; the kid from Mid-America. Rick would call me in the evening with a singular question. I would show up the next morning for a cup of coffee or tea. Both Rick and Adel would be there to discuss and always encourage. Rick was a great creative businessman who always tried to give creatives room to grow. Their showrooms were amazing productions, reminiscent of an epic Busby Berkeley production.

Berkeley of course devised intricate musical productions in the 1930s that were highly choreographed orchestrations of showgirls, elaborate costumes, and music. Wolfe said, "Rootstein did for mannequins what Berkeley did for chorus girls."

Rootstein and Hopkins agreed that fashion reflects the world. Together they anticipated reaction to new music, or great art shows at the museum. They both had creative minds and knew how to turn creativity into money. As an illustrator with a keen sense of aesthetics, Wolfe recognized the allure of Rootstein's beautifully sculpted mannequins. "They captured the subtle fashion essence of a real personality. Moreover, the Rootstein line was further elevated by the celebrity connection. It was news every time a new celebrity mannequin collection was introduced."

Wolfe thought of Rootstein mannequins as works of art. He explained, however, "They were not exact replicas of human beings. Instead, they were enhanced and improved representations of real-life subjects. Most mannequins, before and after Adel, could usually be considered as functional forms to display the garment. Adel's mannequins captured the entire 'look' of a fashionable persona, based on a real individual, whether female, male or kids."

As Wolfe continued his mastery of fashion illustration, he notes that it was his early love of this art and his innate flair for fashion that propelled him into the next chapter of a remarkable career. As he turned the page, his creative path brought him to New York where he served as a preeminent global trend forecaster at the Doneger Group. That lofty position provided him with a front-row seat to the runways of New York, Paris, and Milan.

And while he moved on to new horizons, Wolfe's work at Rootstein remained near and dear to his heart. He recalls that Rootstein and Hopkins were very interested in his emerging career shift from fashion illustration to trend forecasting. While still working with Rootstein, he had wonderful meetings discussing where the next trend might be coming from. "I remember getting a phone call from Rick who wanted to discuss the shape of eyebrows on the latest sketches I had sent him. I explained that I'd been inspired by Gertrude Lawrence's sickly-pained eyebrows in the 1930s. He understood immediately. No further discussion was necessary. The next Rootstein collection had those brows."

As a fashion forecaster reflecting back on his association with Rootstein, and the role of mannequins as a reflection of fashion and culture, Wolfe said, "Most workday mannequins seem to be in search of representing the commercial 'mainstream fashion,' aiming to provide the retailer who buys one to make use of it for several seasons or even years. It is rare that a mannequin precedes a major fashion trend. Rootstein mannequin collections dared to venture to the cutting edge of fashion with every collection."

As time went on, Wolfe notes that something happened in retail history. As salespeople went away, mannequins took on an even more important role. Also, while his sister was modeling at a show with other models, all wearing designer apparel and walking up the runway, David thought that mannequins did a better job of modeling than models did.

As time passed and Wolfe's momentous career unfolded, he remembers his return to America, and living in New York.

> While strolling in Chelsea one day, I found myself looking in a fabulous store window at a grouping of Rootstein mannequins. I went inside, introduced myself, and explained my Rootstein connection. I was shown into a big office and there on the wall were huge blow-ups of my illustrations from the long ago past. It brought back wonderful memories of a wonderful time.

References

1. Eric Feigenbaum, "The 1960s: Kaleidoscope of Inspiration," *Visual Merchandising and Store Design Magazine* (August 7, 2001).
2. Marsha Bentley Hale, "Lasting Impressions," *Visual Merchandizing and Store Design Magazine* (November 1985).

CHAPTER 8
THE TRANSITIONAL YEARS: 1970–1980

Changing times and values fostered a considerable rethinking of mannequin design as a new sense of social awareness demanded a heightened level of realism. The customers of the day wanted to see mannequins that more realistically represented them. In 1972, Henry Callahan designed the "Contessa" mannequin for Saks Fifth Avenue's windows. Callahan's vision was a dramatic departure from the aloof, unblemished beauty of past mannequin creations. She represented a woman in her mid-thirties who, although elegant and of regal bearing, looked totally human.

As the decade proceeded, a major shift occurred. While the Contessa at Saks Fifth Avenue garnered a great deal of attention, and some were still using the glamor girls of the '60s, there was a definite move away from the identifiable celebrity-inspired mannequins. Soon, mannequin designers began taking a more artistically rendered or abstract approach. In addition, headless and faceless mannequins became increasingly popular toward the end of the '70s.

During the transformative years of 1968 to 1972, a disgruntled youth culture dissociated itself from bygone eras, values, and traditions. As the '60s slipped into the '70s, a growing counter-culture produced a new couture and the streets produced a new anti-fashion.

As the decade began, the war in Vietnam was raging on, Washington was mired in the corruption of Watergate, and long lines at the gas pump became the new normal. As society was still reeling from assassinations, riots, and civil unrest, young people looked eschew at traditional retail, considering it uninspiring, frivolous, and unimportant. The younger generation gravitated toward a new music laced with thoughts of peace and love. A new sexual revolution led the way to the opening of closet doors and the forging of new identities. Anti-fashion called for open attitudes, setting the parameters for a broader scope of understanding and imagination. Changes in fashion were no longer considered cyclical or progressive, but rather avant-garde, revolutionary, and radical.

Looking poor and threadbare became chic and cool. The street emperors of anti-fashion adorned themselves with ragged jeans, long hair, beads, and a cornucopia of vintage clothes. Ethnic pride paved the way for Afros and dashikis, while new waves of diplomacy introduced the West to the style and gear of Chairman Mao. Fashion designers responded to the nuances of the day. Inspired by ethnic tradition, they began to include layers and mixed separates in their collections. Yves Saint Laurent led the way in the early '70s by translating the ethnic and street look into high fashion statements.

The ethos of street-dominated fashion defined the show windows along the avenues and well-travelled retail corridors. In 1976, Rosemary Kent coined the term "street theater" in her New York Times piece on the new trend in fashion windows. With New York "street artists" setting the pace, this window genre soon spread across the country.

At Chicago's Carson Pirie Scott, a window sequence escorted the viewer through a blissful night "Out on the Town." The eight-window progression began with a grouping of beautifully bedecked mannequins anticipating the night out, to the theater, to the bar, dinner, dancing, under the moonlight, and then home alone with a cold compress. Audiences were alternately enthralled and outraged at this new vehicle for social commentary.[1]

STREET THEATER, FASHION, AND ANTI-FASHION

Mannequins took center stage, becoming actors in real-life dramas. High-fashion outfits were in the spotlight for probing social commentary that included murder, drug overdose, and sexual intrigue. The decade's most revealing mannequin innovation was a direct by-product of street theater. Increasingly, mannequins were designed to be sold as sets or groupings. Adel Rootstein was a trendsetter in this new approach with collections of mannequins that interrelated as they appeared to talk, touch, and listen to one another.[2] At Bloomingdale's, Candy Pratts Price raised eyebrows with sensational window presentations that led viewers on a trail of discovery. Displays featured women scrawling lipstick messages to each other across a mirror, suggesting a possible rendezvous; then a satisfied femme fatale lay musing between the white sale sheets. Ignoring architectural constraints, Pratts Price told complete stories that flowed from one window into the next.

When Pratts Price bolted onto the display scene in 1974, men had been dominating the profession. (The historians' ingenuous claim was that this was due to the long hours and heavy lifting required by the job.) However, attitudes were changing and barriers to social injustice were being torn down. It's significant to note that women were discouraged from wearing pants in formal settings, especially in the workplace. As a newfound feminism surfaced, mannequin attitudes assumed an air of self-assurance. "Dressing for success" became the catchphrase for women with visions of the corporate ladder instead of the social ladder. As Saint Laurent interpreted the passion of the streets, he introduced the reefer jacket, the safari suit, and the all-important trouser.

Pratts Price credits much of her success and development as a visual artist to Marvin Traub, the chairman and chief executive officer at Bloomingdale's at the time. A highly respected legend in the retail world, Traub was an impresario of sorts, organizing and directing talent that reimagined Bloomingdale's into a fashion-forward, international showplace and destination. Through brilliant merchandising that included some of the world's best-known fashion designers, and world-renowned windows and interiors, Traub led a team that created a must-see store like no other. "He was the P. T. Barnum of retail," said Pratts Price.

> He believed in entertainment, and he believed in an international approach. He opened countries to do business with Bloomingdale's. I sat in on every single ad meeting and every single project for the store. He was someone who believed we're not just selling shirts, we're selling magic, we're selling a new shirt, we're selling

> Ralph Lauren shirts. This kind of direction was very inclusive. We all learned a great deal from him.

Pratts Price's tenure at Bloomingdale's was an amazing and consequential time for retail. It was also a time of transition with a great deal of political and social unrest that triggered a wave of creativity. With Bloomingdale's as her canvas, she was able to make groundbreaking statements that captured the imagination as well as the essence of the times. As an artist, she inspired all who engaged her work and made them think.

"There was a lot going on in retail in 1975," said Pratts Price.

> Bloomingdale's offered a canvas both outdoors and indoors. There was a great deal of change in retail back then. Although Fifth Avenue was still the hot spot, designers were moving to Third Avenue and Lexington Avenue. As I approached my work at Bloomingdale's, I realized that the arena was tremendous. Marvin Traub got Bloomingdale's to be a destination for designers such as Sonia Rykiel and Yves St. Laurent.

The groundbreaking visual merchandiser is quick to acknowledge the contributions of her team.

> We had an amazing staff of carpenters, electricians, and painters. You could create magic from within the house. It was fantastic. We decided that we could use the talent in new ways without setting new standards. Let's get to work. Let's use all of the magic that's in the house. Create this store as our movie; our center and destination for fashion.

Mannequins were ubiquitous and every retailer was using them. "At that time, most people were using what you would call human-looking mannequins," said Pratts Price.

> Terrible horse wigs and a stick that held them up. We decided to get creative and to have wigs done at this wonderful place, Teresa Wigs. We introduced some feathered hair and other contemporary looks. We got rid of the pole and tried to use our set designer mentality to balance the mannequin in a particular way. A subtle twist or position could make all the difference. It could be done with wire, fishing wire, or a small nail to hold the mannequin in place. We were very concerned about safety. We had a very talented staff. If I wanted the mannequin to lean against the wall, they would figure it out. We wanted to be sure she wouldn't fall in the night. The mannequin totally influenced the work and functioned as a conversation in the window. They created a dialogue.

Like so many others before and after, Pratts Price absolutely considered mannequins to be an art form. She used both realistic and abstract mannequins.

> We used all of them as best we could. Nothing was thrown away. We knew we could paint and refurbish. We worked closely with Adel Rootstein. We created the Toukie Smith mannequin after the model. We changed a skin color, we had a make-up person come in to do make-up that wasn't permanently painted on a girl. As we saw the beauty business changing, we wanted the mannequin to reflect this phase, from glossy face and glam sheen to skinny brows. We were very engaged with society, or with what the culture was doing.

Looking toward the future, Pratts Price recognized the tremendous change in retail and in windows.

> We must be very grateful for window art having their constant competitions. Everyone following how windows are done. Hands down, Louis Vuitton is spending and absolutely entertaining me on Fifth Avenue and 57th Street. I strongly believe the future must include digital media and at Louis Vuitton, they have learned to do it so well. What they have been able to do is beyond the scope. It's what a Hollywood studio used to do. It reminds me of Francis Ford Copula. It's key to include digital media in today's window. You can still do what I did, but if I was still doing windows I would be obsessed with artificial intelligence and digital media.

References

1. Eric Feigenbaum, "The 1970s: Street Theater and Anti-Fashion," *Visual Merchandising and Store Design Magazine* (September 20, 2001).
2. Feigenbaum, "The 1970s: Street Theater and Anti-Fashion."

CHAPTER 9
SEARCHING FOR IDENTITY: 1980–1990

The advancing decade began to obscure baby boomer idealism. The Hippies of the 1960s and '70s had become the Yuppies of the 1980s—materialistic, narcissistic, and acquisitive. The 'Me' generation was reaching its earnings peak and trading beads and flowers for power ties and dress-for-success outfits. Shopping became a sport, with fashion as the ultimate prize.

Unbridled over-optimism however, fueled over-spending, over-borrowing, and over-expansion—ultimately leading to over-storing. A rash of liquidations, acquisitions, mergers, and restructuring plagued the department store world. 1986 proved to be a year of monumental change. A Canadian real estate developer created a wave of uncertainty by acquiring Allied Stores Corp., Gimbel's folded, and May acquired Associated Dry Goods Corp.

Specialty retailers such as Gap, Guess, Limited, Benetton, and Esprit began to offer their own brands. Large retailers tried pushing back with unique environments of their own, but the brands they were promoting—Ralph Lauren, Liz Claiborne, Perry Ellis, Calvin Klein—took on a life of their own, assuming a dominant role on department store selling floors. Ralph Lauren's flagship in New York's Rhinelander Mansion was opened. Soon, large retailers were struggling to grab back their identities.[1]

As visual merchandising adapted to change and continued to progress, the job description changed dramatically. Creativity was still paramount, but business acumen and merchandising skills became necessary accompaniments. The leading mannequin designers and manufacturers helped a new breed of visual merchandisers balance the need for creativity, store identity, and the bottom line.

A PURVEYOR OF POSSIBILITIES

Entering Ralph Pucci's mannequin showroom in New York City is a transformative experience; taking visitors to another place, another point of view, and another state of mind. While not an artist in the traditional sense, Ralph Pucci is a purveyor of possibilities, transforming abstract ideas into creative realities. His medium is people, and his brushstroke is his ability to push the limits of their talents. He has inspired a wide range of artists and creative thinkers to articulate the attributes of their art into a dynamic collection of mannequins that are quintessentially Pucci.

A lover of music, he performs his job as a master conductor; an impresario bringing together multiple forms of artistic expression. He will quickly tell you that he is neither artist nor musician; and yet, as a master at melding artistic disciplines, he will move you through rhythm, harmony, and a beautiful simplicity of line. He built a successful career by daring to be different. While Pucci has his finger on the pulse of the times, he doesn't follow trends, he sets them.

In 1954, his parents, Nick and Leigh Pucci, started a mannequin repair company in the basement of their Mt. Vernon, New York home. The impetus for the new start-up business came from the outgoing and personable Nick Pucci's return from World War II, and the little plaster shop run by Leigh Pucci's parents. The Bronx-based plaster artisans specialized in statuary and decorative bird baths. At the same time, Leigh was working as a wig stylist for Mary Brosnan, one of the most important and successful mannequin houses at the time. Given their backgrounds and personalities, the move into the mannequin world seemed like a natural progression. The two aspiring entrepreneurs seized the opportunity and opened what was to become a thriving business.

Ralph's aunt, Maria Pucci, was the secretary for Dorothy Shaver, the president of Lord & Taylor, and the first woman in the United States to lead a multimillion-dollar company. When Maria told Shaver about her brother's new mannequin repair shop, the Lord & Taylor executive instructed the head of her display department to give the fledgling company a try. A call was placed to Mt. Vernon, and Nick and Leigh Pucci's mannequin repair company got their first order. Other orders soon followed, and before long the operation moved from the Pucci basement in Mt. Vernon to a 2,000-square-foot facility on West 20th Street in Manhattan.

Twenty-two years later in 1976, after graduating from Northeastern University in Boston, a young Ralph Pucci joined the highly successful mannequin repair shop run by his parents. "We had everything," said Pucci. "We had a sprayer, a packer, a sander. We had everything except ideas." Brimming with new ideas, unbridled enthusiasm, and a piecing vision, he asked his father, "Why are we repairing other people's mannequins; why don't we make our own?" Nick Pucci was an open-minded man; without hesitation, he said, "Let's give it a try." Ralph was ecstatic. He knew that the industry was growing in leaps and bounds; stores were opening everywhere, and everyone was trying to out do everyone else. He knew the time was right to enter the market and take his shot. He surveyed the competition and analyzed what others were doing. He realized that competing mannequin manufacturers were designing very elegant, lady-like mannequins. His assessment was that what they were doing was good, and wondered why he should do the same. True to his creative instincts, he thought, "If everyone goes to the left, we're going to the right."

Fashion was changing dramatically at the time. The direction of the day, as seen in stores from Barneys to Armani, was a more casual and relaxed look. Exercise became an important driver of men's fashion. It was the beginning of a new life-style that included jogging, running, and guys with sexy physiques. "I wanted our mannequins to be more sculptural," said Pucci. "So we started with action poses; a bicycle rider, a jogger, and a hand-standing pose. They were all male mannequins that we painted black, white, and red. They were a big hit. Before long, stores were asking us to do the same thing with female mannequins." Schlappi Mannequins contracted with Pucci to sell the new abstract action poses in Europe. Pucci's New York showroom featured eight of the new bicycle riders in the same pose, each with a different sculpted hair style, and all standing in a

Figure 9.1 Ralph Pucci Mannequins, Girl 2, 2008. Abstract mannequins in a graphic black and white grouping. Photograph by Antoine Bootz.

straight line. The presentation was dynamic. Bill Withers, the visual director at Macy's San Francisco took one look and said, "This is great." He then promptly placed an order for twenty mannequins painted in a high gloss black finish. A few days later, Andrew Markopoulos, the visual director at Dayton Hudson, came into the showroom and asked for an exclusive. Pucci said he couldn't do that, but he could give him an exclusive color. Markopoulos took thirty mannequins and had them painted a metallic hunter green. Jim Elliot from Marshall Field's came in next, also asking for an exclusive. Again Pucci offered an exclusive color. Elliot purchased fifty mannequins in red. The abstract action line was off and running.

The next wave of vision and creativity focused on reimagining the lingerie mannequin. Always driven by the arts, Pucci turned to the likes of Michelangelo and Rodin for direction and inspiration. Once again, Pucci's approach was to differentiate his company from all of the others. It wasn't merely to be different for the sake of being different, but rather, being different in an attempt to be new and invigorating. Pucci fully understood Albert Einstein's memorable quote, "Logic will get you from A to B. Imagination will take you everywhere." And it was with imagination that Pucci led visual merchandisers to rethink the lingerie mannequin, and in fact, all mannequins. The new lingerie mannequins

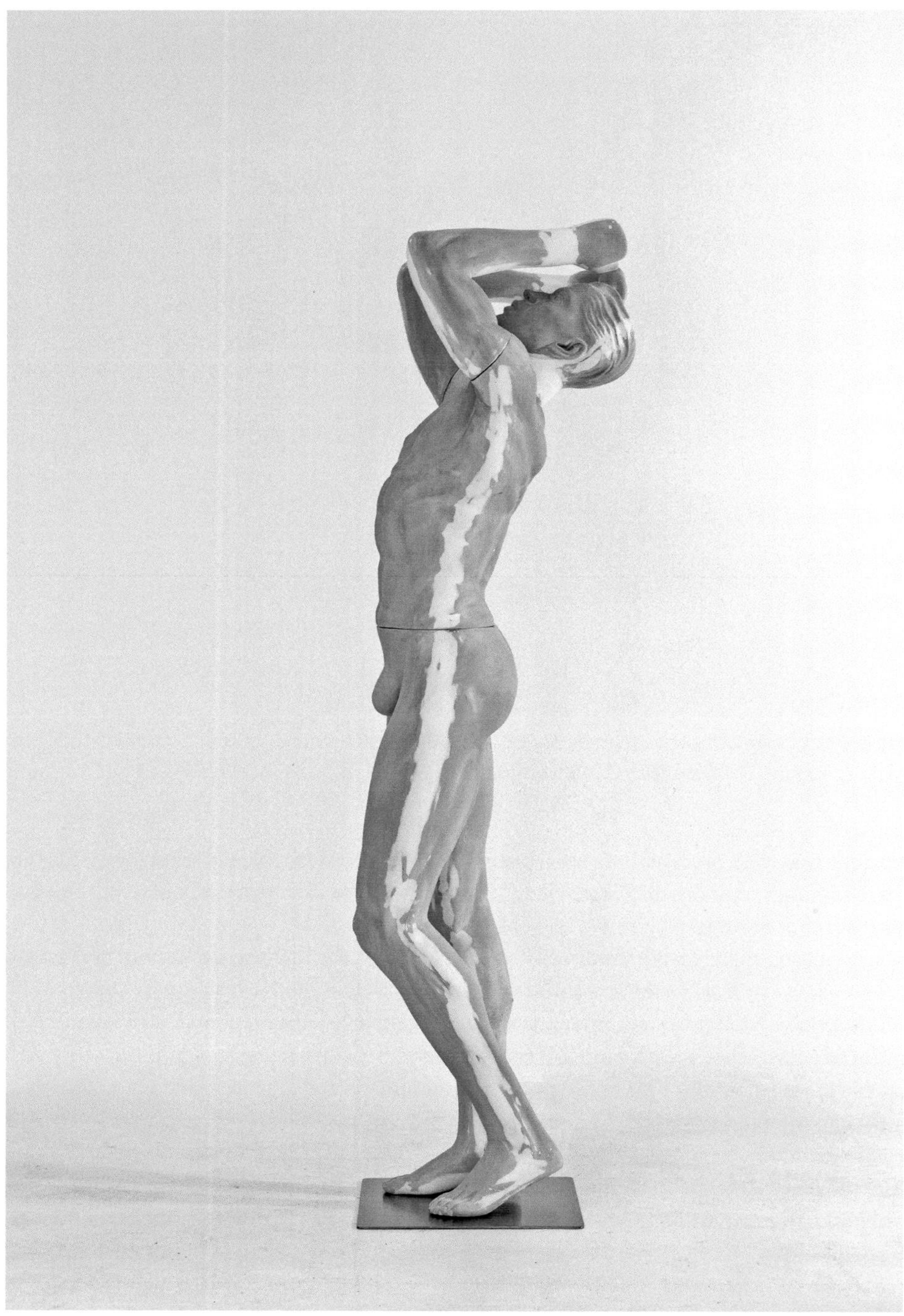

Figure 9.2 Ralph Pucci Mannequins, Olympic Gold, 1989. Lowell Nesbitt, designer; Photograph by Antoine Bootz.

were shown in pairs and made to look like marble or stone. Pucci's mannequins were not merely fancy clothes hangers, although they wore clothes well, they were works of art.

Always in tune, Pucci responded to the groundbreaking events of August 1, 1981, when the music world changed forever. It was soon after midnight on that memorable date that MTV first hit the scene. The words, "Ladies and Gentlemen, Rock and Roll," punctuated the airwaves, welcoming in a new platform for music videos. The careers of soon-to-be musical icons from Madonna to Cyndi Lauper were catapulted to the moon along with new imagery and associated dance moves.[2] Inspired by the MTV phenomenon and his love of music, Pucci developed a new line of abstracts, all striking dynamic dance-like poses. The action figures were finished in reds and yellows, and all sported wigs that celebrated the new pop culture. Before long, the Pucci *Mysteries in Motion* mannequins were dancing in Juniors Departments in stores across the industry.

Pucci's next big innovation and subsequent mannequin success came in 1986 when he met Andrée Putman, the world-renowned French interior and product designer. Barneys was expanding at the time, opening a new women's store at their existing 17th Street location in the Chelsea section of Manhattan. Putnam was hired for the interior design of the multi-story store. In designing the interior, she made a significant impact, as one of the architectural signatures of the new environment was her magnificent spiral staircase. Concurrently, Putnam was working on the design of the Morgans Hotel in New York. This, along with other high-profile projects such as the interior of the French Concord, and salons for Azzedine Alaia, Balenciaga, and Karl Lagerfeld marked a new meteoric rise in her illustrious career. It was the design of the new Barneys store, under the direction of Putnam and architect Peter Marino, which nudged Pucci's imagination, getting him to realize that there was a market for a different kind of mannequin.

While still working on the Morgans Hotel, Putnam teamed with Pucci to design a new mannequin for the store opening called the "Olympian Goddess." Putman wanted the mannequin to be God-like, muscular, and strong. The resultant design featured big shoulders, big breasts, and even a bigger head than a typical mannequin. The design was also Art Deco inspired with flipped-back sculpted hair. The Olympian Goddess was a major change in direction; a total pivot from anything ever done before in a retail environment. This was an eye-opener for the visionary and enterprising Pucci. He immediately recognized that retail was ready for something new; retail was ready for an artistically rendered mannequin that was reflective of a new fashion direction.

With visions toward a new day, the Pucci showroom featured the Olympian Goddess. The statuesque mannequins were dramatically positioned and dressed in black by the up-up-and-coming fashion designer, soon-to-be fashion icon, Isabel Toledo. The opening was a true New York happening. Putnam brought Andy Warhol and Keith Haring to the event, while Pucci brought retail's brightest stars and luminaries. The showroom was buzzing with fashion people, artists, writers, and creatives of all kinds. The press corps covering culture and the arts was ablaze with excitement as the opening was covered on *Page Six of the New York Post* and in a two-page spread by Nina Hyde of *The Washington Post*. Every relevant magazine covered Barneys' new mannequin designed by Andrée Putman and produced by Ralph Pucci.

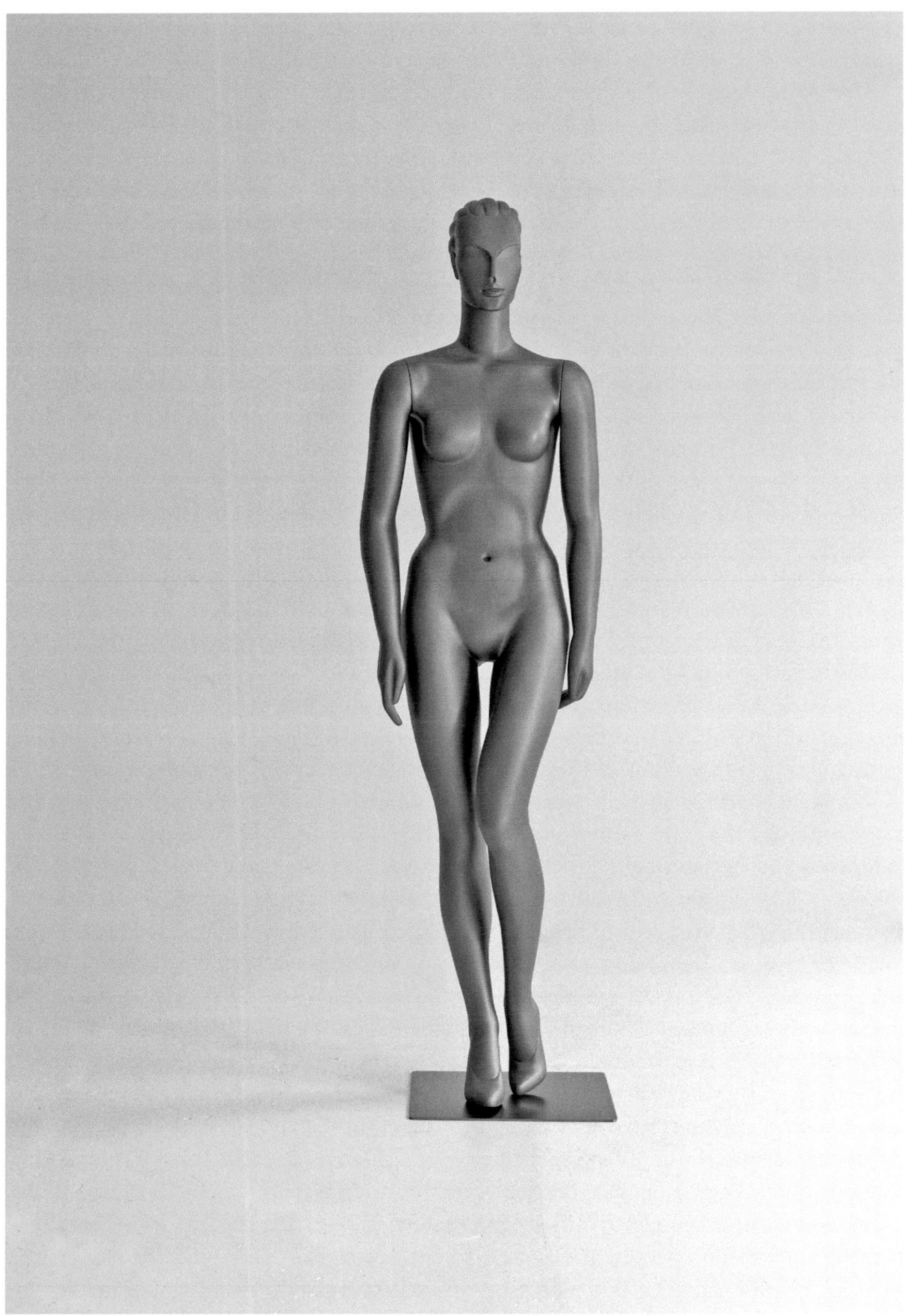

Figure 9.3 Ralph Pucci Mannequins, The Olympian Goddess, 1986. Andrée Putman, designer; Photograph by Antoine Bootz.

Figure 9.4 Ralph Pucci Mannequins, Birdland, 1988. Ruben Toledo, designer; Photograph by Antoine Bootz.

Working with Andrée Putman lit a fire in Pucci; it was as if a light bulb went off. Inspired by her vision and willingness to push the boundaries of convention, he knew that he could work with other creatives from a variety of disciplines to make mannequin magic. Next, he turned to the emerging Cuban American artist, Ruben Toledo. "The body shapes in his illustrations were so relevant. They were where fashion was going," said Pucci. "Inspired by his wife Isabel, Toledo used flat whites, grays, and blacks to create compelling forms and images." Pucci thought that Toledo would be the perfect creative to produce a new line of mannequins. The results of the collaboration made a significant statement to retail and the mannequin industry; everyone wanted the Toledo mannequin. After the success of his first mannequin collection, Toledo went on to design five or six more lines.

Through his collaborations with a wide range of artists working in many different mediums, Pucci demonstrated that his mannequins were truly an art form. More often than not, the catalyst for great art is our response to the events of everyday life. Inspiration is drawn from our challenges, problems, concerns, failures, successes, and joys. Among Ralph Pucci's most cherished joys was reading bedtime stories to his two young children as they were growing up. Among their favorites, and Ralph's as well, was the charming work of author and illustrator Maira Kalman, whose portfolio includes a dozen children's books such as *Max Makes a Million*, *Max in Hollywood: Baby*, *Next Stop Grand Central Station*, and *Fireboat: The Heroic Adventures of the John J. Harvey*.

"My kids loved when I read to them, and they particularly loved *Max Makes a Million*, and *Max in Hollywood: Baby*. I was so moved by their reaction to her stories and to the corresponding imagery, that I cold called her," remembered Pucci. "I asked her if we could take the heads from her illustrations and use them on mannequins. Without hesitation, she said absolutely." What resulted was Pucci's most successful mannequin line. "We created a whole fantasy world; animated mannequins with orange and blue hair. There was a dancer, a baker, and even a shoe cobbler. We drew upon anything related to New York in a very creative and inspirational period of time." Visual merchandisers across the industry admired Pucci for taking chances. Ken Smart, the visual director at Saks Fifth Avenue loved it. He enthusiastically said when seeing the new mannequins, "This is a big hit." The Kalman mannequin line was indeed a big hit. It started with women and men, and then the success and the creativity continued with a line of children's mannequins that included pink hair, pig tails, and spotted puppies.

Perhaps the most successful program involving the Maira Kalman mannequin was developed by Andrew Markopoulos at Dayton Hudson. "Everyone in retail at the time was trying to find and define an identification, a face of their own," said Pucci. "Consumers were also gravitating toward a workday casual look, but Andy knew that they were getting it all wrong."

Markopoulos understood that workday casual wasn't ripped jeans and old sneakers. He thought of it rather as John F. Kennedy on a Saturday in Hyannis Port. As such, he wanted to do a major promotion that would get this message across. He proposed a massive program to Dayton Hudson management that included a grouping of ten men's, women's, and children's mannequins positioned as greeters at every Dayton Hudson store. Markopoulos was ready to purchase five hundred mannequins for the promotion. Management told Markopoulos to come back with another idea. Undeterred, the visual merchandising legend came back with an even bigger program based around the Kalman mannequin. His new vision involved a thousand mannequins for stores across the Dayton Hudson chain, with their unmistakable images printed on shopping bags and billboards. Markopoulos even went so far as to develop a TV commercial with the mannequins coming to life. Markopoulos's persistence paid off; management loved it. The promotion was one of the biggest and most successful in Dayton Hudson history. Ten years later the chairman of the board of Dayton Hudson happened to come into Pucci's furniture showroom looking for furniture for his home. Ralph asked him what he did for a living. When he told him that he was with Dayton Hudson, Ralph told him that he supplied the Maira Kalman mannequins used in the workday casual promotion ten years earlier. The former retail leader responded by saying that the promotion was the biggest success of his career. He went on to say, "It didn't need much. The mannequin created the experience and the wow."

Pucci's relentless drive to stay ahead of the curve brought more creativity and continued success. In 1993 the Metropolitan Museum of Art in New York was looking

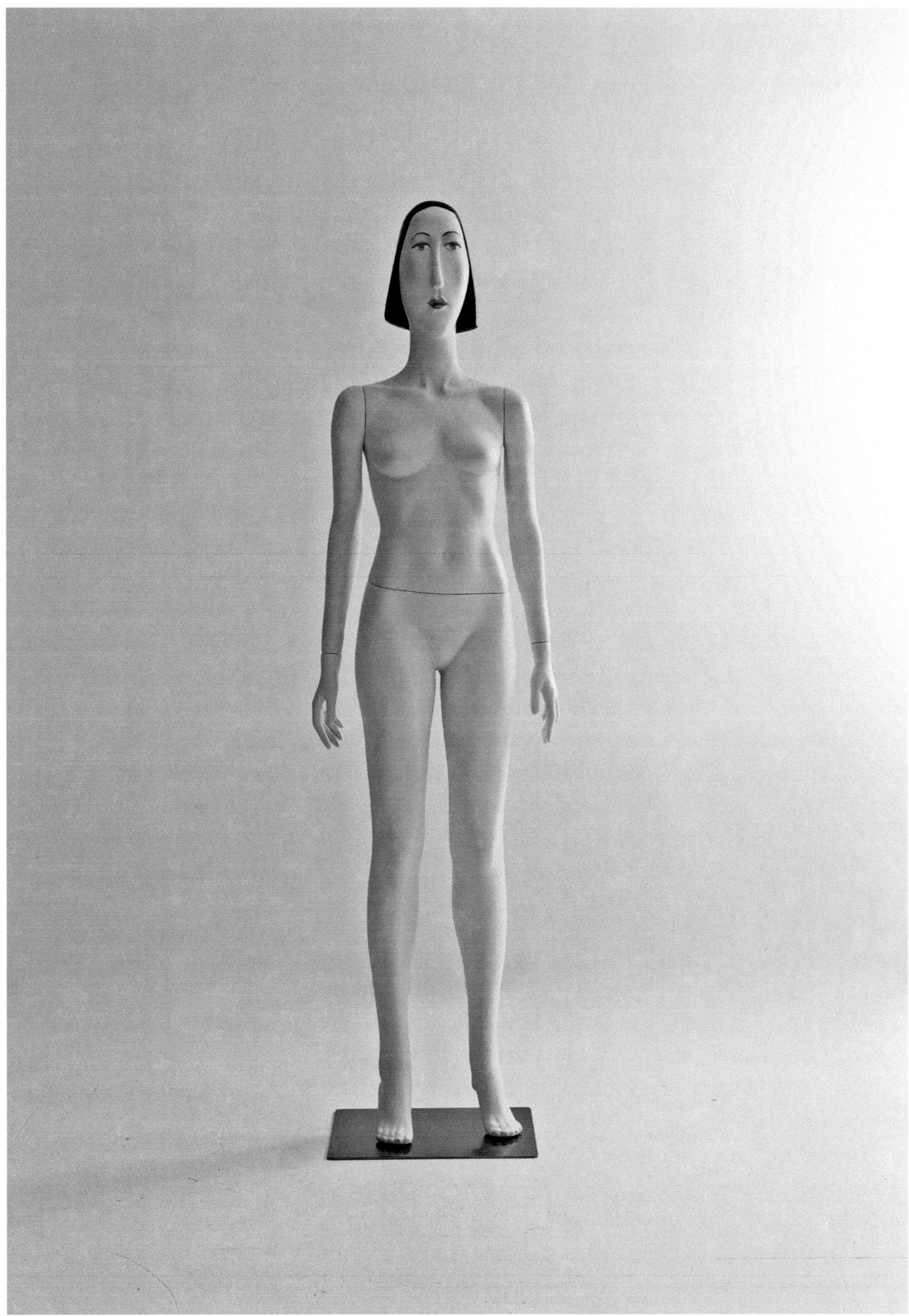

Figure 9.5 Ralph Pucci Mannequins. Maira Kalman designer; Photograph by Antoine Bootz.

Figure 9.6 Ralph Pucci Mannequins, Christy Turlington yoga mannequin. Photograph by Antoine Bootz.

for one classic face to launch the first installation at its new Costume Institute Galleries. A year earlier, supermodel Christy Turlington was recognized as the new face of Maybelline Cosmetics. The curators and stylists at the Met were so taken with her timeless and universal look that they proclaimed Turlington to be the "Face of the 20th Century." A rising star at the time, Turlington attributes her captivating visage to her mixed ethnicity. She credits her El Salvadoran mother for her rich olive-toned skin, and her American father for her classic bone structure.[3] In recognizing her star power and appeal, it was decided that all of the mannequins for the opening of the Costume Institute Galleries would have one common thread. Whether a men's, women's, or children's mannequin, they would all share Christy Turlington's timeless face.

The Metropolitan Museum of Art collaborated with Pucci International to produce 120 mannequins, all with the face of Christy Turlington. Excitement was in the air at the launch of the new mannequin. The opening reception at the Pucci showroom in New York featured 40 fiber-glass mannequins in the likeness of Turlington, with the real flesh and blood supermodel walking about. The Christy Turlington mannequin received a barrage of accolades from all quarters, including prime coverage in *Vogue Magazine*.

Pucci's relationship with the supermodel didn't end there. In the mid '90s as yoga was gaining in popularity, Turlington designed a line of yoga clothing. As her fashions garnered attention, she worked with Pucci to develop a collection of mannequins in yoga poses, including the iconic lotus pose. Naturally, all of the mannequins sported Turlington's now-famous face.

With the success of the yoga mannequin, Turlington suggested that she and Pucci collaborate every ten years. Pucci recalled that when she returned ten years later, she didn't want the mannequin to be too skinny. This compelled Pucci to consider a range of sizes. Instead of making mannequins only in the idealized size 2, he created "Line Sizes," a grouping of mannequins with a mix of sizes 8, 10, 12, and 14. Another success and more accolades from the press quickly followed.

When considering his longstanding career as a leader in the mannequin industry, Pucci said, "It's all about fun, being different, and taking chances." Along those lines, the mannequin mogul always sought out new people to work with; people who had something new to say. As Memphis Design, a movement inspired by a blending of Art Deco and pop art, began to pick up steam in the 1980s, Pucci thought about creating a mannequin with someone who was instrumental in the development of the genre. After sending many letters, Pucci finally got a response from Aldo Cibic, an influential Italian architect and one of the founders of the Memphis Design movement. Cibic was very interested in Pucci's proposal to design a new mannequin in the Memphis style. When Pucci received Cibic's first sketches, he was surprised to see that the designer wanted to work with metal. Pucci went along with Cibic's vision and produced the metal mannequin with associated Memphis colors of red and blue. The result was a new Pucci mannequin inspired by one of the most important movements in 20th-century design history.

Pucci worked with a wide variety of creative people over the years, most from different disciplines. He recognized their vision and saw how their creativity could elevate the retail experience. All of them went on to great careers in the design world. "The industry is hungry for new ideas and new concepts," said Pucci. "The mannequin is a great way to get new ideas out there. I was never caught up with trends, but rather, timely, beautifully sculpted pieces of art."

FROM REALISTIC TO STYLIZED

Soon after Mark Goldsmith's grandfather, Rabbi Meyer Goldsmith, emigrated to the United States from Russia, he started a small mannequin company at 330 Broome Street in New York City. When he founded Goldsmith & Sons Display Fixtures in 1927, he never intended to personally participate in the business. His hope was to establish a company for his family to work in. Like any other father, he wanted to be sure that his sons would have jobs. At the time, the good rabbi had no idea that the little family-owned business would evolve from its humble beginnings and limited technologies to become the country's leading manufacturer of mannequins and one of the top international mannequin and visual merchandising companies in the world.

When Mark Goldsmith assumed the leadership of his family-owned and operated mannequin business in 1977, he embarked on a ten-year mission to change the company's

Figure 9.7 Ralph Pucci Mannequins, Ralph Pucci in his gallery, 2014. Collection of Ralph Pucci. Photograph by Antoine Bootz.

vision and business model. "I was always uncomfortable and embarrassed by the Goldsmith business model," said Goldsmith.

> We had never created an original product. We bought product from the top companies and copied them, selling at less than half the price. When I took the reins of the company, I vowed never to copy a mannequin again. I hired a creative director and together we designed our first line. It's rather ironic, but it took around 10 years for us to lose our bad reputation and become an industry design leader, with our products copied by several other companies.

When Rabbi Goldsmith started the company, there were four Goldsmith brothers, each of whom worked in the company until they were all bought out one by one by Mark's father, Sam, who remained the only Goldsmith left in the company. Sam Goldsmith died suddenly at the age of fifty-three when Mark just started college. "I worked each summer in the company as my cousin Norman ran the business until I graduated," remembered Goldsmith. "In 1977 when I was 26, Norman was killed in an automobile accident and suddenly, it was just me."

Goldsmith readily credits Colin Birch, EVP of Visual Merchandising at Bloomingdale's, for helping to propel Goldsmith Mannequins to its position as an industry leader. "Colin was one of visual merchandising's legendary geniuses. He was one of the first top-tier directors to buy from the newly revamped Goldsmith. He realized our talent, and we became his major supplier."

Shane DeRolf was the Creative Director at Goldsmith Mannequins from 1981 to 1991. During his decade-long tenure, he worked closely with Mark Goldsmith to develop new programs and exciting leading-edge mannequin concepts. As DeRolf's creative vision expanded, he befriended Birch. He fondly recalls, "I first met Colin Birch in the hallway of his second-story office on 59th Street in 1981, across from the Bloomingdale's Mother Ship. He was cradling and petting a plush silver-toned schnauzer." The friendship and professional relationship took off immediately; together they created mannequin magic.

Of all the mannequins ever produced by Goldsmith, Inc. in its long history, the most popular line ever created was "Dani and Abi." The collection consisted of two models; one realistic and one abstract. Dani was the realistic version of Abi, who had softer and more abstract features and quickly became the most popular of the two mannequins. Abi stood out because of her beautiful simplicity and elegant lines. Abi was created based on a grand vision Birch had for a promotional event in Bloomingdale's iconic Lexington Avenue windows.

Every year Bloomingdale's staged a storewide event based on a particular international culture. One year they celebrated Italy, another year China, and then Israel, etc. For each event, the Lexington Avenue windows were decked out in the splendors of the selected country. In 1985, Birch contracted Goldsmith to sculpt, build and, debut Dani and Abi in time for Bloomingdale's upcoming Italian promotion. Birch had a vision of replicating the tricolor Italian flag with several groupings of three mannequins. To do so, he created tightly positioned groups of three Abi mannequins positioned in graphic geometric

Figure 9.8 Goldsmith Mannequin advertisement. Courtesy VMSD Magazine.

patterns. Rather than wearing clothes, each mannequin within each group of three was painted with one of the three colors of the Italian flag. One mannequin was painted green, one white, and one red. When grouped together they formed the Italian flag. One group of three was positioned diagonally in one window, one was positioned sideways in another window, and the other head-on in yet another window. The windows were a big hit; everyone in the industry flocked to Bloomingdale's to see Colin's grand presentation and to see his leading lady, Abi. Traffic on Lexington Avenue was slowed to a crawl as drivers stretched their necks to see the dynamic Italian flags made entirely of Abi mannequins. Mark Goldsmith was very appreciative as he recalled, "Colin credited our company by writing '*Mannequins by Goldsmith*' on the flagship windows."

One of Birch's favorite things to do was to stand incognito across the street on the west side of Lexington Avenue whenever his windows were unveiled. He did this religiously to see how passersby reacted to his street theater. When he watched the reaction to Abi in the Italian windows, he became teary-eyed seeing the response to something that started as an idea.

Used exclusively in the windows for her debut, Abi eventually found her way into the store interior where she became a Bloomingdale's mainstay. And while she didn't wear clothes in the window, what Colin liked most about the "Dani and Abi" collection was how well they wore clothes. "We don't need a lot of animation and attitude in mannequins today," said Birch. "The new mannequins reflect the new clothes. The feeling is soigné, relaxed and more ladylike, as opposed to the standard, realistic, pretty mannequins that have been big."[4]

According to DeRolf, "Colin knew exactly what he wanted. The great sculptor, Michael Katok, sculpted the line and did a truly inspired job. Also, one of the best-kept secrets at Goldsmith was our mold maker, Tony Checci. It was a true team effort. My role in the development of Abi was to orchestrate the project. While I had occasional creative input, my job was to keep the process going." DeRolf proudly said that in his 10 years as Goldsmith's Creative Director, there was never a project that the creative and production team couldn't deliver on.

"I certainly consider mannequins to be an art form," said Goldsmith. "We required top sculptors, artists, and wig makers to produce our products. They were original works of art. In addition to our highly developed aesthetic standards, we were known for our daring design ethic. And while not all new products were best-sellers, they were all the topics of industry buzz." Goldsmith also strongly believes that there is no better way to sell apparel. "The only way a customer can see themselves and imagine how they will look is on a somewhat realistic body."

Another great, timely, and even humorous Colin Birch and DeRolf collaboration was Multi-Man. Birch had an idea to create a robotic superhero with static and even classic poses. The entire Goldsmith team, from Mark Goldsmith and DeRolf to the shop foreman and the sculptor, Alexander Danel, ran with the idea. A sign of the times, Multi-Man, complete with neon eyes or LED light eyes, was a futuristic space traveler made of

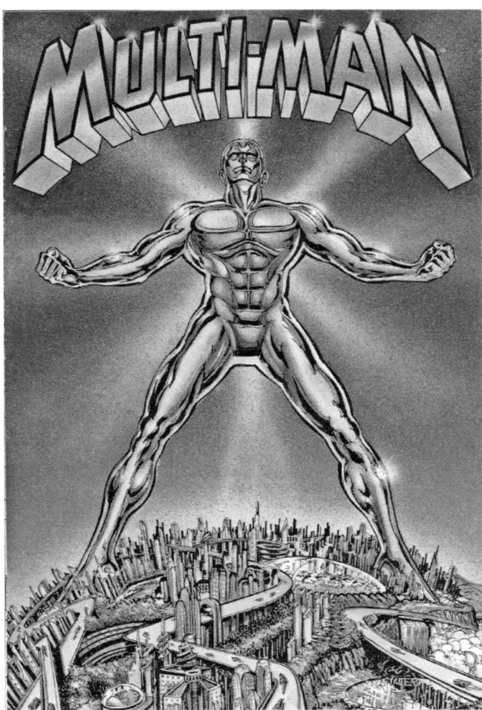

Figure 9.9 Goldsmith Multi-Man, the superhero comic book. Courtesy of Shane DeRolf.

fiberglass with a metallic, high-gloss painted finish. This muscular robotic-looking mannequin was a nod to the burgeoning electronic age and an advancing scientific society. One of DeRolf's favorite and enduring memories was when he was watching the iconic 1988 American comedic fantasy movie drama *Big*. In the film, directed by Penny Marshall, Tom Hanks is seen playing with a ray gun as he hides behind a Multi-Man. DeRolf recalls, "Multi-Man was revolutionary for its time. We were very hot at the time, and we attracted many great talents. Rather than a traditional catalog, our photographer, Michael Bauman, had the brilliant idea to launch Multi-Man as a comic book hero. And so, Multi-Man, the superhero, was launched in a comic book and immortalized in cartoon form."

Goldsmith and DeRolf pushed the limits of their creativity far beyond the retail world. "We designed many products outside the industry," said Goldsmith. "We manufactured the giant toy soldiers that surround the Rockefeller Center skating rink each Christmas, and we made many of the mannequins for the Metropolitan Museum's costume institute." The long list of projects outside the industry continued with all the bodies for the Smithsonian's First Lady exhibit, and all the Victorian mannequins for the original, and all national productions of Phantom of the Opera.

"We threw a legendary party each December at varied and wonderful venues," reminisced Goldsmith. "Over a thousand guests would attend each event, many of whom I didn't even know. Those parties are some of my fondest memories." In 2001 Goldsmith was approached by a venture capital group to buy the company. "They commissioned an industry-wide survey to discover our status," said Goldsmith. "The results said we were the largest mannequin company in the world!"

When speaking of his tenure at Goldsmith, DeRolf said, "No story about the success of Goldsmith would ever be complete without a 'high five' to the adroit leadership of none other than Mark 'Coach' Goldsmith himself . . . the best leader and partner I've ever had the pleasure of working with." DeRolf first met Goldsmith while working as the director of visual merchandising for a small chain called Parklane Hosiery. "We bought mannequins from Goldsmith because they were reasonably priced," said DeRolf. When Mark came by one day on a sales visit, DeRolf asked him if he would like to double his profits in two years. "I'd love to," Goldsmith eagerly replied. "How can I do that?" Without missing a beat, the young self-confident DeRolf said, "Hire me." Goldsmith hired DeRolf. The rest is history.

Retail was evolving quickly in the early 1980s, and store design was changing dramatically with new approaches and new concepts. The department store of the 1970s featured deep departments with layouts that extended far to the rear with little visual access to back wall presentations. Store designers searched for new ways to maximize merchandise exposure while creating clear and easily navigable traffic patterns. To mitigate the problem of merchandise buried within the depths of the department, store designers developed what was commonly referred to as the racetrack floor plan. In this configuration, the main traffic aisle looped around the entire selling floor much like a racetrack. This dramatically reduced the depth of each department and increased frontage and merchandise exposure. Retail, like real estate, is all about location, location, location. And naturally, the best location for merchandise is front and forward. Every merchandise resource wanted their product offerings to be as close to the main aisle as possible. While everyone can't be on the aisle, the new racetrack floorplan gave new power to the perimeter, or the back wall. The back wall suddenly became the most important fixture in the store. It could be seen from a great distance, and it could tell strong merchandise stories. Visual merchandisers quickly realized that they could create dynamic wall presentations that would highlight merchandise and draw customers into the department. They began to look for different techniques to create in-store excitement while showing merchandise conviction. Carol Barnhart, who was an account executive for Spaeth Display, was in the right place, with the right product, at the right time.

For Barnhart, it all began with a simple philosophy and a creative idea. The philosophy was to build a business by satisfying the ever-changing needs of the visual merchandising industry. She wanted to fill any holes that existed in the visual merchandiser's toolbox for presenting and ultimately selling merchandise. The idea evolved out of a discussion she had with Elliot Gerber, the visual merchandising director at Gimbels. Men's polo shirts in a rainbow of colors were all the rage in the early 1980s. They were typically housed in glass cubes running along the back wall of the department. In a casual lunchtime conversation, Gerber told Barnhart that he would love to have some sort of pinnable shirt form that would allow him to easily display a full range of shirts in a full spectrum of colors on the back wall. Upon hearing this, a lightbulb went off in Barnhart's head. "I have an idea," said the young creative with a twinkling of entrepreneurial spirit.

Through her husband's work, Barnhart was familiar with a company that made Christmas trees out of EPS (expanded polystyrene). Of course, selling Christmas trees is a seasonal business. In order to keep their company afloat during the offseason, they produced ice chests made out of EPS. Barnhart's idea was to craft men's shirt forms out of this lightweight pinnable material. She pitched the idea to her boss at Spaeth, which was also a seasonal business needing supplemental offseason work. Spaeth never moved forward with the concept, it never really got off the ground. Undeterred, the relentless visionary went back to Gerber with the idea of making the form out of EPS herself. She told Gerber that she would give him ten percent of everything she sold. Gerber loved it and told her exactly what he needed.

With Gerber's nod of approval and subsequent set of detailed specifications, Barnhart cut up one of her husband's polo shirts and took exacting measurements. The idea became a reality when she hired a Russian sculptor by the name of Alexander Danel to create the form. As Danel continued to work on the sculpting of the piece, retail's fourth quarter selling season was fast approaching. At the time, Barnhart was still in her position at Spaeth, and she faced the enormous task of getting several malls trimmed for the holiday. The job seemed daunting as she was also working to nurse her husband back to health after a debilitating illness. Envisioning the opportunities and ultimate success of her pinnable shirt form, she took a gamble and decided to quit her job at Spaeth. She thought her energies would be better spent devoting her time to caring for her husband and developing her new idea.

Steadfast and determined, she produced her first shirt forms in time for the NADI (National Association of Display Industries) December Show in New York. Together with a small group of artists, she took a booth at the New York Passenger Ship Terminal Pier where NADI held its biannual trade show. Upon seeing the form at the show, Wilmer Weiss, the visual merchandising director at A&S, loved it. He was the first to buy Barnhart's new men's shirt forms with a $20,000 order. Later that week, Barnhart was on the NADI shuttle bus that took buyers and exhibitors to the permanent showrooms in midtown Manhattan. While en route, the display director at Sterns Department Store saw her carrying the form. He also loved what he saw, and Barnhart had her second sale. With those two orders, her molds were paid for. Her new company was off to a flying start.

It didn't take long before more orders started to stream in. Rob Unger, the director of visual merchandising and store design at Burdine's in Florida, wanted the forms, and Joe Powers wanted a female version of the shirt form for Bamburgers in New Jersey. Upon hearing Powers's request, Barnhart went home and cut up one of her own shirts and took exacting measurements. The train was rolling as orders and special requests continued to pour in. Someone wanted a form for swimwear, and then there was a request for a 3/4 form. Next came requests for jewelry forms, and then forms for folded towels. Soon after that Howard Meadows from B. Altman had an idea for a collection of children's mannequins. Meadows drew up his mannequin concept, and Barnhart produced it.

Now with her own company, Barnhart wanted to take on the challenge of expanding into full-size mannequins. This was a big step for the young company, and Barnhart had some trepidations and concerns. And then she met Adel Rootstein whom she credits with giving her the confidence and the will to succeed. "Adel Rootstein changed everything for me. She let me know that I could do this. When I saw the Rootstein mannequins I was in heaven. I told myself that I could do this. I told myself that a woman owns this company, and I can do it too."

As Barnhart continued to build her business around the many new requests she was getting for additional three-dimensional pieces, she called upon her love of sculpting and the knowledge gained in her multi-disciplined education. She studied life drawing and sculpture at the Art Students League in New York, and fashion design at Parsons School of Design. Also adding to her understanding of the structure and movement of the human form was her earlier work as a model.

Upon graduation from Parsons, she took her first job in visual merchandising at Plymouth Shops. One day while walking past the store, she was intrigued when she saw someone doing their windows. She thought to herself, "I can do this." She applied for a job, and with her educational background in art and fashion, she was hired. While she learned the basics at Plymouth Shop, it was the next chapter of her career that truly opened her eyes to the possibilities that the industry offered. While doing a Fifth Avenue window for Plymouth Shop, someone knocked on the glass and told her that he was friends with Bob Benzio, the visual merchandising director at B. Altman's. "This guy, whom I've never met before said why don't you interview with Benzio for a job, you would be perfect." She took the stranger's advice and applied for a job. Benzio interviewed her and hired her. Although she took a $70 cut in pay, she was thrilled with the opportunity. "Benzio had a great taste level," she said. "His aesthetic sensibilities were very lofty and sophisticated. He always tried to elevate everything." Upon being hired, she became the first woman to work in B. Altman's windows. Benzio was so pleased with her work that he sent her to D.G. Williams, a major mannequin manufacturer, to redesign a mannequin exclusively for Altman's. With that, she got her first experience with mannequin design.

Just a few years later she found herself running her own company with the challenge of designing her own full-size mannequins. Always wanting to fill the needs of the industry, she realized that stores wanted active mannequins. There was a request for a basketball player. The caveat was that it had to be lightweight so that it could be hung from the ceiling. Barnhart's EPS was the perfect solution.

Barnhart's mannequin line continued to expand, and she eventually began to produce fiberglass mannequins. As a sculptor herself, she considered mannequins as both an art form and a vital utilitarian tool. "Nothing sells better than a mannequin," she said. "The art comes in the sculpting. No mannequin is a perfect representation of the human body. It's an idealized version of the body. Creating that is an art form."

While it all began with utilitarian shirt forms, and later full-size mannequins, she extended her offerings to decorative props. Her most well-known and perhaps most lucrative decorative was the Carol Barnhart Banana Leaf, inspired by the wallpaper pattern of the Beverly Hills Hotel. At the time Barnhart was developing the banana leaf, Burdine's was positioning itself as "The Florida Store," a holistic marketing and branding approach that proved quite successful for the Miami-based retailer. The banana leaf was perfect, and Rob Unger purchased truckloads of them.

While the Barnhart decorative was a compelling embellishment in Florida's sunny climes, it also offered creative possibilities in New York and New Jersey.

> At the time, I was the director of visual merchandising at Sterns Department Store, based in Paramus, New Jersey. While considering the spring and summer trim for our twenty-plus New York metropolitan area stores, I envisioned the impact the banana leaves would provide on our center core ledges. After I also placed a sizable order for the dynamically sculpted leaves, I wanted to add another level to the presentation. I met Carol in the parking lot of our flagship store in Paramus, where we poured over my detailed drawings of what would become "The Rousseau Flower," the perfect complement to the banana leaf.

In looking back at her career, Barnhart reflected on a trip she took with her father to the Champagne Region of France. While on a tour at a Champagne House in Epernay, her father saw a motion torso in the gift shop. She knew she was a success the moment her father said, "Look Carol, isn't that your form?" Her father beamed with pride knowing that his daughter's mannequins and forms could be found all over the world, even in a remote champagne winery in the small town of Epernay, France.

MANNEQUINS AND MUSIC

Born and raised in Toledo, Ohio, Ronald Gosses always had an enduring love of music and art. Even at the tender age of sixteen, young Ronald was a true Renaissance man. His first job while still in High School was a gig that he truly loved, playing piano and organ in a local Toledo restaurant. At the same time that he was displaying his musical talents, he was also showing his paintings around town. A fellow by the name of Paul Powers, a friend of the young artist, bought one of Ronald's paintings for his home. Herman Van Etten, a neighbor of Powers, was the manager of the new Tiedtke's, a local department store in Toledo's Greenwood Mall. Gosses recalled, "When Van Etten saw my artwork, he said if I could paint like that, he was sure I could do display. He offered me a job as head of the display department (that's what they called visual merchandising back then) with 3 employees." The opportunity presented by Tiedtke's opened up a new world for the young artist, providing yet another stage for him to share his creative spirit. It also marked the beginning of a long and rewarding career as a leader in the visual merchandising industry.

"Tiedtke's was unique in so many ways," recalled Gosses.

> It carried everything from sturdy overalls to furs and elegant evening gowns. It had dry goods, groceries, fresh fish right off the boat. People used to say if you couldn't find it at Tiedtke's, it probably didn't exist. The original Tiedtke's on Summit and Adams in downtown Toledo opened in 1884, had a huge bakery, made its own candy, and roasted its coffee beans. There were so many places to eat, just on the first floor; the lunch counter, the deli, Sea Way Cafeteria, soda fountain, buttermilk bar, and more. There was a pipe organ and one of the first wooden escalators that only went up. To go down you had to use the stairs or elevators. The building itself spanned a city block, and then another block deep to Water Street, and the railroad. I was thrilled to get a job at the newly opened Tiedtke's in the Greenwood Mall.

Gosses went on to attend the University of Toledo while also studying at the Toledo Museum of Art. His big break in the visual merchandising industry came when he was hired by David Nichols, president of a three-store group, The Lion Stores. A short time later he was promoted to the 12-store Joslin's group in Denver, Colorado, where he also headed the Fashion Department and the Store Planning Department. When David Nichols became CEO of Mercantile Stores, he brought Gosses with him. "I moved along to Cincinnati as the Corporate Vice President of 118 stores," said Gosses. "At that time, Mercantile had 13 divisions: Bacon's, Castner Knott, de Lendrecie's, Gayfers, Glass Block, Hennessy's, J.B. White, The Jones Store Co., Joslin's, Lion Store, Maison Blanche, Mc Alpin's and Root's."

During the course of his long-term career in store design and visual merchandising, Gosses witnessed fashion's grand evolution as it continued to reflect the social consciousness of the day. Accordingly, he also witnessed the many changes in which fashion is displayed and presented in stores, particularly on retail fixtures and mannequins. "The first mannequins I used when I began my career in 1968 were heavy fiberglass models with stiff fiberglass wigs. Of course, when I started at Tiedtke's in Toledo, bell bottoms and mini skirts were the height of fashion."

As fashion adapted to cultural shifts and responded to changing societal values and attitudes, Gosses turned his focus away from those early realistic figures to more stylized designs and a wider use of bust forms and dressmaker forms. While increasingly favoring the abstract, he still believed there was a place for realistic mannequins when used strategically. "While we were moving toward the abstract, we did like to use 'realistic' mannequins in windows and in situations where they interacted with the customers," offered Gosses.

> We placed them overlooking a balcony or seated in a customer's sitting area in the fashion departments. While heading Mercantile's corporate visual merchandising department, I found creative ways to use mannequins when we changed our department designs. Each area was developed as a distinct environment which included special visuals and different and distinct music. A mannequin could be seen climbing a wall in Active Wear or wearing an apron while taking on the pose and attitude of a chef in the Housewares department.

As a musician and a painter, Gosses understood the symbiotic relationship and the harmonious interactions of the arts. With an appreciation of the French Neoclassical painter Jean-Auguste-Dominique Ingres, who said to his students, "If I could make musicians out of you, you would profit as painters," Gosses held strong to the belief that music and art are spiritually united. With that in mind, he explained, "The musical selections were critical to the overall effect. The mannequins and the music had to be connected in spirit and feeling to evoke the desired emotion. We called the music aspirational; engaging Disney tunes for Children's, Baroque in Cosmetics, Classical Jazz in Men's Suits which shifted to Big Band for Men's Casual Wear, et alia."

In the early 1990s, the children's department at Mercantile was inspired by a harmonious coupling of art, community awareness, and mannequins. Gosses collaborated with mannequin and prop supplier Carol Barnhart to create a line of children's mannequins based on Mercantile's needs and Gosses' creative vision. Taking her cues from their design meetings, Barnhart commissioned a local artist to work on a series of paintings titled "Kids on the Move." The paintings featured children of all ages, from the baby carriage to the teenage years. The children in all of the paintings were in motion, all striking action poses. Barnhart then created a range of children's mannequins based on the children in the paintings. To complete the look, Gosses and his in-house team designed a series of fixtures and props such as baby buggies, bikes, roller coasters, scooters, slides, etc., and had them produced by local sources. When the mannequins were completed, Mercantile purchased all of the paintings and donated them for auction to benefit children's hospitals. To complete the project Gosses produced posters and note cards to sell in all of the Mercantile stores, with a hundred percent of the profit going to the Make a Wish Foundation.

Barnhart explained that she first met the artist at a showing of his work that featured a ballet performance. "The ballerinas danced on a painted canvas. I had my inspiration." When her showroom opened the next season, she featured the dancing mannequins in front of a screen that replicated the artist's work. The presentation was so dramatic that NBC News covered it. Gosses took one look at the showroom and loved it. The rest was history, Gosses found the right mannequins for his children's department, and Barnhart had a great showroom opening.

Great visual merchandising like great music and art, has the ability to move people's emotions. Like any impactful art form, visual merchandising touches people by telling stories they can relate to. An effective method for connecting with viewers through storytelling is the use of found objects. Successful visual merchandisers will see beauty in things that other people don't even see and bring them to life in unexpected ways. As such, Gosses worked on several projects that involved found objects and their interaction with mannequins. While speaking about one of his most rewarding and effective projects using found objects, Gosses recalled,

> We were able to salvage large torchieres from an old Fox movie theater prior to its demolition. Ralph Pucci reproduced them in fiberglass, and we used them on platforms flanking the escalators. Pucci made many specialized forms for us along with associated mannequins. We would send him various 'found objects' which he would then cast into fiberglass. The found objects together with the mannequins, made powerful and memorable presentations.

In addition to being an artist and a musician, Gosses had a bit of the thespian in him. Often seen in a tuxedo and tails, he brought his theatrical instincts onto the retail stage. He fully recognized that fun and theatrics are great design tools. He also recognized that mannequins could be actors on the stage, and much like found objects, could be used in different ways. One memorable Mercantile holiday trim involved mannequins that weren't meant to display apparel. Rather, they were meant to add fun, theater, and excitement to Mercantile's holiday environments. Gosses recalled,

> One Christmas season we made fiberglass Nutcrackers to tie in with the *Denver Nutcracker Ballet* that we were promoting at the time. To add to the fun, we hired a mime to personify a Nutcracker. He was dressed and looked just like the 6ft. Nutcrackers that we positioned throughout the store. He could stand very still for some time. Then, as he came alive, the customers would react with amazement and delight.

Gosses continued his retail career, taking his expertise in visual merchandising and design north across the border. When Mercantile was sold to Dillard's, he was hired by Eaton's, Canada, and moved to Toronto as corporate vice president. After Eaton's he moved back to the United States, to Yarmouth, Maine, where he imported delftware and clocks from The Netherlands and Europe. He set up a successful business selling the glazed earthenware and embellished timepieces to retailers across the country. And while successful and creative in establishing the business, he yearned to get back behind the easel with a palette and brush.

Several years later he returned to Ohio. Once back in his home state his creative instincts and aesthetic sensibilities began to stir. He felt the calling of his original passion for studio art. "I began painting again and eventually left Ohio and moved to Richmond, Kentucky. Within two years the Governor and Secretary of State bestowed on me the honorable and coveted title of Kentucky Colonel." Gosses was also presented to the

Kentucky House of Representatives for his achievements in mentoring and the promotion of young artists in the Commonwealth.

Gosses' abstract paintings have been exhibited internationally at the Seoul National Gallery in South Korea, and in Switzerland, Germany, and The Netherlands. His work has also been featured in major galleries across the United States, from Denver, Colorado to New York City, and has been exhibited at the Whitney Biannual and the Butler Institute of American Art. In addition, the works of the visual merchandiser from Ohio have been featured in newspapers, art books, catalogues, and magazines; and he was the cover/ feature artist in *Art Voices Magazine, 2014 Fall Edition*.

Nicole Gallo, curator of the *Agnes Gund* collection in New York City, said of Gosses, "Your passion in creating sculptures on canvas, and other 3-Dimensional works, is wonderful and we encourage you to continue your groundbreaking work. I commend you, your talent, and your drive in the art world. Your dedication to your field is palpable and I laud your persistence and your faith in the arts as a practice."

Gosses clearly shared that same passion for his work in retail design and one of its most iconic components, the mannequin. He readily notes that mannequins have changed exponentially during his fifty years in retail. In that time he has seen many

Figure 9.10 Hindsgaul Mannequins, "Couture" collection, 1994, designed exclusively for Saks Fifth Avenue. "Waterfall Runway." James Damian concept and exhibition design; Photograph by John Wadsworth.

venerable and iconic retail brands close their doors in the face of great economic turmoil. He has also witnessed retailers adapt and adjust to great technological advances. While no one has a crystal ball, Gosses reflects, "A customer might still want to know what that outfit looks like up close. But who knows, the future may still have room for department store settings complete with mannequins and displays. Another generation may discover this 'new' experience of shopping the 'old' way. The trend is now shopping at small, independent stores. Tomorrow may bring another change."

James Damian, whose career path took him from the windows on Fifth Avenue to the boardrooms of public and private companies, believes the first order for any designer is an understanding of culture before strategy. Damian began his creative journey studying music as a conducting major at Westminster College at Princeton. This experience helped shape his ongoing role as a conductor of diversely talented designers assembled to create awe-inspiring and transformative experiences. "The role of the designer is to bring multiple disciplines together in a safe and collaborative environment," said Damian. "The conductor/designer cannot play every instrument, but their role is to enable the genius within every player. Our role as design leaders is to deliver simplicity through sincerity, grounded with good intent. Love is the answer to everything we do, stirred with the elixir of our dreams, filled with gratitude!"

According to Damian, president of the USA Subsidiary at Hindsgaul Mannequins Worldwide from 1988 through 1995, "The mannequin is a window into the soul of society. It reflects our vision of the times, and society's ideal of beauty through the eyes of fashion and life in a particular time. The body type, stance, and proportions of the figure are a reflection of what society's culture, taste, style, and beauty are of that time."

Damian's introduction to the world of mannequins began with his first job at B. Altman & Company. "I had the great fortune to work and learn from two incredible leaders and collaborators, Mr. Robert Benzio and Ms. Dawn Mello," recalled Damian. "Their working relationship underscored the important partnership between the fashion director and the director of visual presentation."

Damian explained that the relationship between Mello and Benzio was kindred, bound together as arbiters of taste and curators of the collections, exclusive shops, and the unique B. Altman culture.

> This unity had a tremendous impact on our collective teams, inspiring us to work as one tour de force. They modeled the role of the leader, working together for the higher purpose of the organization. They were so far ahead of their time; servant leaders, not top-down dictators; they were mentors and nurturers of young talent. They saw something in us that we could not see within ourselves. They were teachers with the highest standards who taught me that leadership is not about how many followers you have, rather, how many leaders you create.

When remembering Mello and Benzio, Damian is reminded of a poem by Alexander Pope: "Genius creates and taste preserves. Taste is the good sense of genius; without taste, genius is only sublime folly."

Color Plate 1 Ralph Pucci Mannequins, Patrick Naggar designer. Photograph by Antoine Bootz

Color Plate 2 Ralph Pucci Mannequins, Inflate collection; Photograph by Antoine Bootz

Color Plate 3 Color and whimsy at Henri Bendel. Courtesy James Mansour

Color Plate 4 A grouping of white abstract Hindsgaul mannequins. James Damian concept and exhibition design, John Wadsworth, photographer

Color Plate 5 *Ralph Pucci: The Art of the Mannequin*, an exhibition featuring a portfolio of Pucci designs at the Museum of Arts and Design

Color Plate 6 Ralph Pucci: The Art of the Mannequin. Birdland by Ruben Toledo, prominently featured in black. Photograph by Antoine Bootz

Color Plate 7 The "Dress Address" at Lord & Taylor featuring mannequins by Ralph Pucci. Richard Caden Photographer.

Color Plate 8 The "Dress Address" at Lord & Taylor with mannequins positioned directly on the floor. Richard Caden Photographer.

Color Plate 9 Creating a dynamic with one abstract mannequin facing forward and one facing back at Macy's. Courtesy of Paul Olszewski

Color Plate 10 Two abstract mannequins interrelating as they reach upward toward the sky at Macy's. Courtesy of Paul Olszewski

Color Plate 11 A stand alone mannequin celebrating Macy's flower show. Courtesy of Paul Olszewski

Color Plate 12 Playing with angles to create a whimsical dynamic at Macy's. Courtesy of Paul Olszewski.

Color Plate 13 Story telling at The Brooklyn Museum featuring the fashion designs of Thierry Mugler. Exhibition design by Matthew Yokobosky. Courtesy of The Brooklyn Museum.

Color Plate 14 A theatrical setting capturing the essence of Studio 54 captured at The Brooklyn Museum. Exhibition design by Matthew Yokobosky. Courtesy of The Brooklyn Museum.

Color Plate 15 A grouping of three abstract mannequins celebrating the fashion and style of Studio 54 at The Brooklyn Museum. Exhibition design by Matthew Yokobosky. Courtesy of The Brooklyn Museum.

Color Plate 16 A dramatic grouping in an upward projecting triangle featuring the fashions of Pierre Cardin at The Brooklyn Museum. Exhibition design by Matthew Yokobosky. Courtesy of The Brooklyn Museum. Brooklyn Museum Pierre Cardin

Mello went on to become the president of Bergdorf Goodman and then to resurrect Gucci, hiring a young designer named Tom Ford. Benzio went on to reinvent Saks Fifth Avenue, elevating the role of visual presentation and store design.

Benzio, like Gene Moore, was an advocate of the celebrity mannequin. Damian's first window experience was assisting in the unveiling of an exclusive collection of poses showcasing the figure of Allegra Kent, the Prima Ballerina of the New York City Ballet in 1972. That same year Benzio received the Display Man of the Year award, a highly coveted honor.

With valuable lessons learned from his two mentors, Damian selected mannequins based on the fashion designer's vision, attitude, style, and the cut of the clothing. While at Hindsgaul, his goal was to identify the desires of the customer. An example was the realistic and stylized "Couture" collection for Saks Fifth Avenue. "The key for the collection was to find a modeler in clay, one who had a classical training, and a kindred spirit with a shared view," said Damian. "I was fortunate to find such a rare talent in Paris, a man named Cyril Heck." A practitioner of realism and portraiture, Heck designed his atelier to mirror the atelier of Auguste Rodin just a few blocks away. It was truly a beautiful and historical place to imagine and to create.

"Cyril was an important influence in my life. He taught me about the process of creation as a Zen-like discipline. It demanded being on purpose, on time, leading with intent and a clear vision of the goal of being here, now," said Damian. "The atelier was a home and studio; everyone knew their role. It had a full kitchen so we could work, eat,

Figure 9.11 Hindsgaul Mannequins, "Options" collection, 1992. The Modern Woman, " Night at the Opera." James Damian concept and exhibition design; Photograph by John Wadsworth.

and play together at the end of each day." As the work progressed, one assistant would go to market to prepare the menu for the day, another would buy the clay while another would build the armature on a platform with wheels to turn the figure for study. The clay would be watered and pounded for application to the armature, ready for the maestro to shape, with the model in pose. The work day started promptly at 7:30 am and would conclude with dinner and wine in the early evening. The assistants would light candles as the figure was turned under candlelight to show the imperfections. This was the Rodin method of modeling in clay. "The music of a Verdi Opera was always present, Cyril's favorite," recalled Damian.

> He called this his period of reflection at the end of the day. This time set the motivation for the next day. The music, the laughter, the wine, the stories shared were an intimate ritual of our time together, an important bonding agent of the creative process, a celebration of creativity. This was a tremendous leadership model for me that is forever cemented within my being. A method of problem-solving, always aspiring toward the vision of perfection, knowing we will never reach it while on this earth. He was a teacher, who demanded your full self, your commitment, and your contribution to the end, a time when the artist within all of us learns how to let go. It is a constant struggle and an internal conflict searching for resolve.

Together with Heck, Damian developed the "Options" collection. "It was conceived to showcase Cyril's mastery of realism in a time where abstract was prevalent," said Damian. "I wanted to honor and recognize the power, influence, intelligence, elegance, and humanity of the 'Modern Woman.' The books she read, the music, fashion and art that enveloped her personal taste and adorned her being. Her places of interests, the restaurants, cafés and theaters, celebrating the theater of her life, her *True North*."

The "Options" collection honored the Modern Woman and her impact on society at large; her higher purpose. The positions selected celebrated her finer qualities and characteristics. The iconic position of the collection was the stand-alone position with arms extended, anchored on the boardroom table. She was a leader and visionary of her time, a force of strength and inclusiveness bringing people together. The collection consisted of 16 positions launched in an exhibition that celebrated all the elements of her taste and style. "We launched this exhibition with the art, furnishings, photography, videography, music, aroma and clothing of a young female fashion designer," said Damian. "We transformed the gallery into a Parisian town home. This was a tribute to all of the artists in my orchestra, for whom I had the honor of conducting."

Damian appreciated the mannequin as an art form.

> The role of the mannequin is to attract the eye of the passerby, to invite them to stop, take pleasure in the sparkles of magic before their eyes. This private moment allows pause, stopping time, transporting the viewer within the story of the play before them, creating a personal journey bound only by their imagination. The mannequin is not a clothes hanger, it is an art form and should be created as such.

Figure 9.12 Hindsgaul Mannequins, "Options" collection, 1992. The Gallery was converted to her town home. James Damian concept and exhibition design; Photography by John Wadsworth.

Figure 9.13 Hindsgaul Mannequins, "Couture" collection, 1994. The Gallery was transformed to showcase a collection of mannequins walking on water and grass. James Damian concept and exhibition design; Photography by John Wadsworth.

He summed up this conviction with a passage from Catherine Sauvat, Cyril Heck's wife.

A well-known Parisienne author, Damian asked Sauvat to write the forward to Cyril's "Options" collection:

> In a world of appearances, of constantly transfigured reality, the mannequin brings the upheavals of the time before our eyes. The mannequin's project is to unveil or mask, to be forcefully present or discreetly effaced: to re-perform the ballets of our inner lives. The mannequin reflects the dreams and desires of the public that gazes on it, yet, in an invitation to surpass the boundaries of the self, it imposes its own vision of beauty.[5]

Figure 9.14 Hindsgaul Mannequins, "Options Stylized," 1995. Damian with "Maria." James Damian concept and exhibition design; Photograph by John Wadsworth.

AT THE OPERA

In 1980 James Chiao boarded an airplane in his hometown of Guangzhou, China, and headed for Los Angeles to study at California State University, Long Beach. As a foreign student, he was eager to begin his studies at an American university and excited to be taking his very first airplane trip. After fourteen long and exhausting hours in the air, Chiao landed in what seemed to him a strange and very different place. As he left the terminal getting his first breath of fresh air after being confined for so many hours in the cabin of the plane, he was shocked to see the countless number of cars, buses, and taxis maneuvering around the airport or waiting on indeterminably long lines. He was also thunderstruck at the scope of America's documented diversity. "I was amazed to see America as a melting pot with so many races and ethnicities; more than I previously imagined."

Figure 9.15 CNL Mannequins. Designer James Chiao mannequin design was influenced by his love of music. Chiao performing at Euroshop. Courtesy of CNL Mannequins.

Everything was new and very different. Chiao was like a sponge taking it all in; the sights, the sounds, and the people scurrying about. He was over the moon with excitement for his new opportunity in this new land. He began his American education studying computer programming and graduated with a bachelor's degree in business administration. After graduation, he worked as a computer programmer for ten years which included work for two Fortune 500 companies. Little did he know at the time that he was planting the seeds for what was to become a robust manufacturing company. James Chiao would soon become an important contributor to the retail design industry as the founder of CNL Mannequins.

Chiao's road to success as an influential mannequin designer and manufacturer was paved with a rhythmic and perhaps unexpected upbringing. His parents were both professional singers in China, a tenor and a soprano. His father went on to become a famous Chinese composer. Among his more than two hundred musical compositions is the beloved Cantonese lullaby, "The Moonlight." The piece was so popular that it was featured at the 2010 Asia Olympics in Guangzhou as the theme song for the closing ceremony.

Chiao's older brother was also a professional tenor and the deputy director of the Guangzhou Symphonic Orchestra.

Growing up in a musical family, I always loved music and played the Erhu (Chinese violin) and accordion when I was young. In fact, I sold my blood to the blood station in Guangzhou in 1968 to get 30 Chinese dollars to buy an Erhu so I could take it to the countryside where I had to work for six years as a farmer and a fisherman after high school graduation.

One year later Chiao came to America where he spent his hard-earned money as a waiter in a restaurant while still in college to buy an accordion.

Another influential factor in Chiao's future ventures in the mannequin business was his parents' work for the Song and Dance Troupe run by the government of Guangzhou.

> We lived inside the Song and Dance Troupe compound. So every day we saw the dancers walking and moving about. They always kept the dancer's upright posture, very artistic and very fluid. They were graceful and elegant, and this stuck in my mind. Almost every week, as naughty kids, we would climb up to the windows of their dance studios to see their rehearsals. Their dances were diverse and varied; balletic and folksy. From watching dancers for so many years as I grew up, I developed a sense and understanding of body movement. For instance, the dancers' eyes always follow their hand movements. This proved to be an advantage for my mannequin design work. In particular, I designed a few mannequin series in dancing themes: The "La Belle" collection, the "Drama" collection, the "La Dolce" collection, and the "Matador" collection.

Chiao first got the mannequin bug while working for the TransAmerica Corporation in downtown Los Angeles. "Every day I would drive by the garment district there," said Chiao. "There was a small street-level storefront that sold mannequins. Once while stopping at a stop sign I saw all of the naked bodies lined up in the window." This caught the future entrepreneur's attention as he was searching for a new business to start as China's economy was beginning to boom. "One day I walked into this mannequin store and asked where the mannequins were made," said Chiao. "They told me they were made in South Korea." This struck a chord in the aspiring young computer programmer. A bell went off in his mind as he thought that he could possibly be the first one to make mannequins from China. He thought that the sense of body movement he had developed from watching dancers in his childhood and young adulthood should help. He also thought that his sketching and drawing skills would be an asset. This might be the right opportunity.

This inspiration led to the founding of CNL Mannequins. Chiao went on to grow his small business venture, a local mannequin company in Los Angeles, into a well-known mannequin supplier both in the US and around the world. "Becoming mainstream in America was my goal in life," said Chiao.

> To do so I thought when in Rome do as the Romans do. This began with speaking their language, in this case of course it was English. I was fortunate that I was attending a top-3 foreign language university in China, whose students and alumni would become China's diplomats and interpreters or trading officials. Now, when I go to the shopping malls and see stores using our CNL mannequins in their windows, I'm humbled and gratified that I'm finally part of this great country called the United States of America. This feeling is so different from the moment I first landed in the Los Angeles airport some forty years ago. I was then only an

> outsider. Now I am in. Now I'm making an important contribution right here in America.

Invariably, it's been the mannequin designers who have embraced other art forms that have been successful. In Chiao's case, it was his love of music that propelled his career. "You need to be creative to successfully perform music," offered Chiao. "So clearly, the same holds true with designing mannequins. Be creative, be different, be unique and provocative, but at the same time find a connection, something people can relate to and associate with."

Chiao's creativity didn't stop at the design process but also carried over to the presentation of his creations. Always looking for that point of connection, he reached deep into his bag of theatrical tricks at Euroshop in 2002.

> We designed our mannequin/hanger booth in Euroshop around a huge hanger to tell the story of the King of Hangers. We all wore Roman soldiers' outfits rented from a Hollywood costume store and created a short opera performance telling the story of how the emperor searched for the perfect hanger for his glorious robe. My big brother Ping Chiao played the part of the emperor as he sang Aida. I played the general, desperately looking for the hanger. Before being executed, I sang Tosca. When we finally found the perfect hanger, we all sang Turandot's Nessun Dorma. "Victory! Victory" we sang every four hours during the show. Our theatrical performance attracted about a hundred visitors each time.

As a musical artist, Chiao always believed that mannequins, when designed with passion and imagination, were also an art form.

> I always considered mannequins to be a reflection of the human experience. Even though they do not speak, they are communicating in an artistic way while they work to attract customers, complement the clothing, highlight a fashion statement, and build a lasting image for the stores. Just like the dancers, mannequin poses, attitudes and the emotions they project must be designed artistically so they can convey quality messages to the customers. Every time I visit museums, such as the Metropolitan Museum of Art in New York, I spend hours studying the sculptures there, which become the inspirations for our mannequin design.

Chiao steadfastly maintained two approaches to designing a new mannequin line. First, he would listen to the needs of each individual customer. Secondly, he would be inspired by his own understanding of what the current market needed.

> If we initiate a new mannequin line, it is mostly because we understand from the market trend that there is a special need. If the customer initiates a new project for a certain type of mannequin, we would first listen very closely to their needs and

> requirements. We would study and analyze the functionality of the targeted mannequins as well as the artistic message and image they are intended to achieve. We would work together with the customer as a team, always offering our suggestions and expertise. We would try to integrate all of their requirements into a new mannequin line. The intent of a new collection was always to address all of the customer's needs, including the window display, the sales floor, floor-standing fixtures, and the perimeter walls and shelves.

An element of CNL Mannequins that Chiao remains quite proud of is their unique finishes.

> CNL has developed many popular mannequin collections over the years, but one particular specialty is our mannequin material and finishes. At the 2011 Euroshop, CNL showcased our eye-catching cement-like finish mannequins and translucent finish mannequins. As a result, we became a global supplier for Adidas Worldwide for their cement finish sports mannequins. We also supplied Uniqlo's mega stores at both Fifth Avenue and 34th Street in New York with more than 1,000 translucent mannequins. They were a great success, fitting in perfectly with Uniqlo's crisp, clean, and somewhat futuristic environments.

In 2017, Chiao recognized the need to incorporate the latest advances in mannequin production. With new technologies abounding and new demands coming from all quarters, CNL began a fast-track development of 3-D printing and sculpting. "Foreseeing 3-D printing as the future of mannequin design, we purchased 16 large 3-D printers," said Chiao. "Each machine was eight feet high; we could print a full-size mannequin. We enhanced our 3-D sculpting capabilities by hiring in-house 3-D sculpting professionals. Each technical artist could sculpt one mannequin in one day, which is a great advancement compared to clay sculpting a mannequin for 10 days in the past."

"3-D printing is the future for many industries including ours," said Kerry Barry, vice president of sales, Patina V Art / CNL International Inc.

> This is an amazing technology that speeds up the prototyping process and enables stores to get their samples quicker and more accurately. Employing this breakthrough technology is key for us; it has put us on the map as the leading 3-D company in the mannequin business. In addition, we have taken the technology forward and are creating more than just mannequins. We're also using this process to create props and other items used by stores. When it comes to innovation, creative design, and efficiency, this technology offers unlimited possibilities. And the best is yet to come.

CNL's newfound flexible and efficient 3-D printing capabilities quickly opened new doors for them. Soon after perfecting their 3-D printing process, they received many special mannequin orders including two exciting museum exhibitions. One museum exhibition was *Fearless Fashion: Rudi Gernreich* at the Skirball Museum in Los Angeles in

2019. The other museum exhibition was the *Heroes and Villains* Costume Exhibit for Disney in 2019. The Disney exhibition required 70 different custom-made mannequins, all to be designed and made in six months. Each mannequin, designed for a specific "Hero" or "Villain," had its own specific pose and measurement to fit the exhibiting costume. Chiao added, "In the old days, with clay sculpting, this project with its short six-month timeline would be totally impossible. But with our 3-D printing and sculpting, it was a great success for Disney and CNL Mannequins."

In 2018 CNL purchased Patina V Mannequins, a well-recognized brand in the mannequin industry. The move proved to be strategic, broadening CNL's scope of product offerings. "With our established 3-D position in the market, CNL was off to the races," said Barry. "3-D was the perfect match to partner up with Patina V and their highly creative sculptured mannequin selections and plentiful molds."

Ever the performer, Chiao took great delight in showcasing his classical musical background while he showcased his mannequins at major trade shows.

> I performed at Euroshop and GlobalShop at least eight times. The first time was at Euroshop in 2002. We took it a step further at GlobalShop in 2013 and EuroShop in 2014 when we positioned a grand piano in our booth with a mannequin sitting at the keyboard. As she played, I was dressed in a tuxedo singing *Some Enchanted Evening* and *O Sole Mio*. It was very emotional and gratifying because GlobalShop announced that CNL won the Best-in-Show award. I was holding the trophy given to me as I sang.

Before long, Chiao's highly anticipated trademark performances became major attractions at industrywide trade shows. "After I founded the mannequin company I would sing Italian arias at the trade shows to attract attention, especially at Euroshop where Europeans are more familiar with opera." Chiao's love of music and his passion for the mannequin business compelled him to create a song about a mannequin salesman. In the 2019 GlobalShop and the 2020 Euroshop, after creating a musical titled *Mannequin Man by Day, Tenor By Night*, the musically inclined mannequin designer sang a true-to-life song about a mannequin man selling his creations at the trade show.

> For this song, I borrowed the music from *Figaro* in the opera *Barber of Seville*. I took poetic license in adapting the lyrics about a Mannequin Man, rather than the haircutter in the original aria. The original lyrics talked about haircutting for all sorts of people; kids, young men, women, men, old ladies, and old men. Now for my song, I changed it to become 'selling kids mannequins, male mannequins, female mannequins, fashion mannequins and sports mannequins, and even plus size and petite.' Through the magic of music, I turned a humble mannequin-selling job into an honorable and artistic act. My goal was to help our customers understand that we're not merely businesspeople, but artists. This was an effort to help our customers appreciate what we do and the passion that we put into our jobs while still having fun and being light-hearted.

Although created in a lighthearted manner, Chiao's musical *Mannequin Man by Day, Tenor by Night*, is a true testament to his love of music and his passion for the art of the mannequin. "My musical is a true story mixed with a touch of fantasy," said Chiao.

> It is true that I design and sell mannequins by day. I do it wholeheartedly with a dedicated commitment to my customers. I enjoyed designing new mannequin lines with new functionalities that surprise and excite our customers. I also enjoy making breakthroughs that earn us new customers. That is very satisfying and very gratifying. But only for the daytime. By night, I pursue music. I'm a tenor. My father was a tenor, and my brother is also a tenor. We are *The Three Chiao Tenors*. That is my happiness and joy, at night I sing, sing, and sing. Trying to hit the high note, trying to pronounce the correct Italian phrase for the arias. This is all true. So I always looked forward to the day when I could spend more time making music.

That day came for Chiao when he turned 65.

> I decided to retire and go back to school to learn music. In 2015 I was accepted by CalArts (Founded by Disney) for a master's degree program in its music school. I studied for two years and earned 65 units and graduated in 2017. This is when I decided to write my own musical *Mannequin Man By Day, Tenor By Night*. One year later, I wrote a play script for the two-hour musical, composed 25 songs with original music, and wrote lyrics with my wife. We mounted the productions in two theaters in Los Angeles and Orange County with ten nearly-sold-out performances. The fantasy part is mannequins can come alive. They come alive through my tenor voice.

In the fantasy story, Chiao is kicked out of the house by his wife because of his excessive non-stop singing. As the story continued, he moved out of the family abode and took up quarters in the mannequin warehouse where he continued to sing.

> In the story, my voice woke up the mannequins one night. After that, we had a "Mannequins Got Talent Show" every night in the warehouse. My wife was curious and concerned. One night she disguised herself as a new mannequin and came to the warehouse to check up on her husband. As the drama continued, the wife / mannequin was sold away in the mannequin trade show.
>
> Chiao's favorite mannequin story has to do with his musical.
>
> In early March of 2020, we were planning to mount our musical in the Cerritos Performing Arts Center. We were concerned that we might not have enough show-goers to fill the 1,400-seat theater. We were joking that if that were the case, we would put mannequins in the seats on the second and third tiers to make the theater look full. But later, we actually decided, since it is a show about mannequins, we were going to put six mannequins in the theatre seats as

> audience, to attract people as part of the aesthetic of the musical extravaganza. Two would be put in the middle seats, two in the balcony, and two in the back seats. We were even planning to put one male mannequin in the men's room facing the toilet doing his thing. We almost did it, until the pandemic killed the show before it started.

Chiao's unique and exciting mannequin story told in a musical form attracted many people and critics.

> We were planning to take it to Off-Broadway in 2020 and hopefully, Broadway going forward, until the pandemic hit. But my dream is still alive. In some way, I feel my musical is a manifesto on behalf of all mannequin makers that we are not just selling mannequins for money. Rather, we are artistically equipped artists with a passion for art and music but equally passionate for supporting fashion.

A FLAIR FOR REPAIR

Frank Glover is an icon in the mannequin world; a friend to all who've anguished over a minor mannequin chip, a missing hand, a scuff, a scratch, a crack, or major damage caused by a drop, a fall, or general mishandling of the precious but fragile beauties. Glover wistfully recalls the early days of his New York-based business when he would drive his brown Volkswagen Rabbit Hatchback to branch stores around the greater metropolitan area, from New Jersey to Long Island, collecting mannequins to repair. With logic and determination (and all passenger seats removed), he would dismantle and pack as many as ten mannequins into the back of the diminutive, front-wheel-drive, road-running hatchback. He was so efficient at cramming the mannequins into the small vehicle, that he once thought it would be a great commercial for Volkswagen to film him unpacking and reassembling all the mannequins.

While the mannequin road warrior covered a great deal of territory in the early days, his highway to success had been paved with many twists and turns along the way. He spent five years as an apprentice studying to be an engineer in his native Sheffield, England. All the skills learned there became useful later in his mannequin journey.

His introduction to mannequins began in the late 1960s when he met a young woman who was the display manager at Walsh's, an independent department store located on High Street opposite the Castle Square tram stop in the heart of Sheffield. A popular store at the time, Walsh's opened in 1875 and by 1895 there were 36 departments selling a wide range of goods.[6] Glover was so intrigued with the young display artist's work that he married her. Little did he know where this journey would lead him.

His first real encounter with the mannequin world was through a company called Modreno (Model Renovation), a small mannequin repair shop based in London. Their logo was a vulture with wings spread wide, ready to swoop down to whisk the mannequins away. The owner of the company, Len Harvey, was a former warehouse manager for Adel Rootstein Mannequins. Harvey later hired a man named Ronald Kirkland to be his sales manager. Kirkland, a Scotsman, began his career as a Mini driver, (the Uber of the day), and one of his regular clients was Adel Rootstein herself. The trend-setting Rootstein so loved Kirkland's gift for conversation that she convinced him to work for her as a salesman. After a few years with Rootstein, he left to join Modreno where he traveled around the country on calls to stores in cities such as Sheffield, Newcastle, Edinburgh, and Leeds. The repair team from London would drive to the appointed stores and haul the mannequins up to the roof where they set up a workbench with a portable compressor and spray gun. The damaged mannequins were then repaired on the spot.

Following in their trail was the makeup artist, known affectionately to all as "Bin Man" because of an earlier job as a garbage collector. In reality, he was a true Renaissance man; a poet, a photographer, and a painter, who eventually started a popular rock band (Ultravox). The band would actually practice at the mannequin factory when the workers went home.

Without going into too much detail, Glover said the introduction of Modreno and crew into his life eventually broke up his marriage. Sometime after the breakup, Glover received a phone call from Kirkland to inform him that Len Harvey the owner of Modreno was accidentally killed. Kirkland then asked Glover if he would like to join Modreno in London. With a "What the hell, if you can't beat them, join them" attitude, Glover accepted and moved to London. This was a giant step backwards in his career (sanding mannequins and spraying mannequins) but when the current manager left Modreno to set up his own repair company, Glover became the new manager at Modreno.

Glover and Kirkland became the best of friends. They lived together, drank together, and did just about everything together. It was during this time that Glover met one of Kirkland's old friends from his days at Rootstein. Her name was Sonia, and she was the head makeup artist for Rootstein. Sonia and Glover also became good friends, and one day over dinner she told Glover that Rootstein was looking for someone to set up a New York refinishing studio. Glover called Rootstein and scheduled an appointment to meet with Adel and her partner Rick Hopkins. The pair told Glover they would let him know. A year passed when he received a call from Rootstein informing him that they were ready to start, and they asked him if he was still interested. Two weeks later he was off to New York to set up a refinishing studio at Rootstein's new premises on Varick St, close to their showroom on West Broadway. While at Rootstein, Glover got to work with the legendary Nellie Fink who ran the New York showroom along with Michael Southgate (who also moved to New York from London). Michael was the creative force behind all of Rootstein's iconic showroom displays.

At the time, a company named Mayorga was making mannequins for Rootstein in New York. This eventually presented another opportunity for the enterprising Glover. His friend Sonia joined Rootstein in New York from London and became friends with Bill Mayorga. They all subsequently became good friends. Four years later over dinner one night Mayorga said he was thinking of closing his business and asked Glover if he would be interested in any of his equipment. Glover saw the potential to start his own company and jumped at the opportunity. He stored the equipment and began the process of forming a business plan. A year went by when he found the ideal property, a 3,000-square-ft loft with a loading dock on North 8th Street in Williamsburg, Brooklyn. It was now time to 'put up or shut up,' there were no more obstacles or excuses. He borrowed $5,000 from the bank, and Frank Glover Productions was born in the spring of 1982.

The new mannequin repair shop's first client was Robert Benzio, vice president and director of visual merchandising at Saks Fifth Avenue. Glover had a 10:00 am appointment with the influential Benzio. He said to Glover, "come back with a sampling of makeup masks, and then we'll talk." At the time, Glover worked with makeup artists Barbara Graff and Tom Lyons, an accomplished artist who for 40 years filled sketch pads with drawings of hands, feet, and naked men. They made a half dozen masks to show Benzio. When Glover returned to Saks with the newly created masks, Benzio took one look and gave Glover the job. That $4,000 order gave Glover's new company the boost and recognition needed to survive.

Glover credits his expertise in mannequin repair to the people he met along the way, and to his early training and apprenticeship in engineering where he and his colleagues were literally tasked with making all the tools they used including the toolbox. He equates the process of repairing mannequins to automotive bodywork. "We use the same components. The only difference is that we use water-based paints. Some damages are brutal, while some just need small cracks or chips repaired and smoothed." Glover takes pride in the fact that he can look at a breakage, and know exactly how to repair it.

"The role of the mannequin will never go away," said Glover. "They will always be an integral part of retail, but perhaps without the same pizazz and flamboyance seen in the past.

Retailers will want simpler silhouettes that exude the elegance and practicality needed for the job to be done." The renowned "mannequin doctor" knows that mannequin repair will always play a vital role in maintaining a functional and effective regiment of dedicated silent salespeople.

References

1. Eric Feigenbaum, "The 1980s: Search for Identity," *Visual Merchandising and Store Design Magazine* (October 24, 2001).
2. Steve Peake, Liveabout.com (March 8, 2017).
3. *People Magazine* (May 3, 1993).
4. Enid Nemy, "New Breed of Mannequins," *New York Times* (July 22, 1983), section A, page 12.
5. Catherine Sauvat, "Belles Lettres," Brochure for the "Options" collection, Hindsgaul Mannequins, 1991.
6. "Turn Back Time: Memories of Walsh's store in Sheffield," BBC News, Sheffield & South Yorkshire (December 14, 2010), available at http://news.bbc.co.uk/local/sheffield/hi/people_and_places/history/newsid_9286000/9286367.stm.

CHAPTER 10
AN AGE OF AWARENESS: 1990–2000

Rike's was a full-line department store with a venerable seven-story flagship in downtown Dayton, Ohio. Tracing its roots back to the 1850s, it continued on to become an integral part of Dayton's bustling business community. In 1959, Rike's joined Federated Department Stores, becoming a part of a large national retail conglomerate.

In the early 1970s, a young man fresh out of the University of Dayton with a degree in commercial art was looking to jumpstart his career in an art-related field. The classified ad from Rike's read "Display Trimmer." Ignaz Gorischek had no idea what that was, but it sounded interesting. After interviewing for the position at Rike's, the display manager hired young Gorischek to build props for the windows and the selling floor. Gorischek was delighted with the opportunity as he loved to build things and he loved a creative challenge.

After a few weeks of successful prop building, the manager recognized his new protégé's creative ability and asked him to dress a mannequin. The supposition was that if he was so creative, he would certainly be able to funnel his inspiration into a stunning mannequin presentation. Somewhat overwhelmed, but ready for the challenge, the newly appointed display trimmer sized up the situation. A realistic mannequin with a realistic wig stood posed and poised on a four-foot, square platform. Then the struggle began as he lifted the mannequin off the platform and tried to undress her. After fuddling about, the ensuing scene on the selling floor in the women's department wasn't pretty. Arms and legs were strewn about after the intense effort to detach the aforementioned body parts. But alas, the fiberglass beauty was undressed. Next came the somewhat daunting task of picking clothes. Not knowing where to start, the resourceful young artist walked around the selling floor asking salespeople what to put on the mannequin.

With the help of the opinionated sales staff, the outfit was selected. And now the fun truly began as he wondered how to put the mannequin together, dress her, and position her on the platform. After much trial and tribulation, the static beauty was whole once again. There she was in all her glory, totally undressed. How to dress her? How to approach her? How to even pick her up? Where to hold her? Not to be outwitted by the beguiling beauty, Gorischek struggled, but got her dressed. Next, he wondered what to do with the wig, he never styled a wig before. He reached deep into his artistic sensibilities and coifed the hair. Finished, the lady was dressed. All that remained was to put her back on the glass base and then onto the platform. Every time he attempted to lift her onto the platform, the shoes kept falling off. Finally, Gorischek persevered, his first mannequin was trimmed and positioned. Looking back he recalled, "She looked like a street person." And thus began a legendary and inspirational career in the visual merchandising and store design industry. Gorischek went on from an entry-level display trimmer, to become one of the industry's most influential voices. "As I grew up in the industry, I learned that

I was in control of the mannequin," said Gorischek. "The mannequin was not in control of me."

Prior to his work at Rike's, Gorischek never paid much attention to mannequins. As a creative spirit, his overarching interests were in the art of airbrushing, having employed the technique for everything from T-shirts to customized vans and cars. Once entrenched in his new position at Rike's, however, his artistic interests began to pique and expand. He was beginning to learn the tools of the trade in addition to the many shortcuts involved with the art of the mannequin.

As time passed, Gorischek wanted to leave Ohio and its brutal winters behind. He loved spending time at his parents' second home in Sarasota, Florida. As luck would have it, Burdine's, another division of Federated, had a branch store in Sarasota. Gorischek was happy to learn that company policy allowed him to transfer between divisions. Based in Miami with its flagship store in the Dadeland Mall, Burdines had a similar mannequin philosophy to Rike's. Both stores used all realistic mannequins with no abstracts.

The Florida chapter of Gorischek's career began as a branch store display trimmer at Burdines in Sarasota. From there he went on to spend two and a half years as a display manager in the retailer's downtown Ft. Myers store. His career path began to take focus when he was moved to Miami and promoted to regional director of visual merchandising. In that capacity, he was responsible for all of the Burdines stores from Homestead to West Palm Beach. Even in that capacity, however, he still was not that interested in mannequins. He viewed them as a necessary evil. That point of view was all to change with his next career move.

For part of his tenure at Burdines, Gorischek worked under the direction of Joe Feczko, who held the position of vice president, and director of visual merchandising. After a few years of working together, Feczko left Burdines for a position with Neiman Marcus based in Dallas, Texas. In 1993 as Feczko began to build his team at the high-end Neiman Marcus, he called Gorischek and offered him the position of creative director. Gorischek accepted the offer and moved to Dallas. From that point forward everything changed, including his appreciation of mannequins. As he assumed the reins of his new position, he developed a newfound vision and philosophy relative to the mannequin.

"Then my eyes opened up," recalled Gorischek. "And it was mainly because of Ralph Pucci. There were many mannequin manufacturers at the time supplying the retail industry. Ralph was doing something different, he elevated the mannequin by turning it into an art form. He brought people from various artistic disciplines into the mannequin world who knew little or nothing about them."

With a keen interest in art, Gorischek saw the possibilities of developing the mannequin. Seeing what Pucci was doing excited him; it opened up a whole new world of creative endeavors. He asked Pucci if they could collaborate. Mannequins were no longer a mundane utilitarian tool to Gorischek, but rather a necessary tool to elevate the customer experience.

> In my mind I now saw mannequins as a dynamic vehicle to connect our brand to our customers by using them as an art form. The vocabulary of the mannequin

changed for me, it became a real opportunity to move forward in promoting the Neiman Marcus brand and philosophy. In the past I just shopped for mannequins, sometimes straight out of a catalogue. Now I was creating mannequins.

While Gorischek appreciated the mannequin as an art form, he also recognized its importance as a vehicle to present and ultimately sell merchandise.

In the retail world, the mannequin is a selling tool. In museums the mannequin is a presentation tool. In retail we often change poses so people take notice. In museums the mannequins are more static. The lines between selling and presenting are the same. In retail you want to sell, but to sell you have to educate. Once I understood this I changed my point of view and pushed my mannequin philosophy and vocabulary to another place. I wanted to create my own. I wanted to explore the possibilities presented by the art of the mannequin rather than merely flipping through a catalogue.

Gorischek then sat with Pucci's sculptor in long and inspired creative sessions. Together they visited the visage of a typical mannequin. They redefined the nose, the lips, and the eyes. The head began to take on a more abstract look and feel. As the two worked together, a new mannequin began to reemerge, breaking out of its more traditional and expected form. As he worked with Pucci to further define the mannequin, he realized that abstraction was about referencing or suggesting a form or shape rather than an overt representation. He also realized that both abstract and realistic mannequins had their places with both offering different but desired results.

I bought realistic Rootstein mannequins for my windows. I wanted more drama in the windows because outside the store you only have seconds to capture the customer's attention. Realistics provided eye-catching drama that would turn the heads of even the most preoccupied passersby. In the interior of the store I wanted abstracts because you have more time to engage the customer once they are already in the store. In the window you capture the eye with drama. In the store you capture the imagination with art.

Together, Gorischek, Feczko, and Pucci developed mannequin imagery that best represented the Neiman Marcus brand. Pucci had commissioned artist Rubin Toledo to design a mannequin that was unique to the artist's aesthetic sensibilities. Gorischek and Feczko wanted to restyle Toledo's headless mannequin into a Neiman Marcus mannequin. Putting their creative vision together, they fashioned a sensual tulip-shaped neck and a static pose with one mannequin having both arms to the side, another with arms on the hips, and a third with one arm at the side and the other arm on the hip.

In 1995, Gorischek became the vice president of visual merchandising at Neiman Marcus, and in 2005 he was promoted once again to vice president of store development, responsible for visual merchandising, store planning and design, corporate graphics, and the corporate art collection. As his career evolved, he continued to develop his mannequin philosophy. With an understanding of the compositional "rule of three" and the artistic insight that an odd number of elements is more impactful than an even number, he began to work with groupings of three. As he developed mannequin programs for all of the Neiman Marcus stores, he also used the rule of three as a matter of practicality. "I wanted to send my stores a foolproof kit of parts," explained Gorischek. "The concept was that no matter how you put the elements together, the end result will work. Each store was sent groupings of three mannequins. No matter how they were grouped, whether lined up or back to back, the grouping always worked. It became an architectural grouping that had balance, structure and impact."

As Gorischek continued his collaboration with Pucci, Neiman Marcus mannequins went from mere selling tools to art pieces worthy of museum presentation. With an understanding that an integral role of the successful retailer is to educate, Gorischek worked to develop a mannequin language that best articulated the nuances of the Neiman Marcus brand. "We wanted a mannequin vernacular worthy of carrying the designer names of the clothes they were wearing. With the right mannequin, nobody ever questioned the quality of the fashion presentation."

Gorischek retired from Neiman Marcus in 2015. In looking back he said,

> When we released the results of a Neiman Marcus collaboration with Pucci in his New York showroom, people came from all over the industry to see the new mannequin. Once I had an opening at Ralph's, I knew I had arrived; there was nothing higher in the industry. Both Ralph and I were driven by the same desire. We strove to be in front of a new norm, not to follow a new norm.

The mannequin, much like retail itself, is always evolving. "It takes vision to shape the future," said Gorischek.

> It goes back to history; sometimes you have to look back in order to move forward. I perceived the mannequin as a necessary evil, and then came to see it as an object of distinction. Going forward, leaders will have to reinterpret. Visionaries will create mannequins that stand for something. If you can tell a story that transcends fiberglass, that is about vision, intent and purpose, then you are going to win. True leaders will see the mannequin as a differentiator, not merely as a tool.

PROVOCATIVE INSTALLATIONS

In the early 1980s, James Mansour began freelancing retail displays to support the meager earnings he was making in pursuit of another creative outlet, staging avant-garde theater in San Francisco. The young designer gained experience and developed a visual style and language that was uniquely his while working for exclusive boutiques in Beverly

Figure 10.1 Sculpted heads at Henri Bendel. Courtesy of James Mansour.

Hills and San Francisco. A few years later he began working as a visual merchandising consultant for one of the progenitors of fast-fashion; the 200-store Limited chain. His reputation as a hard-working, risk-taking provocateur, earned him the privilege of working directly with Limited founder, and renowned merchant prince, Leslie Wexner, to develop a series of groundbreaking specialty flagship stores across the US.

"What distinguished these stores was their ambition," recalled Mansour. "Wexner's vision was to create world-class customer experiences in his affordably priced fast-fashion stores. The goal was to exceed the expectations of customers and shareholders alike by rivaling the sensationally exclusive designer boutiques on Via Spiga in Milan, the Marais in Paris and Tokyo's innovative shopping districts."

As Wexner began to expand his retail empire, it was unheard of for a chain store to operate anywhere but in a mall environment, and it was jaw-dropping for customers accustomed to shopping for the Limited's affordable fast-fashion, to step into these exclusive locations on prime shopping streets in major cities.

Wexner's first entry into a highly trafficked and well-recognized retail street was on Wilshire Boulevard in Beverly Hills. For this important unprecedented strategy, Wexner chose a 4,000-square-foot free-standing modernist building that originally housed one of Ben Thompson's ground-breaking Design/Research stores. It became store #283 in the Limited chain and was unlike anything that had come before. Wexner was deeply involved in every detail of the new concept, working closely with Richard Himmel, a

Figure 10.2 James Mansour with mannequin installation at Henri Bendel. Courtesy of James Mansour.

multi-talented interior designer based in Chicago and Palm Beach, Architect, and James Mansour.

"The 30ft soaring ceilings were rimmed with open narrow mezzanines visible outside and inside and barely high enough for me to line with nearly 100 mannequins that I installed in the store," said Mansour. "Visual merchandising was changing dramatically in those days, and many were pushing the limits, taking visual communication to another level. Among others, I was greatly inspired by the wryly ironic, situational windows of Candy Pratts Price for Bloomingdale's in New York. Through Wexner's vision, I was given free reign to break through the third wall." From that point forward, Wexner and Mansour distanced Limited from the rest of the field.

"The lunatics had taken over the asylum: mannequins were not confined to platforms and windows," recalled the young upstart visual merchandiser. "At the live DJ station, mannequins danced on a complementary juice bar, customers sat next to mannequins on designer stools, and the entire store was invaded with unexpectedly intrusive, provocative mannequin installations, all which had less to do with selling clothes than making an impact."

These flagship store environments were Mansour's canvas, and his creative instincts were his brushes as he painted the store with mannequins in unexpected poses and situations. "Some mannequins might be mistaken to be employees opening boxes of merchandise, displaying product on walls or sitting behind the cash wrap, while others became customers on the sales floor talking to each other on a sofa, leaning on a fixture, sitting on a table or seen disrobing in one of the many dressing rooms."

Figure 10.3 Mannequin with sculpted head in front of mural at Henri Bendel. Courtesy of James Mansour.

Figure 10.4 Decorative mannequins at Henri Bendel. Courtesy of James Mansour.

Recognizing Mansour's important contribution, Wexner presented his designer with a choice, or an offer he couldn't refuse: leave his pied-à-terre overlooking San Francisco's Castro and Haight districts and move to Columbus Ohio to work with him as director of design of Limited.

> Wexner wanted me to lead the Limited team in transforming the fast-growing store chain from conventional displays to something more akin to what we were doing in the flagship stores. I somewhat reluctantly accepted his offer. The company's stock provided unrivaled return on investment and I was further rewarded with unfettered creative opportunities. First on the agenda: develop a program to retrain the display team and fill all 400 stores with mannequins.

GROUPINGS AND MATHEMATICAL PROGRESSIONS

Thermopolis, Wyoming is a unique and rather remote corner of America's vast western expanse. The largest town in Hot Springs County, Thermopolis, is known for the largest mineral hot springs in the world, ancient petroglyphs carved into its sandstone cliffs, dinosaur fossils unearthed in working archeological dig sites, and its enduring cowboy spirit. It's also the boyhood home of one of the visual merchandising industry's most influential leaders. Jack Hruska spent his formative years in this gateway town to the great Yellowstone National Park. There young Jack would enjoy pastoral afternoons swimming in the hot springs until he was ten years old when his family moved to Billings, Montana.

With great creative instincts, Hruska enrolled in Eastern Montana College with the hope of becoming an art teacher. Fate of course has interesting ways of determining one's career path. It was just an ordinary day in the railroad town of Billings when Hruska accompanied his sister and nephew to a medical appointment in one of Billings' grand old buildings. When faced with the prospect of being poked and prodded, his young nephew suddenly bolted from the doctor's office in a panic. When Hruska tracked his nephew down in the building's long hallway, he saw a door with the name Hart-Albin Co. printed in bold letters. He knew of Hart-Albin as an upscale women's store, comparable to Lord & Taylor. After returning his unhappy nephew to the medical office, he went back down the hall and knocked on the Hart-Albin door.

When the door opened, Hruska announced that he was looking for a job. He was told to come back in half an hour, which he dutifully did. Upon returning he again announced that he was looking for a job, something creative. He was shocked when asked if he could start the next day. Excited, and surprised that he was offered a job, he asked what he would be doing. Knowing Hart-Albin had a grand bank of 27 windows, his heart started to pound with anticipation as he was told he would be starting out in the store's windows. And so began a glorious career in visual merchandising.

His first responsibility was to paint the windows, make blackout pads, and adjust the lighting. While he never got to touch a mannequin, he quickly noticed that they had stiff poses, typical of the late 1960s. He also took note that the presentations were rather simplistic; two mannequins, with little consideration to positioning, placed around a few bottles of cosmetics. "How uninspiring," he thought.

At about the same time, Hart-Albin hired Peter Glen, a well-known retail design consultant, to assess and evaluate store design and product presentation. After auditing the store, Glen told management that they really needed to spruce up their presentations. Hruska quickly rose to the occasion telling his immediate supervisor that he could make props for the windows. Wanting to respond to Glen's suggestions, they let Hruska do a few windows, but still, no mannequins. He worked on windows with distinct storylines and had the company's illustrators follow up by creating illustrations for the local newspapers. It all began with a bank of Valentine's Day windows. With spring not far behind, Hruska convinced his display manager to get a large quantity of tulips from a local nursery. Although only eighteen years old, the young display trimmer was confident and convincing. Hundreds of tulips were purchased and used in the windows and the interior of the store. When Glen returned to assess the progress he said, "Wow, things have certainly changed. What happened?"

When Hruska was introduced to the New York consultant, Glen said to him, "There's a whole world out there for you." Hruska's response was, "Really, I'm just having fun." Glen quickly responded, "You should look into it, you're quite talented." After hearing Glen describe the industry and the possibilities it offered, Hruska put together a portfolio of his work and headed for California to visit his brother. Upon arrival, he asked his brother what was the best store in Los Angeles. When his brother told him about Bullocks, he packed his portfolio and once again knocked on a door. He met with the display manager who quickly offered him a job right on the spot. While delighted, he turned down the offer explaining that he couldn't take it at that time because he was still in school and he was just exploring for the future. He left with the assurance that he would be hired when he finished his education.

He went back after school, and as promised was given a job. Still, there were no mannequins in his responsibilities. He was put in charge of all the pinning and flying of merchandise, a trend back in those days. And while some think of it as an unfortunate trend, it still required aesthetic sensibilities and an understanding of composition. While he soon became a master of the art of pinning and flying, he still hoped to be able to work with mannequins.

He was then transferred to the downtown Los Angeles store where he was put in charge of the children's and fabrics departments. While he enthusiastically embraced the job, still there were no mannequins. Then he was transferred to the intimate apparel department, where he finally got to work with mannequins. "They were quite old," recalled Hruska. "The good ones were in the women's department, probably Grenekers with thirty to forty Rootsteins reserved for the windows. Oh I so wish I could have had those Rootsteins."

The next step in his career happened when his manager was fired for stealing. He was a bit concerned when everyone in the entire department was questioned over his manager's indiscretions except him. He couldn't help but wonder why he wasn't questioned as well. He asked for an appointment with the human resources director to discuss the issue. He was assured that they knew he did nothing wrong, and he had nothing to worry about. A new display manager by the name of Bud Peale was brought in. Peale was a good friend of Bill Withers, the vice president director of visual merchandising for Macy's West. Through Withers, Hruska got to meet all of the visual merchandising directors in California and Seattle. While all offered him entry-level positions, he decided to stay where he was. And then the big break occurred. His new display manager purchased a Christmas trim made entirely out of bread. "There were lacquered muffins, rolls, and loaves of bread. It was interesting, but a little strange." Then the manager hurt his back and Hruska, although the youngest of the staff, was put in charge of the department. His colleagues were not very happy with his promotion, and as such, were not very cooperative.

Soon after the baked goods Christmas trim was installed, the store got a visit from the local fire marshal. Big trouble, the trim was not fireproof and had to be removed. Hruska found himself alone facing a huge problem as his staff, still reeling over his promotion, refused to help him take down the trim. The mark of a good visual merchandiser has always been the ability to solve problems. And so, young Jack Hruska rose to the occasion once again. He called a local fireproofing team that removed the trim, had it fireproofed, and reinstalled it in just two days. Hruska was an instant hero among store management and the corporate office.

When Peale returned to work, Hruska went to human resources and asked, "What's next for me? I want to be a visual merchandising manager in a store." When asked what store he would like he replied, "I would like a new store. I don't want to follow in the footsteps of someone else." He was offered the San Diego store, and so began the next chapter in his climb to the top of the industry.

"In those days, the stores ran pretty much independently. There wasn't much corporate direction with the exception of store design," recalled Hruska. "It was then that I had the opportunity to work with store design where I learned how to read floor plans and I learned about fixture placement and lighting. It was a great education." Store design was in charge of purchasing mannequins. Hruska wasn't very happy with their selections. "They didn't wear the clothes very well at all, but I had no choice, I had to open the store with these very stiff mannequins." Once again, Hruska knew how to solve problems. "My strength wasn't necessarily fashion presentation. My strength was in laying out departments and merchandising. I knew I had to play to my strengths, so I hired a fashion expert to trim the mannequins and bring them to life. It was a great learning experience for me."

Bullocks had an aggressive expansion plan, opening seven new stores in the next two and a half years. After the successful opening of the San Diego store, the fashion office always selected Hruska to merchandise all of the new stores. To his dismay, store design continued to purchase the same old stiff mannequins. Finally, Hruska marched into the head of the fashion department's office and asked, "Why don't we order our own mannequins." Much to his delight, going forward he was always consulted on the purchase of mannequins for all of the stores. And so, Bullocks received its first order of Adel Rootstein mannequins. In those days in the late 1970s, stores wanted diversity. They wanted Black mannequins as well as Asian mannequins. Rootstein of course was the first mannequin company to design an African American mannequin after the likeness of super model Donyale Luna.

The next rung in the career ladder for Hruska was a stint at Goldwater's, a six-store division of Associated Dry Goods with stores in Phoenix and Scottsdale, Arizona. Although Arizona wasn't on top of his list for places to live, he didn't hesitate to take the position as visual director of the six-store chain. It was in this capacity that he started to broaden his perspective on mannequins. He brought in mannequins from Decter and Rootstein along with bust forms from Silvestri. Then he took his first buying trip to New York for the NADI show. There he was introduced to Goldsmith Mannequins. When he saw Goldsmith's Abi mannequin, he was immediately impressed with its beautiful simplicity. "It's the way their hips gently move forward and their backs sway slightly behind," he said. "They're exaggerated in an elongated way. The Abi really held outfits gorgeously."

After two and a half years at Goldwater's, he received a call from Robinsons in Los Angeles. The LA retailer was planning a big expansion campaign, and they were very interested in the talents of the twenty-seven-year-old Hruska. It was then that he met Michael Gould, the CEO of Robinsons, who would later have a huge impact on his career. Hruska accepted the position and immediately started to bring a lot of mannequins into the Robinsons stores. "I became the biggest buyer of Rootstein mannequins and Silvestri forms, with a few Goldsmiths as well." As his relationship with Gould began to grow, he developed another strong relationship with Adel Rootstein. "I always visited her every time I went to London," recalled Hruska. "She was charming and exciting to talk to. She always bought a table at the Met Gala and always invited me to sit with her at the table. I have such fond memories of Adel."

Hruska's career was really starting to blossom at this point. At just twenty-eight years old he was inducted into the National Association of Display Industries Hall of Fame. His work was being widely recognized across the industry. In 1987 he left Robinson's and went to work at the Broadway in LA as vice president of visual merchandising. Then in 1992, he got a call from Gould who had moved across the country to accept the position of chairman and CEO of Bloomingdale's. Soon after speaking with Gould, Hruska was heading to New York as vice president, director of visual merchandising and store design for the legendary New York department store. The next stop for Hruska was Lexington Avenue and 59th Street in New York City. Not long after his move to the Big Apple, he was promoted again to executive vice president of creative services.

Once at Bloomingdale's, he developed an even deeper affinity for his chosen profession. "I loved the business and I loved visiting the New York showrooms." At Bloomingdale's, he never really bought the more artistically rendered mannequins. He viewed the mannequin as a vehicle to hold merchandise. His approach was to hire "great fashion people" who could bring the mannequin to life. He was always approached by mannequin companies to customize mannequins exclusively for Bloomingdale's. For the most part, he typically turned down those proposals saying, "You do it. That's your job." He also felt that by customizing mannequins he would be locked into working with that particular supplier. Rather, he would collaborate with his stylists to find out what worked the best, with the ultimate goal being the strongest presentation of the merchandise. He would take the suggestions of the fashion stylists, and then ask the mannequin companies to make small adjustments.

There were two times in his career when he designed a mannequin particularly for his store. "I created a wire mannequin when I was at Robinsons and had it made by D&S Industries, a west coast fixture company." A short time later he saw his wire creations in another store and asked about them. He was told they had a hundred of them in each of their six hundred stores. "I never made a dime off of that design." Another time he worked with Vogue Mannequins, a resource based in Los Angeles. It was a custom abstract mannequin with a distinctive sliced chin. The mannequin became quite popular, and once again he saw his creation in stores across the country.

While Hruska liked to experiment, he didn't do so with mannequin design and customization, but rather with mannequin placement. While still at Robinsons, he developed a mathematical patterning for the placement of mannequins within the store interior. "It didn't really matter what the mannequins were, but rather how they were used and positioned to create interest." His concept was based on a mathematical progression of two–three–five. The outer edge or aisle perimeter of a department would feature two mannequins. The center of the department would feature two sets of three mannequins, and the back wall would feature five mannequins. The theory was that this would form a triangle in the minds-eye, encouraging the viewer to move forward into the department. This mathematical pattern was applied to everything from mannequins and bust forms to sock forms.

When other stores began to copy his patterning philosophy, he changed the mathematical equation to a more asymmetrical formula. While the asymmetrical approach favored one side, it worked because of the balance of negative and positive space. It created a noticeably dynamic presentation based on a three–one–three–two progression. The three mannequins would strike one repetitive pose, and the two mannequins positioned behind would strike an opposite repetitive pose.

While at Bloomingdale's in New York, with inspiration everywhere, he continued to experiment. "When Prada opened in SoHo, they did an incredible army of mannequins," he recalled. "I loved it. We were going to do armies." With the understanding that repetition is a great design tool, he began to strategically position his armies of nine to twelve mannequins in key locations throughout the selling environment. As he developed the concept, one out of the group of repetitive forms would be a prop that would help enhance the product shown on the grouping of mannequins. As he continued to deploy his armies, he began to make each grouping bigger. "We had hundreds of mannequins in the stores. We used the armies to make major merchandise statements or thematic statements such as Chinese New Year."

Under Hruska's direction, Bloomingdale's was for the most part a Rootstein house. "While we used mostly Rootstein, we employed different mannequins to help define different areas. Goldsmith's Abi was the most distinctive and we used it on the contemporary floor. Designer bridge was strictly Rootstein. We also began to use more and more alternative mannequins and forms."

No matter the maker, and no matter the store, Hruska was an innovator in mannequin placement and usage. Whether it was his mathematical patterning or the strategic positioning of his repetitive armies, Hruska advanced and elevated both the science and the art of the mannequin.

CROSSING INTERDISCIPLINARY BOUNDARIES

Most people have portraits of their families hanging in their homes. Rachel Arnold, however, has vintage portraits of old Greneker mannequins adorning the walls of her Brooklyn Heights abode. Her early exposure to art and design clearly led to her lifelong affinity and love affair with mannequins. Raised in New England, her artistic parents instilled in her at an early age the value of living a life full of artistic expression. Her father always quoted Rene Magritte, who said, "Art evokes the mystery without which the world would not exist." An industrial designer, her father taught her space design while she was still in grade school, and her mother, who was a painter and sculptor, often took her to New York City to visit galleries and museums. She loved her trips to New York where as a young girl, she was captivated by the paintings of The Impressionists and the sculptures of Degas and Maillol. These early lessons and experiences were the foundation of a rewarding career in retail design.

Like so many successful industry leaders, a career in visual merchandising wasn't even a consideration. Most got into the retail design industry with very different aspirations and goals. Some even came from totally different disciplines to go on to notable careers in visual merchandising. Arnold studied art and music in Boston, then spent four years in England where she studied art history at Oxford for a summer term and then went on to Trinity College in London, studying music as a classical singer while also attending art school. After studying in England she came back to the States hoping to follow a career in music. While continuing to study at Boston Conservatory, she landed a part-time job at Filene's in Boston. "I was working on the floor in the accessory department, but was fascinated with the windows, mannequins and the floor displays," she recalled.

> I would beg the Display Department to let me help on my off hours. I was fascinated by the mannequin room with its rows of perfect, very realistic, figurative sculptures, that you could make up and dress into any character. To me, it was like giving them a script to play out. I envisioned them on stage acting out their scripted roles.

Great visual merchandising often crosses interdisciplinary boundaries. Studying music can only enhance one's design acumen. Arnold left her job at Filene's and moved to the West coast, where she put her art and music background to good use. While still studying both art and music, she landed a job in display at JC Penney's. In those days, store-level visual merchandisers were autonomous, not reporting to a corporate office. "We had free range to express whatever we wanted," she recalled.

> I remember it was the Fall Fashion launch, and I rigged up groups of mannequins in Fall Fashions falling from the ceilings of the windows, with the title *Falling into Fall*. Someone from the corporate offices of May Company saw the windows and found out who had done them. Two weeks later I was one of the regional stylists for the May Company. So in an ironic twist of fate, it was my mannequin friends in the window of JC Penney that got me promoted.

After The May Co. she was hired at The Broadway Stores as the corporate visual designer for women's fashion, and soon after was promoted to the lofty position of vice president of visual merchandising. In that capacity, she quickly filled the Broadway stores with Rootstein and Greneker mannequins. "They were beautiful realistic mannequins, with wigs that needed to be styled. We placed them as if they were in a real-life setting, interacting with one another." At that time, Rootstein was sculpting the faces of famous models and actresses. When seeing the celebrity-inspired mannequins, Arnold was quick to recognize the role mannequins could play as storytellers and the ability they had to connect with customers by tapping into their aspirations. "When I wanted to show women's 'power suits' I put them on Joan Collins mannequins. Management knew that what ever story the mannequins were telling, was the story the customer wanted to buy." In the early '90s, Arnold landed her dream job as vice president creative director for Greneker Mannequins. This opportunity marked the beginning of a new era for Arnold; she was joining a company that was on the rise as the '90s were the beginning of a new era for mannequins. As Greneker was adapting to change, both industrywide and internally, they were searching for someone with a great deal of retail experience to assume a creative executive role. Arnold already had a good working relationship with Greneker, having used many of their mannequins at The Broadway. She was the perfect fit. Greneker began to specialize in custom-sculpted mannequins, offering retailers the opportunity to differentiate themselves from their competition. This was a game changer in the mannequin business. Retailers were the first to speak about branding. They began to recognize the power of the right mannequin to make a clear and defined branded statement. As retail moved deeper into the '90s, more and more visual directors wanted the nuances of their specific brand to be represented by strong statements throughout the store, especially through visual displays and dynamic mannequin presentations. To achieve this, they wanted mannequins that were theirs and theirs alone. Greneker soon became the go-to resource for mannequin customization. Nordstrom launched an advertising campaign in search of "The Nordstrom Woman" who would become the "Face of Nordstrom" in all of their advertising. It was a brilliant marketing endeavor with the goal of connecting with their customer. They wanted "The Face of Nordstrom" to be one of their customers. After a much-hyped search, a winner was selected and flown to Los Angeles to be sculpted by Greneker. It was a stroke of brilliance and great holistic thinking to have the in-print advertising match the mannequin face in the stores. Greneker sculpted "The Face" for several years, with a new customer's face every year. While Greneker was establishing itself as a customization house, it recognized another important trend. The retail sports industry was booming. Stores specializing in all things sports, from apparel to shoes and equipment, were popping up everywhere. It quickly became apparent to the visual directors of these stores that they couldn't use regular fashion mannequins to accurately communicate the attributes of their brand and of their core offerings. Recognizing the need, Greneker jumped into the business of doing life casts from the bodies of real athletes. This became a strong, branded statement and a major enticement for customers who were sports enthusiasts. "We did basketball players, football players, tennis players, baseball players, soccer players and runners," said Arnold. "Some were cast in uniform to be used as decorative pieces, while others were done as regular mannequins; some in action poses, to wear merchandise. Mannequins were evolving from statuesque fashion models to real-life representations of different lifestyles." As Greneker continued to grow and assume an even larger and more recognized role as an important mannequin resource, they opened a grand two-story showroom on 25th Street in Manhattan. "It was a vast open space that gave us the opportunity to create vignettes where we told lifestyle stories with the new mannequin lines," recalled Arnold. "Of course, we held big parties in the space where the attendees mixed with the mannequins. At times you couldn't tell who was real, and who was a mannequin. I was on a platform once, fixing the mannequin's dress, when someone pulled on my hemline. I turned around and she shrieked in surprise thinking I was a mannequin." Martha Landau ran the New York showroom. Landau was known and respected for being the mannequin historian; she knew everyone and could recall all the great fashion designers who would come in to order mannequins for their showrooms in the '50s and '60s. Many of those notable designers would spec certain mannequins to be used for their designs in the stores. At times they were even involved in the sculpting, to make the mannequins more specific to that designer's lifestyle brand. As Greneker continued to grow, Arnold further developed her expertise and working knowledge of mannequins as she became a recognized and highly respected authority on the subject. The most important lesson that she learned at Greneker was that all retailers regarded mannequins as the ultimate selling tool. "Retailers would order around two hundred and fifty mannequins for a new store. It was a great, highly profitable business." In her work at Greneker, she also learned it was not simply any kind of basic body that made a good mannequin. The slightest twist of the pose would make the clothes hang better. She understood that there needed to be a variety of arm poses to handle all types of fashion in each line.

We had to exaggerate the pose of the human body to best show off the clothing. The legs were longer, the torsos shorter, and the arm poses exaggerated to be more dramatic. We would design bodies that worked together, looking at each other, or even holding one another for a more dramatic effect. Mannequins represented the current cultural lifestyles. The females became softer in their body type, instead of hourglass figures; the men a bit more muscular, but more relaxed in their poses. The women didn't have feet that only wore stilettos, they began to have flatter feet to wear Birkenstocks and sneakers. The make-up became softer, more natural, if they were realistic. If abstract, the heads would sometimes mimic a famous sculptor or artist to have a more elevated aesthetic.

While at Greneker, Arnold loved working with the mannequins everyday. She spent most of her time in the sculpting studio developing new mannequin lines to show at the biannual visual merchandising show in New York City. "Rootstein was the Queen of the high fashion mannequin, and Greneker was The Queen of the customized mannequin." Then a new opportunity presented itself to Arnold, one she couldn't refuse. She was offered the position as vice president of visual merchandising at Bloomingdale's in New York. "It was hard for me to leave Greneker, but I had always longed to return to the East Coast, and Bloomingdale's was the premier fashion store, 'like no other store in the world.' I had to go. So in 1996, I moved to Manhattan." The timing was perfect. Bloomingdale's was about to expand to the West Coast, opening five new stores at once, just in time for the Christmas season. Bloomingdale's was known internationally as an ultra-contemporary lifestyle store. As such, the new stores were going to be designed on the cutting edge of contemporary architecture by Arnold's boss and visual merchandising icon, Jack Hruska. As time continues to move, fashions change and mannequins evolve. The early to mid-'90s were a turning point for mannequins as they evolved from the realistic to the abstract. Visual presentations were becoming more direct and to the point. They were simpler, with fewer props and fewer distractions. Mannequin design was becoming more minimalistic with greater emphasis on the clothing rather than the personality of the mannequin. "At Bloomingdale's, we did groupings of headless mannequins or mannequins with abstract heads in addition to forms that blended in with the architecture," said Arnold. "In the windows on 59th Street, however, we still used realistic mannequins to tell a more dramatic story with the hope of attracting attention and ultimately luring customers into the store." Arnold was at Bloomingdale's for several years when another new opportunity presented itself in 2005. She was asked to work with RYA Architects in Dallas to develop the visual merchandising concepts in several stores they were designing overseas. "Visual merchandising was just being discovered in Southeast Asia, and they were starting with a total re-model of a major Department store in Kuala Lumpur. So I seized the moment and opened my own retail design business, packed my bags, and headed for Malaysia," recalled Arnold. "Working overseas was the ultimate adventure. I took teams of visual merchandisers with me to teach merchandising concepts to the in-house staff. Mannequins were always the focal point." In Malaysia, the women covered their heads, so Arnold bought shades of metallic mannequins with abstract heads from Ralph Pucci. Every fashion statement was shown with a coordinating scarf wrapper around the head. The abstract mannequins were very well received; customers loved the metallic accents that brought an elevated fashion presence to a moderate department store. Arnold's international work with mannequin specification continued. From Malaysia she traveled to Seoul, South Korea, to work on the opening of Shinsegae, and then to Doha, Qatar, to work on 51 East. Both were high-end department stores that mixed world-class architecture with local culture to create extraordinary experiential retail environments. In Doha, she used Bonaveri mannequins made from horizontally positioned wooden slats to present handbags and accessories. In Seoul, she specified sleek elegant Schläppi mannequins to show high-end designer fashion. In both cases, she integrated a great deal of local art into the environments, and in both stores, the mannequins were clearly considered to be part of the showing of contemporary abstract art. The globetrotting visual merchandiser's international work continued, traveling to countries both East and West to share her knowledge of mannequins. "I worked on stores for DFS / LVMH in Cambodia, Macau, and Venice Italy," said Arnold. "In Cambodia, the store was simply called T Galleria, while in Macau it was T Galleria, City of Dreams. The store in Venice was T Fondaco Dei Tedeschi, T Galleria. These were elegant free standing high-end stores, that were works of art in and of themselves." These stores were mostly accessories, beauty, and gifts, rather than ready-to-wear. To showcase the accessories, she worked with Atrezzo, a Spanish mannequin supplier founded in Barcelona in 1990, to create forms with abstract heads in harlequin patterned velvets and articulated arms. "The articulated arms and hands let us animate the fashion displays so they showed bags and jewelry. It also allowed the forms to hold shoes in an expressive high fashion manner." Arnold has very definite thoughts about the future of retail and the continued efficacy of the mannequin.

> As the events of the day continue to impact retail, we will always see a reinvention of the shopping experience. Higher levels of technology in e-commerce allow for a smaller footprint, where the customer can come in and virtually try on

> clothes and instantly buy and have them delivered or they can pick up at an in-store pick-up kiosk. Another available option is for the customer to have a video conference from her home with a concierge who knows her profile. The concierge, or personal stylist, will then recommend several outfits that she superimposes on the customer's Avatar. All the while, the customer can scan the web and look for better deals, and send her findings to her friends for a thumbs up or thumbs down.

As technology and e-commerce continue to grow and evolve, Arnold recognizes the potential but still sees the importance of brick-and-mortar retail.

> The physical store will always have the advantage of personal service. The in-store experience gives the customer the ability to touch and to create an event or experience with the product that on-line shopping can not. But what will this experiential retail look like? Will there be more interactive displays, will the traditional fashion mannequin display be a thing of the past? Will the mannequins become more robotic? A lot of concepts are in the working stages, and we shall see what theories become successful. For me, nothing sells better or gives more character to a store than mannequins.

A STANDARD BEARER OF THE STORE

For many of the leaders in the visual merchandising profession, it was the early lessons learned that helped shape and influence their vision and creative sensibilities. It was these seminal experiences and exchanges that guided them throughout the course of their successful careers. This was certainly the case for Brian Preussker, a young display trimmer for Alexanders Department Store in New York. While working in the windows at Alexanders, assisting the lead stylist, he was positioning two female mannequins in what he thought was the best location in the window. While Preussker was behind the glass the stylist was outside on the sidewalk directing him on the precise mannequin placement. "Well, with all the arm waving and shouting through the glass, I just couldn't get the mannequins where he wanted," remembered Preussker. "I could see he was getting frustrated with me, and while he was feverishly gesticulating I was thinking to myself, what's the big deal? I'm sure he was thinking, don't make me come in there and do it myself." Sure enough, the exasperated stylist had enough and he came storming into the window. "I think the five-minute walk to get around to the interior entrance cooled him off a bit. When he came into the window he turned back into the nurturing mentor I knew." What he said to the young trimmer really struck a chord and remained with him throughout his career. "Brian, make believe they are lovers, never wanting to be apart." The stylist's direction had an immediate impact. "The expression on my face made him roar with laughter! He was right, it was a dramatic difference and one I never forgot and always passed on: Keep the placement tight!"

Preussker learned those early lessons and they served him well as his blossoming career path took him from coast to coast beginning with his entry-level position as a display trimmer at Alexanders. The next stop along the way was Bloomingdale's where he spent ten years, advancing from a stylist to a branch store visual merchandising manager, and then to regional director of visual merchandising. After Bloomingdale's, he accepted a position at Macy's East/Bamburger's as a regional director until he was offered the position of vice president of visual merchandising at Bullocks, a division of Macy's West. This was an offer he couldn't refuse, so he packed his bags and headed for California. After Bullocks, Preussker further solidified his position as a leader in the industry with his twenty-year tenure in San Francisco at Macy's West as senior vice president of visual merchandising and store design. During the course of a notable career, Preussker witnessed the reshaping, transformation, and evolution of fashion and its impact on the form, function, and application of mannequins in the retail environment. "Fashion changes every day and mannequins are not far behind in keeping up with those changes," said Preussker.

> In the beginning of my career in the late '60s and early '70s, I worked as a display trimmer at Alexanders dressing a hundred and fifty-seven mannequins every two weeks. I had help from one other trimmer and a fashion coordinator. I knew very little about mannequins but even back then I was seeing how fast the industry would react to the latest trends. I quickly learned how certain mannequins were better suited than others when it came to fashion trends.

With the many mannequin resources available at the time, it was critical to select the right one to not only project the attributes of the retailer's brand but also to best communicate the nuances of the latest fashion trends. "In the '70s and '80s and beyond, Adel Rootstein was the innovator when it came to setting trends as well as promoting them," recalled Preussker.

> Her use of movement in poses of dramatic expression set the pace and challenged the status quo. In the '80s, mannequin selection started to deviate from realistic to abstract. Then there was the introduction of what I call a hybrid abstract. Mannequins were designed with realistic features that included molded hair and shoes. This development responded to and drove fashion trends while also reacting to the financial considerations of the day.

Wearing his historian's hat, Preussker added, "I'm sure the molded design was inspired by Pierre Imans' 1931 mannequin modeled after Josephine Baker." During his twenty years at Macy's West, Preussker recognized that in addition to being utilitarian, mannequins are also an art form. "As both retail and fashion evolved, mannequins began to be used more sparingly so they have become more important than ever before," offered Preussker. "Placement is strategic, and the right style of mannequin is key to evoke and move the customer's emotions. Ralph Pucci showed us many times over how his mannequins should be considered as an art form, and also as dynamic tools for featuring apparel. A leading example of this was Pucci's collection, *The Olympian Goddess*." Moving the viewer's emotion is an integral element of any art form. "Mannequins in the right environment and with focused staging can evoke almost any emotion from the viewer," said Preussker.

> Christmas presentations are the perfect example of how visual merchandisers move emotions. Another mannequin manufacturer that comes to mind who clearly has the ability to evoke a strong emotional response is Hans Boodt. Their "Sports" collection of action and movement are handsomely sculpted and inspire the viewer to feel the need to get back to the gym. To me, this is art at its finest.

Brick-and-mortar stores are tools of communication used as instruments to convey quality messages to the targeted customer about the nuances of the brand, company philosophy, and fashion point of view. Mannequins are an integral part of the retail dialogue; the appropriate mannequin will provide an inflection and tone of voice that reflects the nature of the organization. The evolution of the mannequin has brought about many changes, all inspired by fashion trends and movements, which in turn have been inspired by current events and changes in society and culture, both local and universal. With many mannequin choices available and many issues to consider, Preussker felt that the apparel itself was a prime factor that dictated mannequin choice and selection.

> Very rarely would I let the mannequin dictate the choice of apparel. With that said, however, it was always exciting to be the first to present a new mannequin line in your flagship store windows. Companies were always competing for market share with exciting new mannequin lines twice a year. The hope was that this could be the show-stopper for the new season!

The late 1980s and early 1990s presented many options for visual merchandising directors. More and more were promoting the use of abstract mannequins. "Personally, I favored realistic mannequins over abstract because I feel the customer can relate to that image and expression more closely," said Preussker. "Then Ralph Pucci International showed us the way to use abstracts not only to highlight the apparel but to compliment the design of the environment. Abstracts were also quickly becoming a viable option due to financial considerations. They were practical and made a lot of sense if the retailer couldn't retain a fashion stylist to do hair and makeup." Beginning with his early experiences in Alexander's windows, mannequin positioning was always a critical consideration for Preussker, whether in the windows or the store interiors. "Groupings have their place in windows as well as the store interior. What better way to create excitement and a celebration in the entrance or center of space than with a grouping of ten or more mannequins." Preussker, like many other visual directors of nationally branded retail organizations, had the need and the opportunity to develop a customized branded mannequin as a standard bearer of the store and as a fashion statement. Of course, one must have enough stores to amortize the tooling cost of mannequin development to make this fiscally feasible. "Over the years I have worked with several mannequin companies on mannequin development," recalled Preussker. "I generally stayed away from a complete mannequin design process based on my first experience with mannequin development." Preussker recognized that mannequin development is a precise and delicate process. "At first it seems very straight forward. First you select images of the model you prefer. Next you edit the selection and take direct sketches of poses you would like and discuss your vision with the sculptor." What follows is a painstaking process that goes from inspiration to fruition; and for the visual merchandiser, inspiration is everywhere.

> When celebrity models were the rage, I was fortunate enough to be involved in the development of the DG Williams mannequin inspired by the actress and fashion model Renee Russo. She was all the rage at the time appearing on the covers of both Vogue and Cosmopolitan. The ensuing process of developing the Russo mannequin was very time consuming. Most of the time you just watched the sculptor create. I did get to meet Ms. Russo, but contrary to what I thought, she didn't spend much time sitting for the sculptor as a body double was used. The end result was fantastic but it was what the sculptor had envisioned. Being an artist myself I understand that collaboration can be limited and you have to trust your partner. We opened our fall windows with a chorus line of Renee mannequins to celebrate the opening of Radio City Music Hall's new show featuring the Rockettes.

In late 2000 and early 2001, yoga became a major trend as its popularity rapidly spread across the country. This of course had a significant impact on fashion. Apparel specifically designed to be worn while practicing yoga became a leading focus for most retailers. Shops were requested by retailers across the retail spectrum. While there was a great demand for yoga shops, they weren't easy to design and execute. "The merchandise didn't lend itself to our current inventory of mannequins or fixturing," remembered Preussker.

> Our action posed mannequins weren't right, and hanging the apparel didn't do it any justice. Folding on tables and in cubicle units were used mostly instead of hanging. Fortunately, Ralph Pucci, already ahead of the curve, sculpted a mannequin in a Lotus position, inspired by supermodel Christy Turlington. All you needed was Christy and your shop was complete. Merchants couldn't keep up with the sales! To this day Christy's Lotus mannequin is still the standard.

While most of his illustrious career was spent in San Francisco at Macy's West, Preussker said it wasn't the California vibe that influenced mannequin selection, but rather current trends and the merchandise assortment offered by Macy's.

> While one may think the West Coast would have its own individual look being so far from New York, that wasn't necessarily the case. The fashions and trends weren't that different in most cases. Most of the influencers on the West Coast came from the East Coast and we at Macy's both East and West, agreed on most trend subjects like mannequins.

"From the East Coast to the West Coast and all places in between, the evolution of mannequins will continue to set new standards for the industry," offered Preussker as he waxed poetic on the role of mannequins past, present, and future.

> Mannequins have long made their presence known, from the discovery of a wooden torso in King Tutankhamen's tomb to today's designers creating new images to spark the customers' emotions and capture their interest. Garments never look good on a hanger. Mannequins bring life to a garment that can evoke a dream or fantasy for the viewer on how he or she may see themselves.

LIFESTYLE, ATTITUDE, AND FASHION

George Talbott Martin's meteoric rise in the visual merchandising industry as a mannequin designer skipped a step when he went directly from a branch store position as a visual merchandising manager at Robinson's in Southern California, to creative director at Greneker Mannequins in Los Angeles. After graduating with a degree in architecture from the University of Southern California, young George Talbott Martin, born in New Orleans to a Honduran mother and an American father, took a job at an architectural firm in Newport Beach. While his educational background in art and architecture was impressive, he didn't envision himself sitting behind a drawing board detailing architectural blueprints. After a short time, he left the position with the architectural group to travel to London where he spent two years studying interior design and fine art, in what he calls his "finishing school years."

Then opportunity knocked with a position that seemed to offer a great deal of creative possibilities. He was hired by John Boydston, the visual merchandising manager at May Company's iconic store on Wilshire. At the time he didn't consider this to be a career move, but rather a temporary position. Still, he approached the opportunity with enthusiasm and gusto. The Wilshire store's celebrated Art Deco and Streamline Moderne building had a huge bank of windows. After designing and installing several window presentations, Martin felt that he found his true calling. "I loved doing those windows."

While at May Company he met Wilmer Weiss whom he credits as someone who unleashed his creativity by understanding his vision and point of view. "I was greatly influenced by Wilmer. He had such flair and presence. He could easily take control of a room of executives, buyers, or merchants. He had charisma." Weiss eventually took a position at I. Magnum. When Martin visited him, Weiss gave him a guided tour through the store explaining what he did and why he did it. The two became very dear friends, and as Martin explains, "He was extended family."

After a few short years at May Company, he was hired by Jack Hruska, who at the time was the visual merchandising director at Robinson's Department Store in Los Angeles. It was there that Martin developed an even greater affinity for the profession that allowed him to create a whole environment and a whole world in just one day. "Visual merchandising provided me with the opportunity to use my background and gave me more of an open book on design," said Martin. He credits Hruska as his mentor, and lessons learned at USC as his guiding light. "USC taught me how to think and how to solve problems. The ability to solve problems is a vital component of a visual merchandiser's skill set."

Then in 1981, he received a call from Greneker, offering him a position as creative director. And so began George Martin's illustrious career as a well-respected and accomplished mannequin designer. Once he accepted the position, there was no honeymoon period, everything was fast paced. In his words, "I was thrown immediately into the kettle." The NADI (National Association of Display Industries) show in New York was coming up in six months. He had never been to a NADI show as a buyer, and now he was being thrust into this world as an exhibitor.

Martin honed his art as a mannequin designer at Greneker for six years. Then in 1987, he received a call from Irwin Hochberg, who owned a successful fixture company that did a great deal of custom woodwork for many notable retailers such as Ralph Lauren. Hochberg told him he wanted to start a mannequin company and he would like Martin to join him in the endeavor as the company's creative director and vice president of design and presentation. Hochberg also called on the talents of Norman Glazer, the president of Greneker, to help him build the company. Both Martin and Glazer accepted the offer, and a new mannequin company was born.

While setting up the Greneker showroom shortly before leaving the established mannequin maker, Martin received a phone call from Hochberg asking him to come up with a name for their new business venture. The idea of Patina was floated about, but they couldn't get the rights for that name. Someone in the fledgling organization suggested Patina Visual but Martin said the word visual was too overused. He suggested the name Patina V, and the new company had its name. While some people thought it meant Patina Five, everyone loved the name. The letter V seemed to add a bit of a mystique to the company. Once he moved over to Patina V, he had six months to design several new lines of mannequins in addition to designing the permanent showroom for the next NADI show in New York. Once again he was being thrown into the simmering kettle. He met the challenge head on, and Patina V opened with great success in New York in December of 1987. Soon after, Glazer bought the company from Hochberg, and Patina V became a major mannequin resource.

While recognizing that mannequins, like the fashions they present, are all about change, Martin's approach always remained consistent; think about what is needed in the market. What are they missing? There will always be new body images, attitudes, and of course new merchandise. What are the needs of the merchant? Also consistent in his approach was a belief in creating drama and illusion. "If you have a new line consisting

Figure 10.5 Patina V Boheme mannequin. Courtesy of CNL Mannequins.

of eight mannequins, two of them should have dramatic poses while the other six should be more versatile poses."

For Martin, the design process always began by pouring through myriad images, from which he would collect an assemblage of tear sheets for ideas and inspiration. Then he would bring in a real model and watch the way she moved and the way clothing draped on her body. A hundred and fifty to two hundred photographs would then be taken. As he developed this process he quickly realized that every model he brought in had her own style and attitude. If two girls wore the same clothes and struck the same pose, he would get two distinctly different looks. Like any three-dimensional sculpture, Martin always insisted that every mannequin he designed had to work from any angle from which it is viewed. Every mannequin had to have a built-in versatility with the possibility of being used in any given physical or architectural condition. The next step in the design process was to tweak the concept until it was just right.

Once satisfied with the direction the design was going in, a sculptor and a body model were called in. "We would always start with the simplest pose and then develop the style. After that, we would get more detailed and complicated. We would learn as we went through the process; what is the right waistline, what is the right bust line." At the same time that the body was being perfected, a face sculptor would begin work on the face from the selected models chosen for the collection. It was a two-day process to sculpt from a model, and then an additional week to complete and perfect the head. Upon completion, the clay head would be put on the body, and then once approved, dozens of photographs would be taken. After pouring through the photographs, small adjustments would be made.

As a designer, Martin always considered mannequins to be an art form. "They are three-dimensional sculptures. A talented sculptor can capture the nuances and the nature of a girl. No one is perfect. An artist looks for the essence or the quality of a face that makes it unique. They may take some liberties or poetic license with the face that make it bigger than life." Mannequin design, as in any art form, requires a great deal of editing. The next step in the design process was to edit until the concept was just right. When totally satisfied, the completed sculpture would be sent to the mold maker.

Martin always recognized that it takes a team to create a quality mannequin. "A mannequin company is like a family. The production of a mannequin requires a great deal of labor, and everyone involved plays an important role." It involves the sculptor, the model, the mold maker, sanders, painters, the make-up artist, packers, and finally sales people who service the customers. While the end result may seem glamorous, the task can be arduous and dirty. The sanding process alone takes hours of dusty and grimy work. Martin always had an open-door policy and tried to make everyone along the way feel as though they were part of a team. Out of respect and concern for his staff, he worked hard to establish a more sophisticated and environmentally sound process. Partitions were added to work areas, paint booths were installed, and other clean air initiatives were implemented. After much research, the company also converted to water base paint.

The work of a mannequin designer is quite fast paced. Mannequins are true reflections of society and of fashion movements around the world. The evolution of the mannequin is an anthropological study of cultural movements throughout the decades. As such, change is the hallmark of mannequin design. The mandate of any mannequin designer

Figure 10.6 Patina V Adagio mannequin. Courtesy of CNL Mannequins.

is to continually develop new products that stay ahead of the inherent changes in society at large and the requisite changes in fashion. There are always new fashion proportions to consider, and new societal values. "In the '80s, the body of a woman wasn't about mannequins with breasts encased in bras. We had to recognize this and design accordingly," said Martin. "Mannequins are a reflection of lifestyles. We always had to come up with collections that had different attitudes and were reflective of the times and changing fashions."

Every year, and every season, brings change. "There are always new influences and new ideals. People aspire to be part of these new concepts and lifestyles," said Martin. "We were the dream makers. We would portray a fantasy world, a world of dreams. If you wore these clothes, your dreams would come true." As the 1990s nudged past the 1980s, a slimmer and more assertive mannequin attitude was needed. Women became more active with strict regimens at their local gyms. As such, Martin recognized the need for a more chiseled body type. Prior to this new social movement, bodies were fairly basic. Now they had to be more detailed and defined.

Politics and political correctness also played an important role in mannequin design in the '90s. It happened suddenly, almost overnight. Mannequin designers had to be nimble with quick responses to the wants and needs of their clients. "Everyone wanted different ethnic groups," remembered Martin. "Customers demanded diversity. Retailers thought it important to have Caucasian, black, Asian, and Latino mannequins on their platforms and in their windows." Another big demand of retailers was for special sizes, plus mannequins and petite mannequins. The industry realized this was a large market and they wanted to take advantage of it. Martin responded to both industry demands with new mannequin collections.

Along with the importance of the mannequin design is the equally important stage or showplace in which the mannequins are presented to the retail client. While most showrooms are theme oriented, Martin always shied away from that approach. Due to his architectural background, he thought of a showroom concept as a presentation of what was happening in design at the time. Always a season ahead, he wanted to show potential customers what their stores could look like in the coming selling season. Toward that end, he always incorporated architectural elements. This led to an offshoot of Patina V with the creation and development of Patina Arts. The new division of the company featured lines of furniture from classic to mid-century, and decoratives including urns, sculptures, and the new essential mannequin alternatives. This approach provided customers with a variety of options; they could purchase urns for their ledges or full shop concepts for strong merchandise statements. "When people walked into the showroom, I always wanted to give them options and alternatives. When they looked around, they wanted everything they saw in the showroom, even if it was just a prop. Because of that, we had to price everything. It was all about inspiring people."

Under Martin's direction, Patina V offered clients a great deal of versatility. Twice a year he would create four to six new mannequin collections. And unlike many other mannequin companies, they gave customers the option to choose a body with any head in the collection. "We built in the ability to adapt to whatever the customer desired."

The mid-'80s and early '90s were the pinnacle of realistic mannequins and the high point of the display industry. Everything was robust and fast paced. There were two markets in New York, one in December with everyone flocking to the Big Apple to see the windows and the interior holiday trim, and one in the spring. There was also an annual show every March in San Francisco called WAVM (Western Association of Visual Merchandisers). They were all grand productions and exciting events complete with dinner parties and dynamic showrooms with elaborate lunches and freely flowing fine wine. In the evenings there was dinner, and they weren't just anywhere. They were at places like La Cirque or Bouley's, and not just at any table, but at the best table.

Retail designers all over the world, especially in New York, London, and Paris, were creating fantasy and magic with big window and display staffs. Then suburban malls became more important and windows less important. With the exception of places like New York and Chicago, which still held onto the theatrical approach to brand projection and product presentation, the magic of display and visual merchandising began to be somewhat diminished. Store interiors still featured grand presentations with glorious groupings of mannequins, particularly at the top of an escalator landing. It was the big wow! As time went on, however, interior real estate was at a premium and retailers scrambled to use every square foot of space for merchandise. Mannequin platforms went from grand 10' × 10' stage-like statements to 4' × 4' accents and afterthoughts. Everything in the store shrunk, including the visual merchandising budgets and staffs. To a large degree, this led to a gradual shift to abstract mannequins and mannequin alternatives.

There have long been rumors, if not hopes among some quarters, that realistic mannequins would make a comeback. Martin thinks of realistic mannequins as a saving art form. "There is a market where they are coveted, among collectors and traders. Realistics are becoming a type of art form. There is a real passion for them." He points out that in addition to an economy of effort, abstract also became popular and a strong design statement because upscale fashion designers, who considered their creations to be an art form, didn't want any distractions from highly detailed realistic mannequins.

He also points out that some mannequin collections can take a few seasons to become viable. At times, mannequins that are twenty years old become relevant again. "Sometimes mannequin presentations go back twenty years." He recalled the time when Victoria's Secret mixed mannequins from 1988 with mannequins from 2005. "Many old collections have been revived when people saw them in our catalogue and said wow, this would look great in our window."

With his background in architecture, Martin always maintained a certain level of discipline. "I would strive toward the high mark, and then keep examining the possibilities. I would continue to edit until the time grew short. Part of the art is knowing when to stop. I stopped when I knew I had the best solution." Martin always credited his team of sculptors, including Michael Zadowics, Tanya Ragir, Justine Poole, and John Jebb, for the company's success. "It was the unnamed team members that allowed us to change dreams into reality." After an illustrious and influential career, the much admired and mild-mannered designer retired from Patina V in 2011. He made his mark on the industry he loved.

Figure 10.7 Patina V Belle Monde mannequin. Courtesy of CNL Mannequins.

Much like Martin, Paul Wolff's career was also impacted by his time at Greneker. He was destined to enter the mannequin industry in some manner or form; after all, it was a family affair. His grandfather, Bill Decter, started the Decter Mannikin Company (note the spelling) in the late 1930s in a small one-thousand-square-foot shop in Los Angeles. It was there that Bill carved out a niche for his growing company, initially offering papier-mâché bust forms to the visual merchandising industry on the West Coast.

Bill was widely known and respected as one of the nicest people in the industry. And while many stories abound about the affable Bill Decter, to this day people still talk about Bill's famous encounter with one of his biggest clients, Coles of California. Bill supplied Coles with hundreds of papier-mâché female swim forms. One day toward the end of his career in the early 1960s, a representative from Coles told Bill about the latest sensation, plastic body forms instead of the tried and true papier-mâché forms that Decter was producing. Bill dismissed the idea of using plastic forms calling them garbage. Six months went by when Bill called the Coles executive and asked him to come to the showroom. He told him he had something new and exciting. When he arrived at the Decter showroom, Bill brought him to the roof and produced a beautiful plastic body form. The Coles executive laughed, "Bill, six months ago you said they were garbage." Bill responded, "They are all the rage. This is the future." He then dropped the form off the roof to prove that it was unbreakable.

After attending USC, Bill's son Jerry, a decorated war veteran having served in the Pacific Theater during World War II, joined the company. Later on, he was joined by his sister Joyce and her husband, Jim Wolff. As the family business grew, Decter moved to a significantly larger sixty-five-thousand-square-foot space on 8th Street in LA. Jerry

Decter along with Joyce and Jim Wolff, took the reins of the growing family business. When they landed the JC Penney account, the business really began to flourish and became one of the industry's larger mannikin producers.

Joyce Wolff assumed the position of vice president. In that highly visible capacity, she went on to become a much-beloved industry icon. Well known, admired, and widely respected as an intelligent, elegant, and empathetic executive during the course of her thirty-plus-year career, she mentored many young people as they climbed the ladder in the visual merchandising industry. It was clear to all who met and got to know her that she took a sincere interest in others and graciously gave of her time while sharing her expertise. Joyce was a true champion of the industry, devoted to raising the professional bar and thereby furthering its future. She was known to recognize someone at an industry function who looked star-struck and somewhat out of place. She would graciously introduce herself and then bring the newcomer to meet some of the industry's most recognized and influential leaders. She loved opening a door to a new and exciting world for those first entering the field. Moments like this came naturally to Joyce Wolff as everyone around her was honored to be recognized by her, whether they were new to the industry or were seasoned professionals.

Paul Wolff, Joyce and Jim's son, worked during the summers with the Decter facility on 8th Street in Los Angeles when he was in high school. After attending UCLA, Paul entered the business full time. "The business was really thriving at the time, and I had a MacGyver-like knack for materials and solving problems." (MacGyver was an American action-adventure television series whose title character had an amazing resourcefulness for solving any challenge that came his way using his wit and any materials he had on hand).

After his father retired from the business in 1986, Paul managed the company until early 1991 when he left Decter to find new opportunities outside the family business. In July of that year, Russ Richardson, a top executive at Bon Art called Paul, telling him that he heard Paul had left Decter to pursue other possibilities. Richardson told him that Cliff Sobel, the owner of Los Angeles-based Greneker Mannequins and their parent company Bon Art, based in New Jersey, would like to speak with him. Sobel was looking for someone for Greneker and he thought Paul might be a good fit. The two spoke on the telephone for two hours. After the call, Sobel was convinced that Paul had an interesting perspective of the industry and the customer experience, as well as a sense of future retail. Paul was interested in the opportunity but understood the complexity around his family business and the possibility of taking a position with a competitor. This was beyond a simple discussion with his family and he assured Sobel that he was flattered by the offer and that he would get back to him.

After discussing the offer with his parents, Paul called Sobel and told him he couldn't take the offer. Sobel, still impressed with Paul's background and customer experience philosophy called Paul again three months later. "I've spoken to a number of people and you're still our first choice to fill the position," said Sobel. Paul, married with two children, got on a plane and flew to New Jersey to discuss the opportunity further. He was intrigued with Sobel's plan to grow his company and the importance he placed on the customer and how he might fit into that future. He was the third generation in his family's business and the competitive component was not easy to get beyond. Paul told Sobel he would accept the position on the condition that Greneker could not market or take any Decter Mannikin customers during the term that Paul was with the Company—this was accepted by his family and Decter management. The rest was history, Paul went on to become President of Greneker Mannequins.

Paul learned a great deal about other aspects of the mannequin industry and the many changes it was beginning to undergo during his six-year tenure at Greneker. Coming East and working for another company was an eye-opener, as were the lessons learned under the tutelage of Sobel. "Cliff told me that everyone thought I was a really nice guy," remembered Paul. "But they didn't know if I could close. I asked Cliff what was close? And then I said I would learn to close if he would teach me." Sobel said, "I'm not sure I can teach you." Paul's response was, "then don't expect me to learn." A great team was developed at Greneker and the company doubled its sales in two years.

Entertainment retail was becoming a game changer at the time. In response, East 25th Street was lined with industry showrooms including mannequin houses, fixture manufacturers and decorative prop resources. "It was a grand time for the industry," said Paul.

> Rachel was our creative director and the vision of the new Greneker. She really had the ability to tap into and translate what the industry wanted and what the industry was doing. The showroom was designed with entertainment in mind with an homage to the Bendel's concept of shops within a shop. Our showroom was huge, with large aisles and many compelling and varied vignettes showing mannequins in lifestyle settings, or the way they were intended to be used. Our mannequins were created by the hands of our sculptor based on the information Rachel supplied.

One of Paul's most interesting and innovative projects was a collaboration with Tony Mancini, the visual merchandising director at Herman's, a sporting goods store based in Carteret, New Jersey. "Herman's had a big push to renovate its Manhattan flagship," remembered Paul. "We decided to use live casts of well-known athletes to create a new mannequin line. We had boxers, track and field runners and basketball players that were live-cast. The program was a big success for Herman's."

As time went on, the industry continued to evolve. Paul recognized that the business was changing from a creative center to a cost-per-square-foot strategy. The days of the merchandiser were gone. From Paul's perspective, strategies were no longer inspired by the philosophies of a Stanley Marcus or the creative vision of an Andy Markopoulos or a Bill Withers. "The concept of wide aisles and legions of dressers was not needed. The margins were no longer there, and innovation was devalued." With this understanding, Paul decided it was time to move on and find a new category where he felt his talents and philosophies had greater value. "I wanted to move on to a place where innovation and the transaction were based on relationships and trust rather than an online bid."

After six years as president of one of the retail industry's leading mannequin suppliers, Paul stepped down to pursue other interests. Upon reflection after leaving the industry, he graciously acknowledged all the moving parts and the people necessary to make mannequin magic.

> Naturally there were the sculptors and designers whose creativity was front and center. I would be remiss if I didn't acknowledge the people who worked so hard in the factories, all of the sales executives, the showroom directors, the shipping managers, and the people in the office and all of my family members who were such a big part of my experience. At the end of the day, it's always the people that make any industry great. And in visual merchandising, without those creative people, all you would have is a plastic hanger.

In 1996, Cliff Sobel sold Bon Art, the parent company of Greneker, to a private equity firm to begin a career in politics. He went on to serve as the United States Ambassador to The Netherlands from 2001 until 2005 and the Ambassador to Brazil from 2006 until 2009 under President George W. Bush's Administration.

WIZARDRY AND VISUAL MAGIC

Known as New York's "Window Wizard," Tom Beebe has been a visual magician, stylist, and creative consultant in the Big Apple for well over thirty years. His longstanding approach to window design has always been defined by his compelling mantra to passersby, "look in the window and see your fantasy." Beebe's work has graced the windows at Paul Stuart, Bergdorf Goodman, Neiman Marcus, Hickey Freeman, and many others. Over the years, Beebe developed a sure style that is his and his alone. Specializing in men's wear, he created the "invisible mannequin" while working at Paul Stuart, the venerable men's store on Madison Avenue. Beebe explains that Mr. Grodd, the president of Paul Stuart, was in search of the quintessential gentleman to represent his brand and to highlight his high-end merchandise. Beebe felt that there weren't any male mannequins on the market that would quite fit the bill to meet Mr. Grodd's expectations. In fact, the talented window designer said, "male mannequins were the weak link. Whether realistic or abstract, they never really worked for me."

Always a believer in classical bust forms with elegant neck blocks, Beebe wanted to use his impeccable rigging skills and creativity to take these basic forms to another level; he wanted to add an artistic twist. Having a natural love and affinity toward beautiful design, Beebe happened to own a collection of elegant antique eyeglasses. Knowing he would never find the right male mannequin to satisfy Mr. Grodd's desire for that perfect man, and, driven by his own desire for the perfect male attitude, he thought his collection of eyeglasses would give him the solution. He cleverly hung the glasses with wire over the headless dress forms where the eyes of the mannequin would have been, thereby creating the illusion of an invisible man. To further the concept, he wired, threaded, and pinned all of the hems of the garments and dress ties. In doing so, he articulated the merchandise to give it the appearance of flying in the wind. Flying merchandise and invisible mannequins thus became a Beebe trademark. As such, his recognizable window signature was born. He jokingly, but proudly said, "there's no gravity in my windows." In those early days, Beebe had fourteen windows at Paul Stuart. He painted the walls and the floors of all the windows black, and focused pin lighting on the chests of the bust forms to create a theatrical feeling. To further the fun, Beebe placed a box of ties in one of the windows and perfectly positioned an "invisible man" to appear as though it were kicking the box. All of the ties were threaded with wire and articulated with bends and folds. To passersby, it seemed that the ties were flying out of the box. When Tiffany's legendary window designer Gene Moore saw the window he said, "Someone is finally doing great men's windows. Tom Beebe is having fun with menswear."

In further pursuit of Mr. Grodd's quintessential gentleman, Beebe took an even more theatrical approach when Paul Stuart was in the process of opening up the corner show windows to allow customers to see into the store. Beebe, knowing this would create an even larger stage for his street theater, decided to develop a mannequin worthy of center stage. He delved into the company archives to find old advertisements done by the iconic German-American artist J.C. Leyendecker (1874–1951). Leyendecker was of an age, along with famed illustrators Maxfield Parish and Norman Rockwell, when illustration was the internet of the day; the only way for consumers and the public in general to view images and advertisements. In those days magazines and periodicals were used by retailers to show illustrations of their product offerings. The illustrations also hung in the stores themselves. As retail was spreading its fledgling wings, this mode of communication was becoming a dynamic selling tool. These advertisements were part of a golden age of illustration; they were true pieces of art. Inspired by the early Leyendecker illustrations, Beebe brought some of his favorites to a theater design and stage set company that specialized in papier-mâché props. With illustrations in hand, Beebe asked the company to produce papier-mâché heads for his mannequins inspired by the men in the Leyendecker illustrations. With the new open window facade, Beebe wanted to elevate the customer experience by bringing art and theater into the environment and out to the street. Once positioned over their respective mannequins, the papier-mâché heads brought the forms to life as though they were actors on the stage. In describing the Leyendecker mannequins, Beebe said, "you have two minutes to make them stop. Then you have to reward them. When you do this, you will get them back as repeat customers."

In terms of mannequins and windows, Beebe often found inspiration in everyday objects. "I was at dinner one evening in a very chic New York restaurant," said the window wizard. "When the waiter brought a loaf of bread to the table, I noticed how beautiful it was, both in its form and in what it symbolized. I thought this would make an amazing mannequin head." Much like the aforementioned Gene Moore, Beebe was given a great deal of creative freedom while at Paul Stuart. "I just had to give Mr. Grodd a quick sketch, and he would give me the go ahead." After Mr. Grodd's approval, Beebe went to Amy's Bread, a bakery appropriately located in New York's theater district on 9th Avenue between 46th and 47th Streets. He met Amy and told her the concept. Inspired as well, Amy went to work baking loaves of rye bread, pumpernickel, and seven-grain bread. She sprinkled sesame seeds in the appropriate places to emulate eyebrows and mustaches and combed each loaf to look as though they had a full head of hair. Beebe took Amy's baked creations to his windows and excitedly placed them on the heads of his mannequins. This was also a perfect time to once again use his collection of eyeglasses to embellish Amy's sesame seed eyebrows. Once in place, Amy's artistically rendered baked goods offered a humorous look into the world of men's fashion.

Naturally, the overarching goal of Beebe's windows was to sell merchandise. Toward that end, all of the mannequins were holding wicker bread baskets filled with shirts. To take it a step further, he placed a stove in one of the windows with a "bread head" mannequin sitting on the stovetop. With his "no gravity in my windows" approach, he creatively and amazingly had men's ties flying out of the oven. This was street theater at its best.

Another memorable grouping of mannequins was Beebe's neon musicians. This elegantly dressed band consisted of a bass cello player, a violinist, and a trumpet player. The musical trio of invisible mannequins were the central figures used in a Beebe Christmas window for Paul Stuart. The three musical mannequins played their instruments; a neon cello bow, a neon violin, and a neon trumpet. The articulated musicians holding brightly colors neon instruments were immediate attention getters.

Figure 10.8 Male mannequins with papier-mâché heads designed by Tom Beebe for Paul Stuart. Photograph courtesy of Tom Beebe.

Of course, the paisley robe worn by the cello player, the tux worn by the violinist, and the dinner jacket worn by the trumpet player, were wired and articulated to show movement. Beebe recalled that customers wanted the paisley robe in the window rather than the ones offered in the store. Once again, the window wizard stopped customers in their tracks with his artistry and the magic of street theater.

CHAPTER 11
COMPOSITION AND MOVEMENT: 2000 AND BEYOND

Every store strives to develop a brand image that is unique to them; an image that is theirs and theirs alone. Every great visual merchandiser understands this as they live and breathe the nuances of the brand. Paul Olszewski, who served as the national director of windows and internal flagship marketing at Macy's, was certainly no exception. During his tenure at the famed New York-based retailer, Olszewski was a great proponent and articulator of the brand, and his favorite tool for communicating branded messages was the mannequin. His usage of mannequins was very consistent; he had certain principles and standards that he always maintained as he developed a style that clearly reflected the Macy's brand image. "I always like windows to exude a sense of playfulness and unexpectedness," said Olszewski. "Using mannequins merely as a device to present clothing is really just the beginning of it. I always try to create movement and attitude, even attitude among the mannequins themselves, while always having a sense of humor and whimsy."

While keenly aware of the fact that Macy's wasn't necessarily a high-end designer store, he wanted to treat the design of the windows as if it were.

Figure 11.1 Simplicity is the deciding element; one abstract mannequin at Macy's. Courtesy of Paul Olszewski.

> Styling of the mannequins allowed my team to bring a sophistication to the merchandise that wasn't there before; and because of this, the merchandise presentation was elevated due to our studied use and positioning of the mannequins. I felt strongly that great styling and fun sleek mannequins created a unique style that had been previously missing in the store's windows.

Olszewski entered the industry after graduating with a BA degree in studio art. By his own admission, he had no idea that the industry even existed. "I sort of fell into it," said Olszewski. "I sent resumes to every company that had a creative department that I thought would be interesting, including high-end retailers." Fresh out of college, Olszewski was hired by Neiman Marcus as their graphics coordinator, which basically meant that he made signs in the basement of the store by typesetting on an old printing press and using an ink roller. As luck would have it, the sign shop was in the visual department, and he caught on quickly to the principles of visual merchandising. Before long he was the one who painted the windows and took out the studio garbage. He did both well and was given a small area (cosmetics) to test his skills. He quickly moved from cosmetics to stylist for almost every department throughout the store, including couture and designer men's. As he started to do windows, he took an artistic approach. Working with many designers, he eventually became the window person. "I loved the job," he said. "It was like studio classes at college, but I was actually getting paid." From there he went on to become the visual manager of a Neiman Marcus branch store, and then eventually explored other high-end retailers such as Prada, and Bergdorf Goodman. "I think my background in high-end stores is what made a difference in my work at Macy's."

Olszewski's style afforded him the wonderful ability to say a lot with just a little. His positioning of mannequins was never random or haphazard; it was always precise and deliberate. Like the renowned mid-century architect Mies van der Rohe, who coined the phrase "less is more," Olszewski understood and appreciated the challenges and ultimate rewards of making a lasting impression with simple gestures.

"Strong positioning of mannequins is something I feel very passionate about," said Olszewski.

> I would drive my staff crazy by standing outside the glass and making them rearrange mannequin compositions until it felt right. Sometimes I would know beforehand exactly what the mannequin composition should be, sometimes not. After the composition was set, I would drive them even crazier by making them move the mannequins by merely an inch or two, or slightly twist the mannequins' angle a tiny bit. Sometimes they wouldn't understand why I wanted this, and I would have to tell them to just trust me. The viewers know. They may not know that they know, but they do know.

Selecting mannequins for a particular window involves consideration of how many you want and how they are going to interact with each other, and with the audience. Generally, Olszewski likes to have the mannequins either looking at each other or looking at the

Figure 11.2 The rule of three: Grouping of abstract mannequins at Macy's. Courtesy of Paul Olszewski.

viewers. "One of my biggest mantras is 'what's not in the window is just as important as what's in the window.' I truly believe that negative space can create drama. I usually prefer asymmetrical compositions, but balance and rhythm are key to successful execution."

When teaching this, in his role after Macy's as professor and creative director, visual and special projects at FIDM in Los Angeles, Olszewski uses one of his Macy's windows as an example.

> If you divide the window in half and take out all the propping, you are left with three mannequins: One on the left side and two on the right side. I ask my students what makes this a balanced composition. The answer is not only the positioning of the mannequins but the poses. The two that were together are stoic and standing there calmly looking out of the window. One may even be sitting down. The other mannequin is by itself and slightly toward the back. That mannequin is turned to the side with hands on hips in a walking position. This movement gives that single mannequin weight equal to the combined two.
>
> There are many other rules that guide Olszewski; below are his most enduring dictates:
>
> - Keep it clean.
> - Use negative space as part of the overall composition.
> - Pick appropriate poses and mannequins.
> - Use odd numbers of mannequins or grouping of mannequins (i.e. four mannequins should be positioned as three and one by itself in a window, and three mannequins can be grouped together or either as two and one, etc.).
> - Keep stepping outside the glass until you know it's absolutely perfect!

Olszewski had definite criteria for selecting the right mannequin for the right job. A great deal of thought and consideration always went into every mannequin selection for every window or interior display. "Selecting the correct mannequin is crucial to the success of any window; it's good to build a large inventory when one is dealing with a large store with multiple levels and styles of merchandise," said Olszewski. With great emphasis, he added,

> You always, always, always must know the designer's product and lifestyle, and who their target customer is. Is the product aimed at a younger crowd? Then abstract or semi-abstract with glossy finish and fun poses are in order. Is it more of a career-focused product assortment? Then perhaps semi-realistics with less playful poses and more of a hand-on-hip attitude with a matte finish works best. When doing higher-end sophisticated stories, I look for more couture or fashion poses which are usually calm but still can have interesting poses, as if in a photo shoot. For these applications, I usually look for more interesting finishes for the mannequins such as a foundry finish or a customized finish that suits the designer. Due to the reality of store staffing, realistic mannequins aren't used as much these days but there is certainly still a place for them in window design; I would use them for high-end looks or fantasy displays. The challenge with realistic mannequins is the styling of hair and make-up. We would always hire professional stylists to make sure the execution was spot on.

With hundreds of windows under his belt and in his portfolio, Olszewski certainly has his favorites. One that quickly comes to mind is the bank of windows he designed using Pucci mannequin molds. The window team at Macy's, under Olszewski's direction, did a series of windows that were in recognition of a grand New York City fashion event called Sidewalk Catwalk. College students from fashion schools in the greater metropolitan area were asked to design weatherproof outfits to be presented on special Ralph Pucci mannequins positioned up and down Broadway during Fashion Week. "Of course, part of this happened right in front of our Broadway windows, so collaborating with Pucci made perfect sense," remembered Olszewski. "Since I love working in the abstract and Pucci mannequins were such a key to this event, we thought it would be fun

Figure 11.3 Rhythm and flow of abstract mannequins at Macy's. Courtesy of Paul Olszewski.

to create a 'landscape' made out of the molds used to actually make the mannequins." While these windows could have been straightforward with event information, sketches, and mannequins, Olszewski felt it was more important to always deliver the unexpected. With that notion, he sent a truck to Pucci, picked up a large quantity of mannequin molds, legs, torsos, arms, etc., and carefully placed them in the window to create unusual-looking piles. "It became an art installation all created with Pucci's molds. We have done similar installations like this with huge piles of dirt for Calvin Klein and actual trash/recycling for Earth Day." Using the right element can make for a very compelling and attention-grabbing window series.

Olszewski looks back with great pride and a sense of accomplishment at his creative career during his years at Macy's. Of all of his successful award-winning windows, he humorously and ironically recalls the time Macy's changed the names of all the regional nameplates to Macy's.

> We executed a massive campaign in which the marketing was designed to appeal to people of all races, sizes, and ages, and to celebrate our differences. For this campaign, I decided to break the cardinal rule of never mixing mannequin styles in the same window. Thus, I filled all of the windows with mannequins from end to end, with different types: realistic, abstract, semi-abstract, semi-realistic, headless, customized "bizarre" shapes and even forms; all in different colors and finishes standing next to each other. We brought this message to life with mannequin stories in all our six Broadway windows. It was a very dramatic effect that strongly tied in with the marketing campaign. Later, I heard that the fashion office walked the windows and really liked them but said, "It's embarrassing that Macy's doesn't have enough of the same mannequin for a consistent window!" I thought, Really? Wow! Some people just don't get it!

STRATEGIC POSITIONING, REPETITION, AND POSE

Lord & Taylor was a magical place for generations of young girls growing up in New York City. For Roe Palermo, a trip to the venerable department store on Fifth Avenue was like going to the Oscars. "Lord & Taylor was iconic for getting the most beautiful dress for a special occasion," said Palermo. "Any dress from there was a special treat." Little did she know when visiting Lord & Taylor as a little girl that her career path would bring her back to the fabled New York retailer as the vice president of visual merchandising. While studying at the Fashion Institute of Technology (FIT) in New York City, working toward degrees in fashion buying and merchandising, and cosmetic marketing, she got her first job in visual merchandising as an intern at Lord & Taylor. Like so many others in the visual merchandising industry, Palermo didn't know that the profession even existed. "At the time I had no idea what visual merchandising was, or that it would become a passion that I would grow to love."

Figure 11.4 Three mannequins grouped together as "two plus one" at Macy's. Courtesy of Paul Olszewski.

In high school, Palermo was a key holder for a trendy young clothing store. She loved being in the store environment surrounded by all of the great clothes. She was so passionate about the store and the way it looked that she found herself continually rearranging and re-merchandising everything in sight; reworking the wall elevations and moving all the floor fixtures from place to place. "I just loved changing things around," said Palermo. "Maybe I was bored or just had too much energy and enthusiasm at a young age." This early exposure to merchandising whetted her appetite for retail and for her Lord & Taylor internship. Her first visual merchandising experience during her internship at Lord & Taylor was gift-wrapping prop boxes for the holiday decor. Soon after she discovered mannequins. Fascinated by the bevy of fiberglass beauties under the Lord & Taylor roof, she quickly learned the "art" of dressing and styling mannequins.

> Before I even touched a mannequin, I remember learning how to rig men's clothing and dress shirt forms, and the pain in my fingertips from being pricked with so many T-pins. It's almost a lost art, taking thirty pins on a dress shirt form so it fit like a glove. When trimmed properly, you could bounce a quarter off of a form, because they were that tightly trimmed.

Once she mastered the bust form, she graduated to rigging a full-size mannequin. The term rigging refers to the dressing and trimming of a mannequin. "I was mentored on styling a mannequin, paying particular attention to the wigs. It was like going to beauty school," she reminisced. "I was so short I needed a step stool to style the wigs. I still can't use hairspray after years of perfecting a finger wave." The industry changed dramatically since Palermo first began her career as an intern. At the time the average staffing in a typical branch department store for visual merchandising (display in those days) was between three to five members on the team. For a flagship store, teams averaged between fifteen to twenty people. "We weren't so promotional then, the customer paid what was on the ticket and was happy to do so. The stores were welcoming and inviting, hospitality was a prime concern; the stores were always in perfect order," said Palermo.

Figure 11.5 Repetition of mannequins as an effective visual tool at Lord & Taylor. Photograph by Richard Caden.

Merchandising was the perfect balance between art and science. The art was merchandise presentation; the science was driving sales. Mannequins had hair and people specialized in just perfecting the perfect haircut and color depending on the outfit. I remember stock rooms of mannequins in different poses, walls of hair in all colors and lengths, and makeup kits for mannequins. It was fascinating. You were not only styling clothes but creating the perfect model. As the industry evolved, staffing changes and a limited talent pool triggered a new trend. Realistics were being replaced by abstract mannequins including egg heads, sculpted heads, and headless figures.

Palermo's first game-changing experience came with her first mannequin purchase from none other than Adel Rootstein. In 2000 she accepted a position with Mitchells/Richards in Westport Connecticut as creative director. The upscale retailer was about to open a new flagship on fashionable Greenwich Avenue in Greenwich, Connecticut. "We were working with the architects to build a true luxury experience for Greenwich Avenue," recalled Palermo. "I worked with Rootstein to perfect the absolute best look and feel for that store and that customer. We worked to develop the perfect shoe, the perfect sculpted hand, the right pose, and the perfect size for the luxury brands. I even insisted on developing the perfect mannequin base. It was all in the details." Palermo considered mannequins as the foreground to the clothes. Her experience in opening the Greenwich Avenue store proved to be a great learning opportunity, one that she never forgot.

In 2007, Palermo returned to Lord & Taylor as the creative director of the storied department store. Five years later in 2012, her career went full circle from her earlier days as an intern at Lord & Taylor, to being promoted to divisional vice president of merchandising and store visual at Lord & Taylor. In that capacity, she worked on a project that she was most proud of and passionate about, "The Dress Address," a transformation

Figure 11.6 Roe Palermo worked with Ralph Pucci to create the ultimate mannequin for "The Dress Address" at Lord & Taylor. Photograph by Richard Caden.

Figure 11.7 Repetition of three as an effective visual tool at Lord & Taylor. Photograph by Richard Caden.

of the fifth floor of the store's flagship into the largest dress destination in New York. Long a bastion of grace and elegance, the landmark New York flagship building and famed holiday window destination had adorned the venerable Fifth Avenue retail corridor since 1914. Recognizing that customers have always associated the brand's dress department as an integral component of its DNA, the fashion retailer renovated its fifth floor to offer a broad assortment of dresses for every occasion. Under the banner of "The Dress Address," the retailer converted the 30,000-square-foot space into a dress heaven. "The Dress Address was to be the ultimate salute to the Lord & Taylor Heritage. Designing the perfect selection of mannequins was to honor the brand and the icing to a beautiful renovation," said Palermo. "I was passionate about working with Ralph Pucci and team to create the ultimate mannequin for the 'Dress Address.' It was a project near and dear to my heart." Palermo recognized repetition as a great design tool, and that when used graphically it would intensify and elevate any mannequin presentation. She used it brilliantly, inviting customers to travel through the selling zone with the strategic placement of mannequins in a harmonious repetition of pose and posture.

> I wanted the mannequins to be an art installation throughout the store. The concept was that as the customer walked through the floor, it would feel like a wonderful event in your home, a beautiful rooftop bar, a carefully placed gathering of the most beautiful and interesting people, or a group of people that made you feel included and invited. The groupings of mannequins warmed up the room and added energy to the space.

While developing the concept, Palermo referenced the beautiful installations at the Costume Institute at the Metropolitan Museum of Art and the fashion exhibitions at FIT. "The Mannequins enhanced the art of fashion; they defined the look and feel of the space leaving the viewers in awe."

With her many years of experience selecting, purchasing, and in some cases enhancing their design, Palermo developed a personal philosophy and strategy for working with mannequins. "They absolutely set the stage for the store; their strategic positioning will define traffic patterns. They are beacons to guide the customer through the store," said Palermo. "The mannequin will be and always has been the silent salesperson that will sell

Figure 11.8 Repetition of mannequin platforms with groupings of three mannequins on each platform at Lord & Taylor. Photograph by Richard Caden.

a complete look without even uttering a single word." Palermo considers mannequins to be more than utilitarian, but rather an art form. She recognizes their ability to move the customer's emotions.

> The Mannequin is the art piece to the collection and the store; it's the stopping point for the eye. You need the right look and the right pose. They need to embody the profile of the customer you are selling to, and they have to be easy for the staff to update. Moreover, they have to tell a story about the product. A mannequin is like the sprinkles on the cake. A store, much like a cake, is made up of so many different layers; so many different flavor profiles all adding to the experience. The mannequin is the final touch that completes the look and makes everything seem extra delicious.

CHAPTER 12
MANNEQUINS AND MUSEUMS

Mannequins have long been used by museum curators to present and document everything from period fashion pieces to historical movements and events. While the mannequin is the iconic silent salesperson in retail settings, carefully curated, selected, and positioned mannequins speak volumes to museum-goers around the world. When used effectively, the mannequin is a storyteller, engaging visitors in compelling dialogues and informative historical narratives.

Matthew Yokobosky is a true artist in every sense of the term. While he doesn't necessarily work in oils, acrylics, or pastels, his canvas is the exhibition space at one of New York's premiere cultural institutions, the Brooklyn Museum. As the senior curator of fashion and material culture at the Brooklyn Museum, he brings the galleries of the 560,000-square-foot Beaux-Arts-style building to life by creating compelling spatial experiences and evocative environments. Over the course of his twenty-year tenure at the museum, he has imbued its galleries with stories, historical documentation, emotion, intrigue, and color as he designed, staged, and curated numerous world-class exhibitions.

A great storyteller in his own right with a strong background in film studies, theater, and design, he is philosophical about his design principles and ideology.

> One of the differences about my approach to exhibition design is that my background in film and theater got me thinking about the impact of walking through a space and experiencing each object rather than needing 40 feet of wall space. Rather, I'm thinking about what should be the mood of the room, the shade, color, and video. I even consider the contribution of spacing to the overall mood and experience.

As a young man, Yokobosky demonstrated a keen interest in design. When in school at the University of Pittsburg, just two hours from his home, he received a degree in film studies with an emphasis on design. At the time he didn't consider exhibition design as a career option. After graduating, he got a job as a curatorial assistant in the section of film and video at the Carnegie Museum of Art. When he came to New York in 1987 he got a job as a curatorial assistant at the Whitney Museum. With New York as a wellspring of inspiration, his creative instincts intensified. "In the evenings I designed sets and costumes for a theater director, Ping Chong," recalled Yokobosky. "I designed 6 productions for him, mostly at LaMama Theater on East 4th Street. In 1989, I won a New York Dance and Performance Award (known as a "Bessie") for Outstanding Set and Costume. I was then asked by the Whitney if I had considered exhibition design. I had not thought of it as an option." He accepted the challenge and soon worked on a Joseph Stella retrospect at the Whitney. His career in design was well underway.

He worked at the Whitney Museum of American Art in Manhattan for 12 years. In 2009, he received a call from Arnold Lehman, the director of the Brooklyn Museum.

> He saw my work at the Whitney, a Bob Thompson retrospective with yellow and red walls. He loved it and was very interested in my work in exhibition design. The Whitney was twentieth-century American while the Brooklyn was world art. I was eager to expand beyond American Art. I accepted the position and celebrated 20 years at the Brooklyn Museum in June 2019.

Over the years, mannequins played a significant role in Yokobosky's work. Through careful selection and consideration, they proved to be integral components in setting the mood of the many exhibition halls he designed and or curated. They were important tools in the communication and documentation of relevant cultural milestones and events. The long list of the acclaimed exhibitions that he staged in his 20 years at the Brooklyn Museum includes:

- *Hip-Hop Nation: Roots, Rhyme and Rage*, September 2000 (designer);
- *Vital Forms: American Art and Design in the Atomic Age 1940–1960*, October 2001 (designer);
- *Star Wars: The Magic of Myth*, April 2002 (designer);
- *Pulp Art: Vamps and Villains from the Robert Lesser Collection*, May 19, 2003 (designer);
- *Patrick Kelly: A Retrospective*, April 17, 2004 (designer);
- *American High Style: Fashioning a National Collection*, May 7, 2010 (designer);
- *The Fashion World of Jean Paul Gaultier: From the Sidewalk to the Catwalk*, October 25, 2013 (designer);
- *Georgia O'Keeffe: Living Modern*, March 3, 2017 (designer);
- *David Bowie Is*, March 2, 2018 (coordinating curator and designer));
- *Pierre Cardin*: *Future Fashion*, July 20, 2019 (curator and designer);
- *Studio 54: Night Magic*, March 13, 2020 (curator and designer)

The exhibitions that Yokobosky staged were quite varied, from *Pierre Cardin: Future Fashion*, to *Studio 54: Night Magic*. In a museum format, Mannequins are used to display many different types of garments: contemporary fashions, historical fashions, fashions worn by known people, and costumes, to name but a few. With contemporary fashions, the garment size is typically model height and proportions. "For *Studio 54*, while I was displaying modern fashion, they were 'Made to Measure' by Halston, and the proportions were non-model sizes," said Yokobosky. "While you can typically use a standard mannequin, the mannequins for Elizabeth Taylor and Liza Minnelli needed to replicate their actual proportions and heights, approximately five foot two. While there can be standardization, when you are presenting clothing worn by known people, the mannequins need to be custom to replicate the figure to a close degree." In *David Bowie*

Is, his silhouette changed from the 1970s, 1980s, and 1990s. Due to the evolving nature of Bowie's physical appearance, Yokobosky had to have three versions of the Bowie mannequin. "Facially, we varied the look where some mannequins had a 'blank' face while others had replicas of a life mask that was made of Bowie in the early 1970s."

Yokobosky took another approach for the *Georgia O'Keeffe* exhibition; one that he thought was more appropriate. Recognizing that her figure also changed over the decades, he decided that he didn't want to have dozens of O'Keeffes throughout, so instead he chose to exhibit the garments on dressmaker forms, with neck caps.

It must be understood that the use of mannequins in a museum format differs greatly from the use of mannequins in a retail environment. Naturally, those differences pose their own set of challenges. The primary difference between mannequins in a retail situation versus a museum presentation is that retailers are showing new fashions; the fashions of that season. In a museum, the fashions can be recent, but they can also show historic pieces. As such, the curator sometimes has to employ several types and styles of mannequins.

Yokobosky cites the exhibition titled *American High Style: Fashioning a National Collection* as an example.

> In fashioning a National Collection, we were exhibiting clothes from late 19th century through late 20th century. Body shapes and dress silhouettes changed dramatically over this 100-year period. Additionally, there is the element of known personalities, with specific body shapes and measurements. And so, the mannequin becomes an armature on which you create padding and shaping to replicate the dress owner's unique physical attributes, in addition to keeping the garments final appearance in mind. Both the mannequin and the shaping materials must all be sound from a conservation standpoint while still supporting the garment.

Figure 12.1 Mannequins in a museum format. Exhibition design by Matthew Yokobosky. Courtesy of the Brooklyn Museum.

Sometimes though, a garment may be too fragile to be displayed on a mannequin and must therefore be displayed flat. Being fragile, there are dozens of reasons for a garment to require special handling, including deterioration, discoloring from perspiration, make-up or the sun, poor storage prior to admission of the item into a collection, unrepairable tears or fabric buckling, etc. Also of primary concern is the preservation of the invaluable archival pieces. Toward that end, all of the materials used in mannequin production must pass conservation testing. It must be noted that not all garments can be displayed vertically on a mannequin, some must be displayed on a horizontal or angled surface.

For those pieces that can be shown vertically on a mannequin, consideration must be given to their location in the gallery. Can the garment be displayed in the round; is it in good condition from all angles; does it look best in a frontal or 3/4 view; is the back more important or interesting than the front? Does the mannequin's arm and leg position show off the garment to its best advantage; should the presentation include accessories, shoes, hair, or make-up for a more overall look?

And then how will the dressed mannequin appear? On a platform? Does it need to be further than arms-length from view to avoid touching? Does the dressed mannequin need to be in a plexiglas vitrine due to temperature and humidity concerns, or to avoid touching or dust? Is there a large enough plexiglas vitrine to accommodate the dressed mannequin? How do multiple mannequins appear together? Should they appear to be interacting, or should they just be a "hanger" to display the garment? The curator said,

Figure 12.2 Mannequins featuring the times and fashions of *Studio 54*. Exhibition design by Matthew Yokobosky. Courtesy of the Brooklyn Museum.

> There are many philosophies. But you need to choose one that best reflects the subject of the exhibition. For *Studio 54: Night Magic*' for example, I was interested in showing the garments as if caught in movement, or that the group was interacting. So I chose mannequins that would best create those effects. I found that mannequins from Pucci International were perfect for the desired effect. Ralph Pucci has worked with a smart group of designers to think through what a mannequin could be, some more abstract, some more natural, some are straight-forward, some more posed, and some very active. It's this variety, all produced with refined techniques, that allows you to create as much or as little activity in your display as warranted. Also, since each one is custom produced, you can make adjustments as needed. This was the perfect connection for the *Studio 54* mannequin. In the exhibition there was a Calvin Klein lamé ensemble that was very fitted. On a model, she could bend and wiggle into the outfit, but a mannequin is not that limber. So we worked with Pucci to give the mannequin detachable arms and head and reduced the bust measurement to accommodate this classic 1979 look.

Whenever possible, Yokobosky's approach has been to maintain a consistency of mannequin type and profile within each exhibition. At times, however, given the wide variety of garments being shown, size-wise and period-wise, you can end up with a very eclectic, visual situation.

> I prefer that there is a unification among all the mannequins. So for *Studio 54*, although there are multiple body shapes, all of the heads match. I also have one color for the mannequins. For *American High Style*, where we needed to use multiple mannequin types, we had sculptural hairpieces made from formed paper to reflect the hairstyles of the periods. So it was abstract, but they all matched materially.

An overarching challenge in a museum environment as well as in a retail setting, is not to have the mannequin overshadow or overwhelm the fashion statement. Due to this concern, Yokobosky prefers an abstract form for the face; not full features, but a suggestion of ears, eyes, nose, mouth, and chin rather than just an oval shape for a head. This of course allows the option to display earrings or sunglasses, as part of the presentation. Yokobosky cautions that you must be mindful of large groupings. If you have eight or ten mannequins on a platform together, how will they appear side by side with that many heads? "I generally find that when you arrange the mannequins and install them at different heights from several viewpoints, you can harmonize the visual conversation during the installation process."

> The grouping of mannequins presents another challenge when telling a fashion story. Groupings are really dictated by the garments in most cases; which garments you would like to present together. So, you need to think about the spacing between

Figure 12.3 Grouping of four mannequins featuring the fashion designs of Thierry Mugler. Exhibition design by Matthew Yokobosky. Courtesy of the Brooklyn Museum.

> the garments and how each piece will be 'viewable' to the museum visitor. Some garments hug the body; some have wide shoulders or hips, or long trains. These silhouettes indicate the proximity of the mannequins to each other. Having lots of space between dressed mannequins allows for good viewing. When the clothes are slim or close to the body, you can create closer relationships. The mannequins begin to have a visual conversation, and you need to approach it systematically. How are you "staging" the presentation? Are you going to approach the figures like a Samuel Beckett Play, or a Broadway Musical? Ultimately, I believe you need to choose what feels best for your presentation. Is it austere? Is it more of a dialogue?

The selection of pose is a delicate and painstaking process based on the collection to be displayed and the story to be told. Exhibiting clothes at a museum is an extremely collaborative process. The curator works closely with textile conservators, registrars, dressers, art handlers, lighting designers, and couriers. Accordingly, choices are made using information from many museum professionals.

Typically, historical clothing has the most stringent requirements. But it must be noted that contemporary fashions also have their needs. Because most dress samples are made for very tall models, female mannequins need to be approximately 6' tall. Otherwise, dresses would be pooling on the platform; and of course, hemming is not an option for an insured garment that is on loan to a museum.

In most instances, the curator must select a body shape or pose that best displays the garment. If the piece has a butterfly sleeve you might want an extended arm, or if the piece has a split side, you may want an extended leg. If the waist is gorgeous and elaborate, you may want the arms to be bent or in an upward position so the waist is visible. At other times, for historical pieces, you might choose a seated position. After selecting the pose that best displays the garments, you then can think more about how the two, or three, or more mannequins will appear together. At times you might adjust the selection, to improve the display. In most cases, Yokobosky allows the garment to dictate the mannequin pose and the stories to emerge from their juxtapositions. He confirms that it can be a painstaking process!

As with any retail organization, museums also must protect their projected brand image. The Brooklyn Museum is one of the oldest and largest art museums in the United States. It has a storied and venerable reputation as a world-class institution, beginning with its early roots extending back to 1823 with the founding of the Brooklyn Apprentices' Library in Brooklyn Heights, to the splendor of its nineteenth-century McKim, Mead & White-designed Beaux-Arts facade in its current and permanent location on Eastern Parkway. Yokobosky painstakingly maintains a strict set of standards to project and protect the Brooklyn Museum brand image when incorporating mannequins in an exhibition.

> Generally, we aim for a clean, deliberate appearance, which supports the garments on display while not distracting from them. So in that way, the mannequin is really an armature," said Yokobosky. "But, if you choose to use a mannequin instead of a dress or tailor's form, you are also wanting to convey a sense of person, a sense that the garment is worn by a real person, and how that body inside the garment brings it to life.

When working with mannequins, color selection also plays an important role in defining and projecting an image. After many decades of working with myriad types and styles of mannequins, Yokobosky developed a color philosophy or point of view that remains vital to his overall vision.

> Historically, mannequins were a beige or peach to suggest a skin tone. At various times, a true white or a true black was selected to disappear, to be more neutral or to match the wall color. Sometimes multiple skin tones come into play, from dark brown to pale beige, and similarly, multiple metallics have been employed to suggest plurality: Silver, copper, bronze, gold. For Brooklyn, I wanted to make a more universal choice. If you are a make-up artist or a portrait painter, you understand how complex it is to replicate skin pigmentation; there are infinite tones, shades, and highlights. And so for mannequins, rather than pick dozens of colors, I decided on a brown because whether a skin tone is a little brown or a lot brown, the color is always a part of the equation. As such, for the past two exhibitions, I've used a medium brown, which I feel is perhaps the most neutral of all of the options.

Artists throughout history, from Courbet and Degas to the surrealists, have utilized mannequins as subject matter in their work, and as instruments to guide them. They have been used by painters and sculptors as study tools for generations. In the 1930s, surrealists from André Breton and Marcel Duchamp to Salvador Dalí and Man Ray, turned to the mannequin as a subject or a tool to project otherworldly visions. As the curator of one of New York's premiere museums and a passionate student of art history, Yokobosky has certainly been influenced by the use of mannequins in the work of some of the art world's most iconic artists. Among all of the great works of art that have been based on, or have incorporated mannequins, he is drawn to one in particular.

> When I think about mannequins in art, the first artist that pops into my mind is Hans Bellmer. He took the mannequin apart, abstracted it, and eroticized it, created new and provocative forms. Very surrealistic. Also of interest to me is the photographer Pierre Mollinier, who took photographs of actual models but then dissected the images and recomposed them in the darkroom, to create images related to Bellmer. It's not so much the "replacement" of people in artwork by mannequins, which creates an eerie surprise, that I'm fascinated by, but more the intrigue that can be created by the reassembly of the figure. I've also been drawn to the work of the artist Charles Ray, who has also recomposed mannequins in works such as Oh, Charley, Charley, Charley, and Family Romance. To explain, most

Figure 12.4 Mannequins graphically positioned featuring the fashion designs of Thierry Mugler. Exhibition design by Matthew Yokobosky. Courtesy of the Brooklyn Museum.

> mannequins arrive in parts: a torso, legs, arms, head, etc. Some come in halves, some come in a dozen pieces. When you see all the pieces together out of the box, it's a little like an erector set. You are going to build something. For an artist, mannequin parts could appear as a tool kit, rather than parts to be built into one specific form.

As with anyone else who works with or loves mannequins, Yokobosky also has a favorite mannequin story. As a creative whose eyes are always open, and whose radar is always on, he has referenced this story in his own work.

> I think the situation that frequently happens when you are installing exhibitions that have mannequins, is that you turn around and think someone is there, but it's a mannequin. And you can play with that surprise element in exhibitions, depending on how realistic they are. I recall designing and curating a Duane Hansen exhibition at the Whitney Museum of American Art in 1998. Hansen notably makes very realistic sculptures of people, not mannequins per se, but more realistic. His work is most effective when you come around a corner and you are surprised because you think it could be an actual person. It's fun to play with this illusion, to make an exhibition more engaging for the viewer. Position the mannequins to add elements of surprise!

Mannequins have long been the muse of artists and provocateurs, whether working in the 19th-century salons of the Académie des Beaux-Arts in Paris, the show windows of Fifth Avenue, or the galleries of the world's most venerable art museums. The creative process of those who work in this realm is difficult to define; it varies greatly from artist to artist. However, as with so many other creatives, from painters and sculptors to poets and musicians, Yokobosky also moves emotions and tantalizes the imagination of all who experience his finished work.

Phyllis Magidson is both a storyteller and a fashion historian. As the special consultant to the costume collection at the Museum of the City of New York, who previously served as the museum's longtime curator of costumes and textiles, she narrates, documents, and interprets the many phases and facets of fashion in New York City. In her position as curator, she was charged with the organization, management, and presentation of the Museum's permanent collection of over 27,000 costumes and accessories. During her thirty-five-year tenure at the historical institution, she documented and explored the many cultural events, movements, and periods that have impacted both fashion and urban life in the most dynamic and influential city in the world.

The great stages for Magidson's historical reflections are the galleries of the museum's Georgian Colonial-Revival-style red brick building. Constructed in 1929, the museum graces Fifth Avenue directly across the street from Central Park. Founded in 1923, the institution is dedicated to the preservation and presentation of the history of New York and the people who have collectively made it the great metropolis that it is today.

Figure 12.5 The essence of *Studio 54* captured by a mannequin grouping. Exhibition design by Matthew Yokobosky. Courtesy of the Brooklyn Museum.

Magidson has curated and staged numerous exhibitions that featured a diverse and wide range of works from design icons such as Vera Maxwell and James Galanos to Coco Chanel and Yves Saint Laurent, to name but a few. She has also brilliantly taken viewers on engaging walks through history, documenting all of the momentous periods of design and culture, from the Gilded Age to mid-century and beyond. During her remarkable career, she has gifted visitors to the museum with visions of everything from a Balenciaga Peacock gown to a series of dresses designed by Ann Lowe, the first prominent African-American designer.

Magidson firmly believes that every object carries a strong resonance that can only be accurately or most effectively captured in a three-dimensional presentation. She said, "You don't appreciate the physicality of it in a photograph or even in 360-degree art." For that reason, mannequins have been a great vehicle for communicating the nuances, characteristics, and presence of all of the historical pieces she has shown.

Magidson was quick to point out that the use of mannequins in a museum format differs greatly from the use of mannequins in a retail environment. There are particular challenges unique to museum curation when dealing with mannequins. First and foremost, conservation is a major priority.

> When purchasing mannequins for an exhibition, we need all conservation specifications on all of the chemicals used in the manufacturing process. All components must be inactive and inert. Additionally, we need a period of time for mannequins to acclimate or "gas off" so as not to adversely affect the archival fashions. We'll never use anything that's not completely clean. If the mannequin emits any kind of smell, we won't use it.

The first commercial mannequins used in museum exhibitions were supplied by Schläppi, a Swiss company that produces sleek, high-quality abstract mannequins. After Bonaveri, an iconic Italian mannequin brand, bought Schläppi and added it to its high-end mannequin portfolio, museums worldwide have used Bonaveri and Schläppi mannequins in both fashion and art presentations. Gianluca Bauzano points out in *Mannequins: Bonaveri: A History of Creativity, Fashion and Art*, a book she edited for Bodnavari, that, "Since the 1980s, Bonaveri has been creating mannequins that have played a leading role in renowned exhibitions around the world, including some of the most prestigious shows in New York, at the Metropolitan Museum, no less. A virtual consecration, on the stage where it all began.[1] Bauzano summed it up quite succinctly when she said,"Clothes need a human form to tell their own story. More than just a prop, they need the mannequin to have spirit, personality, and character."[2]

According to Bauzano, Diana Vreeland understood the value of the right mannequin when she first stepped into her illustrious position at the Costume Institute at the Metropolitan Museum of Art. She paved the way for others to use mannequins as more than utilitarian objects and props, advocating for "using their soul and quiet personalities to impart a sense of life."[3]

While Mrs. Vreeland used Schläppi and raised them to an industry standard, Magidson, like many of her colleagues in museum curation, works with strict budgetary constraints as museum funds are fairly limited. While Schläppi wasn't always within the budgetary reach, mannequins remained an important tool in her work.

Another challenge and difference between museum curation and retail presentation is the nature of the fashions being presented. The museum curator is dealing with period pieces that call for poses that are representative of the times. For example, the body type and attitude of New York women in the late 1890s differs greatly from the body type and attitude of women in the 1960s. In museum curation, body poses, postures, and positions must be diverse enough to present archival pieces, from the confining silhouettes of the Belle Epoque to the flowing, free-form, rule-bending fashions of the 1960s and 1970s.

Contemporary mannequins don't reflect the dimensions of period fashions. The measurement across the back, running in a straight line from wing to wing, somewhat like a kite shape, in a period piece is fifteen inches. In a contemporary mannequin, that dimension is seventeen inches. Additionally, it's important to note that the location of the waistline shifts dramatically through the 18th to 19th century. Another consideration is that the location of the bust line in 18th-century pieces is totally flat due to boning and corseting. The bodies from different periods have dramatically different shapes. Up until the early 20th century, everything had been radically altered. It wasn't until the 1930s that bodies became more natural. The mannequin maker Mary Brosnan was the first to create a period-shaped mannequin for presenting archival pieces. "We need a range of period-shaped mannequins to contemporary-shaped mannequins," said Magidson.

> Moreover, most of the archival pieces are couture constructions made for a particular person with a particular body type. Unlike retail, for us there is no

> perfect size. We often have to pad the mannequins to replicate the attitudes of particular time frames. Another challenge is the way we pad the mannequins. We must work within the framework of conservation standards. All padding material must not have any acidic properties or other long-term detrimental qualities.

While body shape has been dramatically manipulated and altered over time, Diana Vreeland had a very insightful point of view. When in discussion with the chief fashion restorer at the Costume Institute, she insisted she wanted a Schläppi mannequin for an early 19th-century sheer cotton mull (muslin) dress with a high empire waistline and tiny puffed cap sleeves purportedly worn in Paris during Napoleonic times to reveal a nude body beneath, which might have been the case with a proportion of court ladies such as Mme Recamier and her circle. The dress was also made for a lady of tiny proportions, probably under five feet in height, not typical of the 5' 11' of Diana Vreeland's stable. Vreeland insisted this was all about skin and only a Schläppi would work. The restorer protested saying the body shape was all wrong, the body shape has changed. To that, Vreeland simply said, "Darling, the shape of women hasn't changed since Eve."

With conservation as a top priority, appropriate lighting is also a significant consideration in museum presentation. "We learned that a lot of silks or any organic fiber can't withstand sunlight or natural light. Also, we are careful that we never use direct lighting to highlight our archival pieces. We limit gallery lighting to a range of three-and-a-half-foot candles to a maximum of five-foot candles." Magidson explained that an important century piece was once exhibited in natural daylight. "It was a coral color but turned pink in the light. The pigments are unstable, and in addition, the light also weakens the fiber and bleaches out the color."

Magidson prefers to work with abstract mannequins and at times, headless mannequins. She cites the example of Jackie Kennedy, who was going to be featured in the museum's exhibition, *Mod New York*. While the beloved former first lady was ultimately not included in the exhibition because her gown was not available, Magidson said, "Everyone knows Jackie Kennedy's hairstyle. This is about the clothing. In this instance, we wouldn't have used a head. The head would have been a distraction."

A challenge in the *Mod New York* exhibition was the wide range of body poses, indicative of the tumultuous and ever-changing times. The show spanned the gap between Jackie Kennedy's White House to Pierre Cardin's extra-terrestrial silhouettes and further to psychedelic. "We had to accommodate two different body languages," recalled Magidson. "There were two very different postures from the vertical clear shoulder to the more slouchy stance. As such, we used a variety of mannequins from Hans Boodt to Goldsmith and Patina V. Hans Boodt in particular with their very slouchy and rounded shoulders worked well for the late '60s and into the '70s."

"There are, of course, times when it is absolutely necessary to have a head," said Magidson. "When displaying two masks worn to Truman Capote's Black and White Ball, held at the Plaza on November 28, 1966, heads were obviously necessary. We also had to have a nose and ears to hold the masks in place." One of the masks on display was a Halston design worn by Carol Bjorkman, and the other designed by Bill Cunningham, featured white and black-dyed coq feathers, creating the shape of a pair of intertwining swans.

In an exhibition featuring the works of Valentina Schlee and Vera Maxwell, two highly influential mid-century American designers, Maxwell wanted a retrospective without mannequins. "She wanted dressmaker forms, not mannequins," explained Magidson. "She wanted the presentation to be timeless and classic. A mannequin would have dated it. She wanted the presentation of her work to be totally neutral."

When using mannequins with a head, Magidson rarely used makeup or painted faces. Again, she thought of this as a distraction from the true hero, the fashion. She does recall, however, an instance where she did use a mannequin with natural hair. "We were showing a Stephen Burrows collection, and his muse was Pat Cleveland. In this case, we thought it appropriate to use two African American Rootstein mannequins modeled after Cleveland."

Of course, there are circumstances where hairstyles are important elements of the projected period. Magidson recalls an exhibition featuring the work of 19th-century American couturier Charles Fredrick Worth. Central to the theme of the exhibition was the evolution of style, so it was important to show how hairstyles underscored the period. "In this exhibition, the wigs were taken directly from illustrations in the pages of Harpers Bazaar. We had wigs sculpted to replicate the hairstyles in the illustrations." An additional note on the Worth exhibition was the changing neck length over time. Magidson had to work with the supplier to perfect the forms used, specifically altering the neck length, clavicles, and bust lines. For the 1860s through the early 1890s, they ordered high bust lines. For the late 1890s to 1903, they ordered low bust lines.

When grouping mannequins, Magidson likes to position them as though they are engaged in conversation. "In *Glamour New York Style* we had ballgowns in one section and two really important dresses worn at the Prince of Wales Ball held in 1860 at the Academy of Music on 14th Street in New York." Many eligible young women attended, hoping to catch the attention of Prince Albert. "We had a delicate brocade in lavender and a beautiful cream color dress. Some felt grouping them together undermined their beauty and that they undermined one another. But not only did the mannequins seem to be engaged in conversation, but the garments also related to one another." The grouping of mannequins itself is a delicate art, as a slight turn in one way or the other can make all the difference in the telling of a compelling story.

When positioning multiple mannequins in a museum gallery it's important to note that in most cases there isn't a glazing or glass barrier to protect the archival pieces. When that is the case the curator must have a minimum of forty-inch pullback from the edge of the platform so viewers do not touch. "Sometimes you have to group closely because of space constraints," said Magidson. "We have to determine the best view of the mannequin whether it's back to back, full frontal, or three-quarters. The decision is always based on aesthetics and optimum viewing."

The exhibition *Beyond Suffrage* celebrated a century of New York women in politics. The program featured rare artifacts, documents, photographs, and garments worn by women who made a significant contribution towards equality and women's liberation.

Among them was Congresswoman Bella Abzug, an outspoken advocate for women's rights in the early 1970s. The installation included mannequins that showed the evolution of the garment from the early suffragettes to Bella Abzug. And while Abzug's voice was heard loud and clear in the halls of Congress, particularly when she famously said, "This woman's place is in the House, the House of Representatives," she wasn't one to make a strong fashion statement. Her clothes were rather simple and mundane. Although she wasn't a fashion influencer, she clearly inspired a generation of young women to break through the glass ceiling. As such, it was important to depict the essence of this important figure in New York politics. On display was a hot pink cotton day dress worn by Abzug, complete with clusters of orange and yellow roses within a field of lavender flowers and blue leaves. It was a one-piece dress with an elasticized waist, wide rounded neckline, and above-elbow bell sleeves. It was quintessential Abzug; this was her inimitable style, simple and comfortable with little flair. Accordingly, a simple mannequin was required, one without mannerisms or an extreme pose; one that didn't distract not only from the garment but also from Abzug's robust personality.

During her career, Magidson had the wonderful opportunity to work with beautiful pieces of art. And while she reveres and respects all of the archival pieces she has documented, organized, and displayed, she also holds the art of the mannequin in high esteem, considering it also as a work of art.

> Mannequins are definitely an art form. It's sculptural, it's not the human body. There's an interpretation, an elongation, or a truncation, there's a playing with abstraction. If looking for generalization, there is none. There is the Greek idealization, there is the Egyptian idealization. Each believes they are doing something unique. Every mannequin is a unique interpretation of the human form.

The Museum of Arts and Design (MAD) was founded in New York City in 1956 as the Museum of Contemporary Crafts. The institution's original mission was to recognize the craftsmanship of contemporary American makers. In 2002, the museum changed its name and broadened its scope, highlighting the materials and processes incorporated by a wide range of visionaries and innovators in disciplines ranging from craft, art and design, architecture, fashion, interior design, technology, as well as performing arts and other art and design related practices.

In 2008 the museum moved to its present location at Columbus Circle. A cultural jewel on Manhattan's Upper West Side, the current iteration of the museum explores the ways in which artists and designers reconfigure, reimagine, and restructure the contemporary world around us. As such, the museum's curators examine a broad spectrum of creative endeavors, encompassing a handcrafted artisanal approach to the far reaches of digital technology. MAD is unwavering in its dedication to exploring and documenting the limitless applications of materials and techniques in the world of design. An exhibition celebrating the art of the mannequin may have seemed far reaching, but in reality, it was a perfect fit.

In 2013, Barbara Paris Gifford, a graduate of the Bard Graduate Center with a master of arts degree in the history of the decorative arts, design, and culture; and a business degree from Fordham University, continued her exploration of the history of the decorative arts by obtaining an internship at MAD. After successfully completing her internship, she was hired and joined the curatorial staff. Soon after, she began work on *Ralph Pucci: The Art of the Mannequin*, her first exhibition as a curatorial lead, in consultation with chief curator Lowery Stokes Sims. The exhibition was a study and celebration of Pucci's innovative and artistic approach to the mannequin and how he helped to elevate this familiar utilitarian tool into an art form.

> The museum has been showing New York stories since its inception in the 1950s. The Pucci mannequin story is one that people perhaps did not know about. Most did not even realize that sculpted mannequins are still conceived of and manufactured in New York City. Visitors love learning about these stories and are open to seeing objects in a new light. You can find art in almost anything if you look hard enough, and mannequins are no exception.

After getting to know Pucci and familiarizing herself with his work, Gifford felt very strongly that a presentation of his mannequins fell naturally into MAD's domain.

> As a curator of craft, I felt an immediate connection to Pucci's work. Art objects executed in many different types of materials is my specialty. The superior craftsmanship of a Pucci mannequin is obvious at first glance. And when you dig a little deeper and learn about the stories behind them, they become reflections of our culture and worthy of a museum exhibition. Glenn Adamson, our director at the time of the exhibition, learned about Pucci mannequins and brought the idea of an exhibition to the museum. I was lucky enough to get the assignment as my interests in fashion and jewelry aligned very well with the project.

The Art of the Mannequin was Gifford's first experience with displaying and showing mannequins.

> I had a lot of preconceived ideas about them, some of which were valid enough to bring to the exhibition. Mannequins are a reflection of who we are and what we care about, and Ralph understood this implicitly. I was particularly intrigued by the fact that he was inspired by so many of the artists and designers who shaped American culture. It was clear to both Ralph and me that we should focus on this in the show.

Gifford remembers her first encounter with Pucci in his New York studio.

> He was standing within a sea of naked mannequins! It was quite the sight for someone who did not work in the retail world. I came to understand his

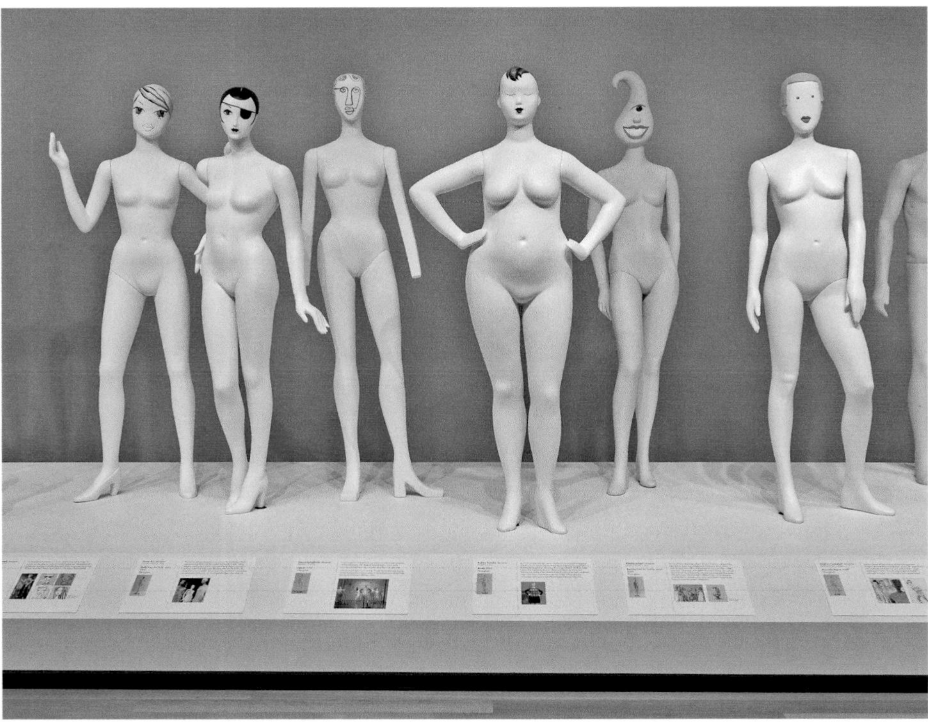

Figure 12.6 Ralph Pucci Mannequins: *The Art of the Mannequin* at the Museum of Arts and Design, curated by Barbara Paris Gifford. Photograph by Antoine Bootz.

nonchalance, though, because to him, these naked female clones were not proxies for fashion models but art sculptures, all with unique narratives.

Pucci explained the stories behind each mannequin and the ones that had the most interesting and culturally relevant biographies were the ones he and Gifford chose for the exhibition. Gifford recalled,

> Ralph has a curatorial eye, he knew which forms he wanted to show, the order in which they should be presented, and how each should be posed. Still, he wanted to display too many for the space we had in the museum. I knew it, but I did not know how to tell him that the checklist needed to be pared down. As our collaboration and friendship grew, so did his trust in me and I eventually told him that some of the mannequins needed to be cut. He agreed and that is how we arrived at our final list.

The newly appointed curator's first major exhibition, *Ralph Pucci: The Art of the Mannequin*, was both exciting and challenging. "In some ways, mannequins were a great way to cut my teeth. No one had expectations of what a mannequin show should look like, so the sky was the limit. I could essentially do what I wanted, and it would have been right," said Gifford. It must be noted that this was not a retrospective on the mannequin form altogether, but rather an exhibition about one mannequin-making family, the Pucci family. Gifford notes that this was her biggest challenge.

> I felt a great responsibility to the Pucci family as they had built their mannequin business from the ground up and were now passing it on to the third generation. Ralph is such a perfectionist, and I mean that in the greatest possible sense. With an understanding of his discerning eye and sophisticated aesthetic sensibilities, I knew I had to do my best job to meet his standards. I had to gain his trust by researching and understanding his mannequins as well as he did, and by presenting them in the best possible light so people would understand them as art objects. In retrospect, it was a very brave endeavor.

Utilizing and positioning mannequins in a museum format is very different than using them in a retail environment. Clearly, mannequins presented in the halls and galleries of a museum, whether to display archival fashion pieces or to feature the mannequins themselves as works of art, pose a different set of challenges. Gifford explained,

> Mannequins are ubiquitous, we encounter them every day. Our eyes are trained to look past them, to notice only what they are wearing. The moment you clothe them, their role is secondary, their bodies standing in for our own, albeit a more idealized version. To display mannequins as works of art in a museum, you have to understand this dynamic and disrupt it. The mannequins are the objects of interest and visitors have to look at them this way.

With that in mind, Gifford elevated the mannequins on a platform and displayed them sculpturally without clothes.

> Visitors' eyes were directed to notice their shapes and to read labels about how each reflected fashion and culture from their time. They were consumed as designed objects. This strategy was essentially responsible for changing how these mannequins were perceived, from retail equipment to designed objects.

Gifford did her due diligence and hard work in researching the Pucci mannequin and understanding the designer's vision and approach.

> Ralph saw the potential for the mannequin from the start. With his *Sport* series, he put form into motion. Mannequins were no longer stiff avatars; they were dynamic, capable of reflecting our lifestyles. This set Ralph on a journey of engaging other artists and designers in making mannequin figures. The designers he worked with (Putnam, Toledo, Veruschka, Sui, Scharf, etc.) were at the center of what was happening in fashion, art, and design, and as a result, his mannequins reflected the

Figure 12.7 Ralph Pucci Mannequins: *The Art of the Mannequin*. A study of Pucci's artistic approach to the mannequin, curated by Barbara Paris Gifford. Photograph by Antoine Bootz.

> driving forces of American culture of the day. Mannequins are a framework for what we think of as ideal, so within Ralph's cadre of mannequins are archetypal feminine figures from the '70s, '80s, '90s, 2000s, and beyond.

Gifford notes that in the late 1980s and into the '90s, retailers across the board were striving to differentiate themselves by carrying cutting-edge fashion and presenting it as part of visually stunning and impactful window displays. Recognizing this industry direction, Pucci's business became even more creative and sought after. "Working with top creative talent and having them sit with Pucci's sculptor Michael Evert to shape their ideas, made Pucci mannequins art," said Gifford. "The mannequin essentially became another artistic medium in which to experiment. What emerged was an expression of our collective imagination as with any other art form."

Since *Ralph Pucci: The Art of the Mannequin*, Gifford, has curated several exhibitions in jewelry and fashion, including *The World of Anna Sui* and *Jewelry Stories*, for which there are accompanying catalogues. Gifford assures that the mannequins she selects for her shows are diverse and represent a range of realities, not just the white cultural norm.

> I respect the representational power of mannequins and want to ensure that whatever I do is not harmful or sending a message that is detrimental to various groups within our community. Ralph's impulse at one point was to diversify his mannequins, so he made likenesses that were young, old, black, white, brown, yellow, straight, gay, heavy, thin, etc. (which we highlighted in the exhibition). He knew the influence his mannequins had, and he encouraged retailers to broaden the types of forms they displayed. Unfortunately, in most cases, they were not willing to walk away from the limiting view of women as white, rail thin, and possessing unattainable physical qualities.

As a scholar immersed in the history of decorative arts, Gifford recognizes what made Pucci mannequins worthy of recognition.

> Not all mannequins are art because many of them are not made with top designer's ideas that are expressed in clay by a professional sculptor. That is what makes Pucci mannequins different. Ralph benefitted from a particular time and place. He attracted many artistic people who wanted to be part of his universe. It was a time when many artists would stop by, hang around, and eventually find themselves engaged in the process of making mannequins.

Ralph Pucci: The Art of the Mannequin was an unqualified success. Gifford's curatorial vision provided visitors to the museum with an in-depth look at a seemingly mundane part of our culture; one that people typically take for granted.

> People like to come to MAD because we show objects that are more interesting and unusual compared with other museums. MAD is comparatively quirky. Showing mannequins was completely natural for us, and it expanded the types of objects we are known for while emphasizing the design aspect of our name. We have since expanded our fashion program in part due to the success of the Pucci exhibition.

References

1. Gianluca Bauzano, *Mannequins: Bonaveri: A History of Creativity, Fashion and Art* (Skira, 2013).
2. Bauzano, *Mannequins: Bonaveri.*
3. Bauzano, *Mannequins: Bonaveri.*

CHAPTER 13
MATERIALS: FROM COBBLESTONES TO CYBERSPACE

The Industrial Revolution in the late 19th and early 20th centuries played a significant role in the development of retail as we know it today, particularly as it relates to the department store. New technologies, such as the steam engine, the harnessing of electricity, networks of communication and transportation such as the telegraph, telephone, and an expanded railroad system, as well as the development of the internal combustion engine, shifted economies from agrarian to industrial. Major population centers across the Western world, most notably in the American Northeast and Midwest in cities such as New York, Philadelphia, and Chicago, as well as in cities across Western Europe, particularly in the United Kingdom and Germany, became manufacturing powerhouses. Agriculture became secondary to manufacturing as factories began to churn out goods in ever-increasing quantities. The factories provided new jobs which bolstered economies and led to higher standards of living. Over the course of time, retail quickly embraced the latest and greatest technologies as it became a dominant business factor and critical component of the newly industrialized world.

From its earliest days, and all the years that followed, retail has always been quick to embrace new technologies, including new materials used in the production of mannequins. Some of the earliest mannequins were simply wirework figures produced in Paris in the 1830s. They were heavy, clunky, and not very flattering. Papier-mâché mannequins were developed in France by the mid-19th century. This was a major step forward beyond the early wirework versions. As time went on, technologies advanced as did creativity and the ever-elusive quest for perfection. Wax creations were the next advancement in the art of the mannequin as designers searched for the most lifelike representation of the female form. Some of the wax creations even sported glass eyes, false teeth, and real human hair. Naturally, wax mannequins had one significant flaw, they melted in the heat of the window.

As time, creativity, and technology advanced, a new mannequin came to life in the 1920s; one that was made of plaster. Here too there were inherent problems. For one, the plaster iteration of the mannequin was very heavy, some weighing in at over a hundred pounds. The other problem was that if dropped, they fell to over a hundred pieces; they were quite fragile.

Experimentation with new materials continued with the introduction of fiberglass, the material of choice for the modern-day mannequin. In addition to fiberglass, plastic mannequins have been developed offering a less expensive option. While more durable, however, the plastic version is not quite as realistic as the fiberglass creations.

ONE WORD, PLASTICS

Jim Talaric was an early proponent of the new plastic mannequin. Talaric began his career in the mannequin industry while still in junior high school. Being an industrious young man, he wanted to find a summer job. At the time, his stepfather, Dick Jachim, was a sales rep for Silvestri Studios, owned by the brothers Mario and Roland Silvestri. Through his stepfather, he met Roland, who lived about a mile from his house in the North Hollywood section of Los Angeles. Roland was kind enough to arrange for him to work in the Silvestri factory sanding mannequins during the summer of 1959. Each morning young Talaric would walk to Roland Silvestri's house and get into the back of his car where he would sleep until Silvestri came out to drive him to work. This was when Silvestri Studios was on Formosa Avenue in Hollywood. Talaric credits Silvestri for teaching him the ins and outs of the mannequin industry. He fondly remembers his mentor as "a peach of a guy, a wonderful man."

After high school, Talaric left Silvestri to pursue other interests. He returned to the mannequin maker in 1978 with visions of the future. With a forward-thinking perspective, Talaric tried to convince Silvestri that the future was in a new material called urethane. "I started talking to Roland about the possibility of manufacturing mannequins and forms in a new more timely and less costly process using a new material, plastics," recalled Talaric. "I had no idea which plastic or how, but I felt sure there had to be a more efficient way to make mannequins." In his excitement, he invoked the iconic words of Mr. McGuire in the 1967 Oscar-winning film The Graduate, when he said to Benjamin Braddock, played by Dustin Hoffman, "I want to say one word to you. Just one word. Plastics."

Silvestri, ever the traditionalist, wasn't convinced; he preferred his family's longstanding fiberglass material. Undeterred, Talaric decided to open his own company with a new material that he thought would revolutionize mannequin production. He took on a partner named Jim Barber. In Talaric's words, "Jim just knew how to make stuff." Talaric and Barber started a new business with the focus of making mannequins in a new, more efficient way. In March of 1986, the two entrepreneurs leased a 6,000-square-foot building in Huntington Beach, California, and began the process of retrofitting it for their use.

> At this point, we had no idea how to re-engineer mannequins, but we found a manufacturer in our business park who was molding car parts out of a rigid urethane foam. He generously showed us his methods and suggested that if we got into molding urethane we needed to contact Thomas Vega, the best mold maker in all of Argentina. As luck would have it, Vega was living in Los Angeles at the time.

Together Talaric and Barber began to make mannequins with a new process and a new material, rigid urethane. The two partners established a new company called Fusion Mannequins.

At the time, most mannequin manufacturers were making mannequins out of fiberglass and forms out of papier-mâché. Talaric explained,

> This new process was more efficient than the long-standing mannequin-making methods, requiring less than one and a half times the labor necessary for the more traditional way of getting the fiberglass into the mold. Making a mannequin out of fiberglass involved the labor-intensive process of hand-laying the fiberglass in the mold. After the fiberglass was laid into the mold it had to set for a few hours before de-molding. Thus, in an eight-hour shift, you could make about two mannequins out of each mold.

Talaric used a high-pressure machine to inject the urethane material into the mold in ten to twenty seconds. Next, they used a spin mold that incorporated centrifugal force to evenly distribute the material to the interior of the mold. Careful calculations of the geometries of the slow spin were needed to perfect the process. According to Talaric, the advantage of this material was that it reduced the time it took to cast a mannequin from eight hours to twenty minutes. Talaric said, "We could make one every twenty minutes and we could make it cheaper and more durable."

Ever the visionary, Talaric thought that in addition to making mannequins and forms, this new process could also be incorporated into other molded products used in retail design. "Basically, we made a mold, injected a certain amount of liquid rigid urethane foam into the mold, closed the mold, and waited for several minutes while the two-part cellular mixture expanded to fill the mold cavity which yielded a solid rigid foam part. It produced a form with a hard skin that we could sand and paint," explained Talaric.

At the time Talaric was working with various Limited divisions in Columbus, Ohio.

> One day as I was calling on Limited Stores, the head of design told me they were gearing up for a big promotion called "Moods By Kenzo." They wanted a molded two-foot-high dimensional letter "M" and a smaller letter "B" on the face of the M, and on the face of the B an even smaller letter "K." The finished piece was to be double-sided. Then she threw down the gauntlet, she needed a few thousand and she needed them fast. I told her we could mold them and meet her time frame. She trusted we would come through for her and gave us a purchase order. I rushed back to our factory and called Thomas Vega, the best mold maker in all of Argentina. He came to see us, and we explained what we needed. He said he could make the mold for $10,000 and it would take him four weeks. He got the order. In week four we called him to find out which day he would deliver the mold. He said he ran into "some trouble" and needed a couple extra weeks. Four weeks later he delivered the mold and wanted his $10,000. I told him first we wanted to mold a part to make sure it worked. The first pull from the mold was great with one exception, the B was on backwards. Needless to say, Vega did not get his $10,000 and we ushered him out of our factory. That was the easy part. Now I had to call my client at Limited and explain what happened. Somehow she understood and Fusion went on to become a major supplier to all Limited divisions for the next 20 years or so.

The new technology that Fusion was using came with certain challenges. The Environmental Protection Agency banned the use of a blowing agent used in the

> process. In 1987 The Montreal Protocol was universally ratified by all of the countries in the world. The treaty was written as a global agreement to protect the stratospheric ozone layer by phasing out the production and consumption of ozone-depleting substances (ODS). This innovative agreement encouraged worldwide investment in alternative technologies that were designed to protect and repair the earth's greatly damaged and threatened ozone layer. The Montreal Protocol was a very significant accomplishment. President Ronald Reagan said of the accord, "The Montreal Protocol is a model of cooperation. It is a product of the recognition and international consensus that ozone depletion is a global problem, both in terms of its causes and its effects. The protocol is the result of an extraordinary process of scientific study, negotiations among representatives of the business and environmental communities, and international diplomacy. It is a monumental achievement.

In 1989, after three years in business and soon after the ratification of the Montreal Protocol, Talaric and Barber knew they needed a bigger factory. "Rent around Los Angeles was very expensive. In addition, workers' compensation insurance was also very expensive, and it was difficult for us to work with the local EPA (Environmental Protection Agency). At dinner one evening we agreed to move the company out of California," said Talaric. After a great deal of searching and researching Fusion was moved to an area around Denver, Colorado.

> We leased a 150,000-square-foot building for much less money per square foot compared to Los Angeles. In addition, our workers' compensation bill was almost cut in half, and the EPA was much easier to work with. The added bonus was it was a much better place to raise our families. We brought 35 employees and their families with us, and they also found this to be a much more desirable place to live.

Just after moving to Denver, Fusion's material supplier BASF, notified Talaric that they could continue supplying their foam but without the CFC Blowing agent.

> They found a way to blow it with water. It sounded fine but the resulting element had a soft skin, like styrofoam. We quickly determined that this would not work in a retail environment, so it was back to the drawing board. Within six months we invented and patented "Cold Rotational Molding." This process involved injecting a certain amount of Urethane Elastomer (we marketed as "E-Flex") into a mold, mounting the mold on a 2-axis rotational machine, spinning/rotating the mold in a certain geometry, and within 15 minutes or so we would de-mold a hollow, almost unbreakable part. Comparing our patented molding method to making a mannequin out of fiberglass meant going from approximately one plus hours of labor to less than a minute and reducing de-mold time from three to four hours to 15 minutes. Hence, we could produce parts eight times faster with a fraction of the

labor cost plus the resulting mannequin was almost unbreakable. This invention put us squarely on the map. We could deliver mannequins faster, cheaper, and of a higher quality than conventional fiberglass mannequins.

This led to another challenge that nobody could have foreseen. When they first started making mannequins and forms with the new process, they received a large order from Limited. With the unique cut of their men's shirts, they were very particular about the dimensions of the bust forms. Talaric spoke of the unexpected dilemma in great detail.

> Our first customer for this new Cold Rotational process was 'Structure' the new Men's division of Limited. Structure's store designers flew to Denver to tell us how they wanted the body shaped for a large order of 3/4 men's bust forms. They had very exact dimensions with no room for deviation. The waistline had to be 31 1/4" in circumference. Accordingly, the chest had a specific size requirement as did the neck and shoulders. There was definitely a sense of urgency as their first store was opening in Cleveland in six weeks. Our sculptors went to work. Two weeks later Limited's design team revisited our factory to tweak and approve the sculpt. After approval, we had to make several molds. This part of the process took about three weeks to complete. That left us with one week to produce 75 3/4 forms. We wound up having to overnight air ship them to ensure a timely delivery. The next day I got a call from their purchasing manager who was quite irate. She reminded me how they had specified the dimensions for the forms. She said the waist was supposed to be 31 1/4". She angrily asked why the ones they received in the Cleveland store had waists with 14" circumferences. I told her I could not understand what she was talking about as I personally inspected the forms prior to shipment, and they all had the specific dimensions they required.

Talaric and his partner were confused and upset. They knew they had meticulously followed Limited's specifications. He explained further,

> The purchasing manager told me in no uncertain terms to get all the misshapen forms out of the store that day. We arranged for someone to go to the store, remove the forms, and transport them back to us. When we received them we measured all the forms. Much to our bewilderment every one of them had a waist circumference of 31 1/4". We couldn't figure it out. Finally, we enlisted the help of an engineering professor at the University of Colorado. We needed an answer, after all, our future of producing mannequins was based on solving this riddle. The professor had a hunch, so we followed his suggestion and rented Ball Aerospace's hyperbaric chamber. The professor was right on the mark. We put some of the forms into the chamber and increased the pressure to sea level. Sure enough, the forms were compressed. We then decreased the air pressure and they re-expanded. When we molded them in Denver we encapsulated our relatively low air pressure due to our

altitude (the Mile High City). When we shipped them to Cleveland, near sea level they compressed due to the much higher air pressure. Lesson Learned: we drill a vent hole in every form and mannequin allowing air pressure to equalize.

Talaric and Barber continued to innovate and move the mannequin industry to new places. One of their most significant inventions was attaching appendages (arms, hands, legs) to mannequin bodies using magnets instead of the customary "Bayonet Fittings." The United States Patent Office provided the following abstract:

> Forms for display of clothing and the like with magnetically attachable parts are provided. The magnetic joints comprise a magnetic assembly with a depth-of-pull sufficient to cause the attachable part to begin to pull toward the form at a distance preferably greater than one-half inch, preferably about one inch. Preferably the magnetic assembly has a depth-of-pull of at least about 120 gauss at a distance of one inch. A metallic plate is arranged in mating configuration with the magnetic assembly. Mating pins may be provided, as well as indexing pins. If the manikin is knocked over, or if the attached part is pulled or bumped, it will come loose rather than breaking off; and the mating parts are self-seeking in use so that they will come together in proper orientation even when being mated beneath clothes. A bump to the manikin sufficient to overcome the on-contact strength of the magnetic attachment may not result in detachment of the limb because of the depth-of-pull strength of the magnetic assembly. The indexing pins allow the limbs to be placed in a variety of positions.[1]

SUSTAINABILITY

Sustainability is not a trend, it's an expectation, a demand, and an approach to ethical business practices and healthy lifestyles. It's an existential concern that touches all aspects of modern life. As stewards of the environment, it's incumbent upon all to protect our fragile ecosystem and preserve our natural resources. Increasingly, retail and the fashion industry negatively impact the environment with a huge carbon footprint. While we strive to fulfill the needs of everyday life for today's generation, we must be cognizant of preserving the health, safety, and welfare of future generations. With the passage of time and heightened senses of social responsibility and awareness, mannequin manufacturers are exploring and developing sustainable and ethical materials for the production of the modern mannequin. As new technologies abound, many manufacturers are striking a healthy balance between business development and social and environmental responsibility. Research and development includes experimentation with natural fibers such as bamboo, coconut, soy, hemp, and flax, as well as the use of recycled materials including textiles and wood. Some enlightened and visionary manufacturers are also looking at the efficacy of sugar cane, while others are working with a bio-based material made from cornstarch.

Figure 13.1 Expor Mannequins sustainable Plex-T mannequins. Photograph courtesy of Expor Mannequins.

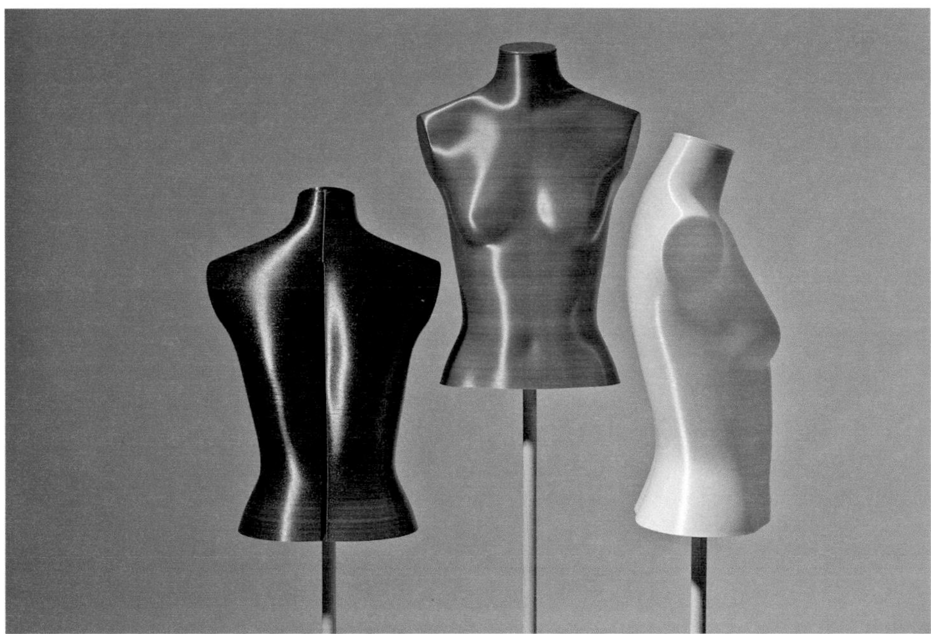

Figure 13.2 Hans Boodt uses a wide range of sustainable materials such as on-demand torsos in coffee, oyster shell, and beer. Photograph courtesy of Hans Boodt.

In addition, several manufacturers are moving forward with recycled materials such as plastic waste. The Nob collection by Hans Boodt (Netherlands), features unbreakable, lightweight mannequins made with recycled plastic, while Expor Mannequins (Brazil), offers a product made with their exclusive Plex-T resin (tested and approved in the market for over two decades). The material is unbreakable, biodegradable, and a hundred percent recyclable. After use, the mannequins can be returned to Expor and transformed into raw materials, thereby supporting a sustainable cycle of continuous utilization.

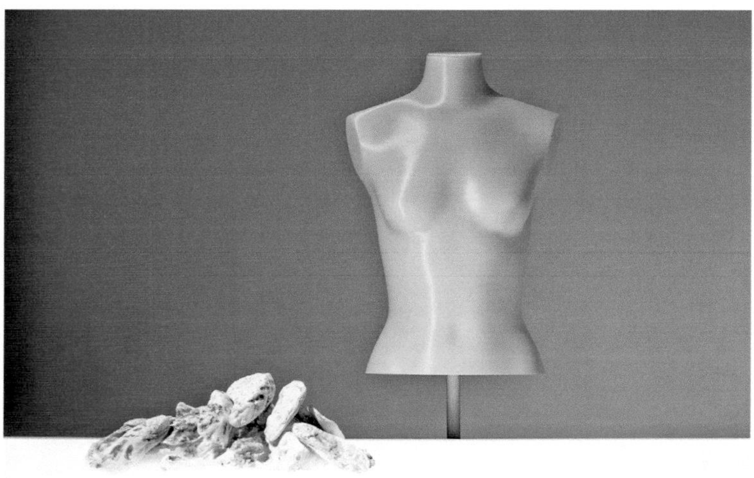

Figure 13.3 Hans Boodt on-demand torsos in oyster shell. Photograph courtesy of Hans Boodt.

Figure 13.4 Hans Boodt on-demand torsos in coffee. Photograph courtesy of Hans Boodt.

With more and more retailers seeking sustainable and environmentally friendly products, some manufacturers are turning to less traditional materials. An example is Hans Boodt, whose innovative 3D production technology offers design solutions in a wide range of sustainable materials such as on-demand torsos in coffee, oyster shell, and beer.

Reference

1. United States Patent (10). Patent No.: US6,705,794B2. DISPLAY FORM HAVING MAGNETICALLY ATTACHABLE PARTS. Inventors: Richard Varner, Longmont, CO (US); James D. Barber, Longmont, CO (US); James Talaric, Louisville, CO (US).

CHAPTER 14
ABSTRACT, CUSTOM, AND UNIQUE APPLICATIONS

Today's consumer gets their fashion information from many sources, including the internet, newspapers, magazines, movies, television, and even the streets. However, they get most of their fashion information from the stores themselves. The physical store is a tool of communication, sending quality messages to customers and educating them about the newest styles and latest trends. In addition, the physical store is the touchstone of the brand. Every gesture that a store makes, including the sign above the front door, the surface coverings on the floors and walls, the nature of the sales associates, and even the stationery used, is a representation of the brand. Moreover, the selected mannequins are as important as any other branded or proprietary element that represents the store.

Mannequins, whether in a window installation or an interior display, are standard bearers of the brand. A store must always be on point with a consistent and holistic message. When selecting a mannequin for a window presentation or an interior store display, the retailer must consider the message that they are hoping to send.

Much discussion has been had in recent years about mannequins representing the true human form rather than an idealized, unattainable vision of the human body. People want to see mannequins that they can relate to; mannequins that look like them. This is an understandable concern if mannequins are used only as a means of presenting merchandise. However, while mannequins are clearly vital tools for merchandise presentation, they also do much more than that. When a store is being designed, and when a branded image is being developed, every retailer must ask themselves three questions: Who am I? What do I have to say? How do I say it? Every retailer must stand for something. Is the message the mannequin is to project simply about the merchandise, or are there other messages to communicate? If it's merely about the merchandise, then perhaps a mannequin that is a literal representation of the human form would be appropriate. If, however, the message deals with a more thought-provoking issue such as the nuances of the brand, or perhaps a cultural movement or even current events, then perhaps a more artfully rendered mannequin would be a better choice for communicating an idea or a concept.

There is a time and a place for realistic mannequins, and a time and a place for abstract mannequins. As mentioned earlier, Ignaz Gorischek bought realistic Rootstein mannequins for his windows at Neiman Marcus. He wanted more drama in the windows with the notion that outside the store there are only seconds to capture the customer's attention. His philosophy was that realistic mannequins provided eye-catching drama that would turn the heads of even the most preoccupied passersby. In the interior of the store, he wanted abstracts because there is more time to engage the customer once they are already in the store. Gorischek said, "In the window, you capture the eye with drama. In the store, you capture the imagination with art."

Abstraction is an enlightened way to represent the reality of any given time or age. It challenges the viewer and compels them to think. It takes them, whether through in-store design or window design, to another time, another place, and another state of mind. Abstraction is truly a commentary on the state of the world, through visions, interpretations, and reflections of the times.

Raymond Mastrobuoni was the window director at Cartier in New York for forty years. In that capacity, he engaged in dialogue with passersby for four decades. Always topical, his windows demanded attention. "Pique their interest, compel them to stop, look and think," was his guiding principle. "Don't present the obvious, encourage them to hunt and discover." While for the most part Mastrobuoni didn't use mannequins in the windows at Cartier, his window themes were eclectic collections of the nuances and subtleties of our lives, using an array of everyday props. A widely celebrated grouping of Mastrobuoni windows featured the Cabbage Patch dolls in 1983. The popular dolls were not an obvious association with Cartier jewelry, but they were on everyone's mind. His antennae were up 24/7, inspiration was everywhere, and everything was a potential subject or medium.

Mastrobuoni did not take "his art" quite so seriously. "Ultimately," he said, "I was a salesman." Although he never collected a sales commission, he knew his window creations enticed people into the store. They were the embodiment of the Cartier image and a three-dimensional representation of the brand. Fifth Avenue and the visual merchandising industry will long be indebted to the creative sensibility of Raymond Mastrobuoni. The overriding message of his remarkable 40-year journey at Cartier is: "To impart mind to medium. Don't be afraid. With a little creativity, you can do anything."

Leigh Ann Tischler, director of window design and special interior events at Bloomingdale's, shares Mastrobuoni's creative spirit. Her work began to get noticed while she was doing window installations at Sony. Much like Cartier's master window designer, Tischler's window creations at both Sony and Bloomingdale's have always been thought-provoking; compelling passersby to "stop, look, and think." Her work at Sony was particularly challenging, as the goal was to transform the Sony Plaza store at 550 Madison Avenue from a tech/museum-type environment into a couture electronic store. "At that time, they wanted to be the Bergdorfs of electronics," said Tischler. "This was the path that led me to Sony. This notion was very intriguing."

After the Madison Avenue store was renovated, the next plan was to open the Sony store in the Metreon shopping center in San Francisco. Metreon was an entertainment mall that housed a Maurice Sendak Wild Things interactive playground, a David McCauley, The Way Things Work interactive museum, a PlayStation store, and the first Microsoft store operated by Sony at the time. "To work closely with the animators, Maurice and his team, and David McCauley was exhilarating and fun," said Tischler.

Figure 14.1 Artistic mannequin interpretation celebrating the beauty floor at Bloomingdale's. Courtesy of Leigh Ann Tischler.

> After Metreon, which was over two years in planning and construction, came the opening of approximately 44 stores across the country. It was an exciting time, seeing our team expand and grow in knowledge on so many levels while always learning from the previous project. This excitement even extended to the use of mannequins in the windows. Of course, it was not every window change, but when we did use them, they were always an unexpected surprise and delight.

Mannequins, abstract and realistic, were an integral part of Tischler's work, both at Sony and Bloomingdale's.

> There are very definite times when the decision was made to use abstract mannequins versus realistic mannequins. During the course of my career, I have used both types of mannequins. At Bloomingdale's the choice can revolve around the fashion trends or if a specific vendor is being showcased. Also, the form and shape of the fashion on a human being can affect the poses chosen so the garments drape realistically. At Sony, believe it or not, we used many realistic mannequins to show lifestyle moments. For example, when we launched our digital frames, we

Figure 14.2 Abstract mannequins in a grouping of three, featuring fine leather fashion at Bloomingdale's. Courtesy of Leigh Ann Tischler.

> used the frames mounted to the head/face of realistic mannequins so their facial expressions were shown on the digital frame.

Tischler believes that both abstract mannequins and realistic mannequins have their own artistry and special qualities.

> Realistic mannequins have always offered a variety of poses, and different mannequin houses were known for certain attributes. One house may be known for ultra-dramatic poses while another mannequin house could be known for more athletic poses. Realistic mannequins provide so many custom opportunities with hair and make-up; the possibilities are endless. I do feel that abstract mannequins have come a long way with variety and the selection of many different poses. And if you have enough lead time, and budget, you can always work with the mannequin houses on custom poses. Abstract mannequins can have sculpted hair and make-up as part of their bodies' material composition or real wigs and make-up that is abstracted. This is a completely different look but just as artistic. It is quite a talent to pull this off without the mannequin looking like an alien . . . unless that is the objective of a particular window theme. Also of note is that many

Figure 14.3 Stand-alone abstract mannequin, graphically featuring a black and white fashion statement at Bloomingdale's. Courtesy of Leigh Ann Tischler.

> abstract mannequins do not have sculpted hair at all. I might add that styling wigs is a lost art and there are not many artists who do over-the-top realistic or abstracted wigs anymore."

Depending on the brand, Tischler believes that in addition to displaying merchandise, both abstract and realistic mannequins can also be a projection of the store's image. Tischler said,

> We are lucky at Bloomingdale's to have a broad selection of mannequins. My talented team is very passionate about always trying to build our inventory of both abstract and realistic mannequins as well as new poses. Some retailers may be known for only using one type of mannequin, but we try to be as diverse as we can so we can be ready depending on the fashion or designer that we are presenting. It is also not uncommon for us to send mannequins, both realistic and abstract, out to be painted for a project. At Sony, abstract mannequins worked very well with the mix of electronics and whimsey we were aiming for. Plus, nobody expected to see a mannequin in a window focusing on a computer or digital camera. We also used mannequins that were not abstract but had more cartoon-like faces. Abstract mannequins can portray street theater in a totally different way than a realistic mannequin does. But it is not whether a mannequin is abstract or realistic. The entire window works as a whole, like the overall composition of a painting. The sum is made up of all the parts. All the elements complete the story together. This

Figure 14.4 A pregnant mannequin celebrating Mother's Day at Bloomingdale's. Courtesy of Leigh Ann Tischler.

includes the fashion, the poses, the environment, and of course the story being told. This is the same for a window or a visual moment inside the store.

As retail continues to evolve, there is a dramatic movement from realistic mannequins to abstract and partially abstract mannequins. The mannequin manufacturers who shifted to the design of abstracts were better positioned to serve their customers and protect the long-term solvency of their companies. An early shift to abstracts saved a lot of mannequin manufacturers. There are of course many practical as well as aesthetic reasons for the success of abstract mannequins. Most importantly, abstracts require less man-power and maintenance. They're much easier to trim, without the concern of wigs and make-up. In the past, many visual merchandising teams included a staff member who was responsible for make-up. Additionally, realistic mannequins require better lighting.

High-end stores seem to prefer abstracts with the notion that it's about the merchandise and not about the mannequin. From their perspective, a prop, fixture, or embellishment should never overwhelm the merchandise, rather, these tools should be used to enhance and communicate the nuances of the merchandise. This principle holds for mannequins as well. Styling the image of a realistic face can carry and support the clothes. However, as is the case with supermodels, there is a fine line not to be crossed, when the mannequin becomes the story and the clothes become secondary.

Some industry professionals doubt that realistic mannequins will ever make a comeback, convinced that their time has passed the point of no return. Many of the stylists and make-up artists have moved on. It seems that only refurbishing studios are really using make-up artists anymore. Also, the mannequin sculptor no longer exists, 3D printing has replaced that function. Some, however, maintain that 3D printing lacks the artistic hand.

As the use of abstract mannequins continues to outpace the use of realistic mannequins in today's retail environment, James Mansour believes that both are valuable tools of communication. "Mannequins are subject to trends, just like everything else to do with fashion," said Mansour. "I think a primary reason that the pendulum has swung towards abstract forms is the ease of dressing and styling them: store associates were able to be trained to dress them, they cost less money, and are easier to repair."

In his role at Limited, Mansour used both, depending on the circumstances. Faced with the challenge of designing for six different brands, he had to differentiate one brand from the other. Mansour recalled,

> It was easy to design the unique look of Victoria's Secret stores because of the merchandise. But for Express, Limited, and Abercrombie and Fitch, I used mannequins as a fun differentiator. Abercrombie was a heritage brand, so it made sense to use traditional men's suiting forms and dressmaker forms. For Express Compagnie Internationale I used antique French table legs as bases that I had cast in fiberglass. Some of the forms had fleur-de-lys's instead of heads. For Limited, I selected realistic mannequins and then placed them in unexpected situations.

In 1984, Mansour oversaw a historical restoration to the exterior of a McKim Meade, and White building in New York. Originally designed in 1927, the 20,000-square-foot flagship at 691 Madison Avenue, is a great example of mannequin selection based on architecture and name brand image. According to Mansour, the space was referred to as a "triplex," divided into three stores: Limited on the ground floor up to the penthouse atrium and Express on the lowest level along with Victoria's Secret.

> In the interior, we did a staircase inspired by Coco Chanel's mirrored staircase in her Paris apartment. I designed a feature that allowed the mannequins to be walking up the same stairs that the customers walked. All of the realistic mannequins leaned on railings, sat on ledges and were engaged with the environment in a way that had never been done in store interiors before.

In the Express store on the lower level that was visible from the top floor, Mansour used white abstract Pucci mannequins arranged in an array around a grouping of video monitors. Both abstract and realistic mannequins played an important role in projecting the nuances of each brand while seamlessly engaged with the distinctive architecture.

There are three levels of abstraction as it relates to mannequins. A totally abstract mannequin offers a suggestion of the human body. While the basics of the human form and shape are recognizable, the figure is clearly stylized and featureless, without discernible eyes, nose, mouth, or hair. Make-up is usually not applied. The projected image is ageless and non-representative of any ethnicity.

A partly abstract mannequin also offers a highly stylized interpretation of the human form but with suggestions of features such as sculpted hair and subtle indications of eyes, ears, nose, and mouth. Make-up is rarely applied, and skin tone possibilities are endless, from a complete spectrum of color to an array of tones, textures, and finishes.

A partly realistic mannequin bridges the line between realistic and abstract with more discernible and accurate indications of facial features. Some can wear wigs and make-up, while others reference hair through stylized sculpting.

While the debate continues over realistic representations of the human form, or abstracted versions, it should be noted that subtlety is a great design tool. An effective window presentation or in-store display should be suggestive of an idea or a concept rather than an obvious interpretation of an idea. If mannequins are considered an art form, as is suggested in this book, it follows that presentations using mannequins are also an art form. Craft enters the realm of art when it moves the emotions of those who engage with it. An effective mannequin, whether realistic or abstract, anatomically accurate or merely suggestive, should touch the soul and impact the way the viewer feels.

In 1987, during my tenure as corporate director of visual merchandising for Stern's Department Stores, based in Paramus, New Jersey, I was involved in the design and opening of five new full-line department stores and five full-store renovations in a period of just thirteen months. While this was a daunting task, I was fortunate enough to have partnered with many visionary and insightful suppliers, particularly those in the mannequin industry.

The new 160 thousand square foot store in Jersey City served as a laboratory, and ultimately a prototype for other new stores slated for opening or renovation. While each individual store displayed some degree of local flavor, all were designed to be strong environmental projections of the company's brand image. A moderate full-line department store, Sterns typically used between 80 to 150 mannequins per store, depending on the size of the store. The Jersey City project provided a great opportunity to push the envelope and take merchandise presentation to another level. When designing a department store our approach was always to define each selling area with its own distinctive feeling, while still having a common thread to pull the entire environment together as one cohesive store.

The underlying connecting threads that provided unity of form, structure, and experience were the rich marble flooring tile that directed foot traffic through the space, the central meeting place and focal point under the grand atrium, and the linear structure of the perimeter walls. One of the most powerful statements that led to a plurality of design was made by a harmonious mix of mannequins. To differentiate each department, and best present the nuances of each merchandise classification, we incorporated mannequins from many different resources including Goldsmith, Patina V, Silvestri, Rootstein, and Vogue mannequins. As we experimented, we learned which mannequins best told the stories that we wanted to tell. A healthy mix of realistic, abstract, futuristic, and conceptual mannequins, served us well in presenting a balanced range of products in a distinctive branded environment.

Silvestri California, a major manufacturer of custom mannequins, forms, and display props, played a key role in the design development of the store in the new Newport Center Mall in Jersey City. At the beginning stages of the design process, I toured the surrounding Jersey City neighborhood hoping to get a sense of the fabric of the area and a feeling for the nuances of its grand architectural heritage. Known for its distinctive facades and elaborate architectural details, ranging from the Gothic revival style to rich period architecture with Victorian references, the location also enjoys amazing panoramic views of lower Manhattan, just across the mouth of the Hudson River. As I ambled about the waterfront, I also found many references to the Corinthian order and classic Greek and Roman design. Wanting a contemporary feel, with but a subtle nod to the area's architecture, I contacted Roland Silvestri, the owner of Silvestri California. I explained my vision to Roland and asked if he would work with me in developing custom display props based on classical forms and structures, and custom mannequins for the men's department of our new store. Roland said yes to both.

During the ensuing months, I worked closely with Roland and came to know him as a talented, empathetic, and open-minded industry professional. He listened intently to my concept of a contemporary fluted Corinthian column. I described an architectural element complete with elaborate capitals and adorned with traditional acanthus leaves. But of course, there was a twist, and Roland understood. I wanted a contemporary feeling with a significantly slenderized profile. After several design meetings, Silvestri produced a series of columns, arches, and porticos that stretched the bounds of historical reference into a sleek contemporary representation of classicism. The architectural forms were meant as a frame, designed to elevate and enhance a one-of-a-kind series of sculpted men's mannequins.

During the course of our discussions, Roland recognized that I wanted a range of mannequins that would project a new style and direction for Sterns. The hallmark architectural element of the new store was a grand atrium with a multi-faceted skylight. The entry-level floor was designed with wide main and secondary aisles clad in a highly veined salmon-toned marble tile. The intent was to invite customers to meander through the dynamic center core under the atrium and achieve maximum merchandise exposure to the adjacent better sportswear and men's clothing departments. The mannequins clearly had to tell the story of the brand and harmonize with the contemporary environment. As the design process continued, it was decided that each mannequin would feature a textured bisque finish and a classic sartorial attitude that served as a perfect complement to the architectural statement and overall ambience of the store. The project was a success on two levels; we installed an exciting men's department in time for the grand opening of our new store, and I got to meet and work with one of the industry's most respected icons.

The welcoming gesture at the main entrance was a synergistic arrangement of strategically positioned abstract Goldsmith mannequins. Customers were greeted by groupings of Abi, one of Goldsmith's most iconic collections. The clean lines of the Abi mannequin perfectly enhanced the merchandise as it drew customers in and through the better sportswear department. Abi's male counterpart, Dani, was featured across the aisle on the left side of the entryway in the men's department. My thought was that Abi and Dani provided a beautiful simplicity with a modern, forward-thinking attitude while the men's clothing department featured the sartorial Silvestri mannequins that were more in keeping with suits, sports jackets, dress shirts, and ties.

The elegance of the dress department was highlighted by the use of realistic Rootstein mannequins, most notably Theona with her long limbs and sensual features. Patina V mannequins were used in the juniors department with a collection of youthful poses and attitudes appropriate to our younger customers.

Wanting to elevate the customer experience by integrating art and references to the work of iconic artists, we took a different approach in the intimate apparel department. We wanted a mannequin that was soft, sensual, and feminine, but we also wanted it to be unique to our store; an artistically rendered mannequin that was ours and ours alone. In brainstorming the concept, the word Venus kept appearing. What better goddess is there to highlight intimate apparel? Naturally, I thought of the Italian artist Sandro Botticelli's *Birth of Venus*. One of his greatest works, completed for the Medici family, the painting celebrates the worldly arrival of Venus as she's born from the sea foam. A depiction of the work of the ancient Greek poet Homer, Venus emerges from the sea as a grown woman riding a majestic seashell to the shore.

I contacted Vogue Mannequins, based in Los Angeles. They were a small company known for pushing the envelope with fun and even quirky mannequins and props. Most of their offerings were Art Deco inspired. They had a mannequin in their line that had a similar bend to the neck and slightly elongated features as evidenced in Botticelli's Venus. Upon seeing this mannequin, I immediately envisioned her with a pearlescent finish gracefully nestled in the embrace of a grand seashell. It was off to the drawing board as I collaborated with the sculptors at Vogue. After a few design sessions that included modifications to the existing mannequin, we were ready to pour the mold on a new form complete with the accompanying seashell. The result provided a suggestion of classic renaissance art with a tinge of Art Deco, in a totally contemporary environment. Years later as I visited Florence, I smiled as I marveled in front of Botticelli's masterpiece hanging on the wall of the Uffizi Gallery. I was proud of the fact that we brought art into the retail environment.

As the design of the prototype store evolved, we looked for other applications of mannequins outside of apparel departments. Goldsmith offered the perfect sentry to stand proudly in front of our electronics department in a welcoming gesture announcing the product within the department. Multi-Man, the brainchild of Goldsmith's creative director Shane DeRolf, was a muscular, robot-like mannequin with hands and arms thrust forward to hold and present merchandise offerings. Painted with a shimmering, silver-gray metallic finish, Multi-Man sported a hot neon tube across his face, looking perhaps like an extraterrestrial being from the far reaches of the future. The ever-present Multi-Man offered a bit of fun to the offerings of cutting-edge electronics. Fun has always been a great design tool.

The Jersey City store opened in early October 1987, a few short months before Christmas. We always celebrated the holiday season with a lush, traditional Christmas trim in all our stores. And now that we've turned the page and entered a new chapter of store design, the goal was to elevate the trim and the customer experience to another level. As such, we stayed with the theme of a contemporary twist on classical forms. Trimco, one of the major suppliers of props for the visual merchandising industry, had a basic court jester in their line. I took one look at the small figure, essentially a diminutive mannequin, about 42" in height, and saw enormous possibilities for an animated Christmas trim complete with harlequins, jesters, festoons, and heralding brass horns. This simple jester provided a flood of inspiration. The jester was going to be the central figure of a new and dynamic Christmas trim. The first step was to redesign the figure and make it uniquely ours. It began with totally changing the fabric covering from a stretch cotton to a smooth and silky satin. Next was a change in the colors of the jester's costume. It went from a basic red and green to shimmering red, gold, and plum. A gold-braided piping was added as an accent. The most important issue was giving the small mannequin the ability to articulate its arms, hands, fingers, and legs. The resultant figure was perfect! I wanted to roll it out to all of our stores. Of course, this would have pushed our 4th quarter holiday budget to the limit. I marched into our chief financial officer's office and told him I needed $50,000. When asked what I needed it for, I told him it was for court jesters. He almost threw me out of the office, but like any other creative, I stuck to my convictions and was eventually given an extension to the budget. With $50,000 in hand, and after much negotiation and insistence on exclusivity, I purchased enough jesters to populate all of our 29 stores. The result was a dynamic celebration across all our stores as jesters cavorted, danced, and played on center core ledges, mannequin platforms, and perimeter walls. This was yet another example of fun being a great design tool. Mannequins both large and small, whether wearing apparel or celebrating the holidays, always appealed to our fascination with the human form.

CHAPTER 15
TECHNOLOGY AND THE FACE OF TOMORROW

As we move ever further into the 21st century, technology continues to impact almost every aspect of contemporary life. From socialization and productivity to healthcare, education, transportation, communication, and everyday household chores, technology is moving minds and bodies through the complexities of an ever-evolving world. Retail has changed exponentially due to the impact of technology. Increasingly, retail of the 21st century revolves around the collection and analysis of data, and the sharing of inspiration, innovation, and information. Technology is not only a vehicle for collecting relevant data but also a great tool for communication. While the physical store remains a stage for disseminating information, new technologies are providing new ways to convey quality messages.

The discussion about online and offline commerce is over; the nuances of the brand however remain omnipresent. It doesn't matter where or how the customer communicates with the brand as long as every gesture the retailer makes is consistent and aligned with brand image, corporate values, and the story the company endeavors to tell.

As we venture deeper into new retail realities, the physical store is more important than ever before. Once the store was a selling stage; it was retail theater with the merchandise performing as actors on the stage. When orchestrated effectively, the store in today's retail model becomes a vehicle for the delivery of the brand message and enhancement of the customer/retailer relationship. Today the store is not simply a place to sell, but rather a curated exhibition designed to capture and engage the heart and soul. Moving emotions and establishing a connection are the keys to establishing customer loyalty. Visual merchandising is the most powerful tool to create and manage the customer connection.

If the physical store is the embodiment of image and brand, mannequins are an integral part of the narrative. Since the early days of modern retail, these fabulous forms have always been the most important tool of successful merchants across all segments of the fashion industry. Today, they are perhaps more crucial than ever before as retailers scramble to entice customers to return to the stores. They are the quintessential silent sales force, everything put on a mannequin flies out the door. But they're not simply fancy clothes hangers. When considered with aesthetic sensibility, and curated as a projection of company values, mannequins are ambassadors, if not standard bearers of the brand.

As integral members of the brand strategy and enticement team, today's visual merchandisers may look to the nuances and subtle qualities that differentiate one mannequin from another. The chief executive officer may however have a different viewpoint and perspective relative to return on investment. While some may simply consider mannequins as a necessary expenditure to help sell merchandise, it's the enlightened corporate leader who joins the visual merchandiser in recognizing that the right mannequin can help define an image. This corporate executive will secure a seat at the boardroom table for their creative visual partner. The leadership of most of today's fashion brands recognizes this. In the retail model prior to the connectivity phenomenon, visual merchandising was considered sales support, an important tool for growing and improving sales. Today it must be perceived as a strategic tool for adding value to the brand.

E-commerce has taught brick-and-mortar retailers the value of analytics. Today, metrics are ubiquitous, while in the past, traditional retailers based decisions on limited information, conjecture, intuition, and emotion. NPD Group, a research company based in New York, has found that mannequins are the second most important factor in fashion sales. The findings revealed that 42% (almost half) of people going into brick-and-mortar stores are influenced by mannequins. This number is only surpassed by the approval and influence of family and friends who accompany the shopper.

"Mannequins remain an important part of retail design, continuing to make an impact in store," says Carly Hagedon, editor-in-chief, *VMSD* magazine.

> Much like trends in apparel, mannequins are being tailored to accurately reflect consumer interests and needs. They will continue to evolve with the trends we see in retail and in society. Moving forward, there will be more societal representation, such as plus-size models and gender-fluid options. Additionally, custom mannequins and forms will become the norm as advancements in 3-D printing and sculpting create limitless possibilities, allowing retailers and brands to make statements in store that are visually aligned with their mission statements. Going forward, more companies will adapt sustainable and biodegradable materials, speaking to the growing importance of sustainability within the retail industry at large.

The first question the CEO and the visual director must ask about mannequins is: Are we taking full advantage of this tool? Meaning, do we have the appropriate number of mannequins, and as importantly, do we have the right mannequins?

And what is right? As ambassadors of the brand, mannequins must reflect the lifestyle and values of customers who shop in a particular store. With this understanding, retailers must align with their internal resources. Are the right people, with adequate training and insight, in place to deal with the task of creating mannequin presentations that are compelling, meaningful, and on brand?

As technology continues its relentless march, smart retailers must recognize that the integration of technology into the store environment must be curated in the same manner that artwork is curated at an art gallery or museum. Technology is now entering the realm of the mannequin, retail's majestic silent salesperson. Due to innovations, however, the queen of the selling floor is no longer silent. A new generation of mannequins can move and even speak. Some, outfitted with artificial intelligence, can engage in ways never before imagined as new technologies are reinventing and reinvigorating a tried and true cornerstone of the retail industry. Over the years, mannequins have gone from wire, wood, and wax, to plaster, fiberglass, and plastic. Now, years into a new digital age with myriad devices designed to make our lives better, digital technologies are pressing forward more quickly than any other innovation in history.

The Fourth Industrial Revolution or 4IR, has been characterized as the next stage of the digitization of the manufacturing process. Increased accessibility to data and analytics, combined with advancements in robotics, has ushered in a new relationship between man and machine. "Technology is pervasive and tenacious; it brings everything into play," said Marco Zanardi, Retail Institute Italy president. "Even in the mannequin sector, the incorporation of technology has changed the way mannequins are perceived, seen, and used."

The mannequin industry, ever responsive to market demands, analytics, technology, and cultural shifts, continues to seek innovation based on its own research and development. Retail has consistently demonstrated its ability to embrace new technologies. According to Zanardi, "Mannequins with embedded technology, virtual mannequins, and digital mannequins are very compelling due to their dynamic nature and incremental innovation." Zanardi cites the example of mannequins with customer behavior detection systems. "Equipped with sensors in the eyes, these mannequins allow for an infinite number of insights into the end customer: what they focus on, for how long, and with what degree of attention, etc."

Virtual mannequins, while not tactile and devoid of three-dimensional form and texture, use pre-recorded videos to impersonate a variety of characters and personalities, creating a compelling and interactive point of customer engagement. Virtual mannequins are well-conceived and designed to serve as attention-getting digital hosts or presenters of institutional messaging and product information.

Robotics is another example that takes the mannequin into another dimension, establishing an interaction between man, mannequin, and machine. A sensor in the shop window can detect the movements of shoppers, and then communicate those movements to a robotic mannequin. The mannequin can then replicate the movements of the viewer. This technology creates a newfound relationship with shoppers, especially younger generations, from Generation X and Millennials to Generation Alpha.

Additionally, creating a digital mirror of the physical store, including its mannequins, presents a new frontier in the use and efficacy of virtual store engagement. This is proving to be a very useful tool for management, market research, and the end customer. "We are heading in a hybrid direction: 85% of sales take place in physical shops and 15% online. Certainly, in the next few years, the online penetration will increase a bit more, 80% and 20%. This will lead to a wide range of mannequins, physical, material, and highly aesthetic," said Zanardi, "The frontiers of the digital mannequin are getting closer and closer, including digital store twins, immersive stores, metaverse retail, Avatars in 3D commerce and evolving virtual worlds, etc."

Beacon technology also offers new avenues of in-store communication. While a well-dressed and well-positioned mannequin can speak volumes to the passing customer, the integration of beacon technology into the mannequin world provides yet another vehicle for conveying quality messages. Increasingly, digital devices are impacting customer behavior and in-store purchasing decisions. More and more customers are turning to their mobile devices for information while they are in a brick-and-mortar environment. Mannequins equipped with beacon technology transmit details to the customer's mobile device about the garments they are wearing, including the price and where they can be found within the store. When a customer approaches, engages, or walks past a mannequin equipped with beacon technology, they receive a message from within a range of one hundred feet. This technology connects the virtual world to the in-store shopping experience by using Bluetooth low energy to connect with customers' hand-held beacon-enabled devices. The retail process, customer engagement, and the shopping experience are constantly evolving. This is due in large part to anthropological, psychological, sociological, and economic conditions. From its inception, retail has always responded to new market demands, and the relentless march of technology.

CHAPTER 16
THE BUSINESS OF THE MANNEQUIN

São Paulo, the largest city in South America, is a sprawling tapestry of diversity and multiculturalism. Its urban landscape crosses many socioeconomic boundaries, producing a pulsating energy that is evident throughout. Far removed from the outsider's romanticized perception of summer sun, sandy beaches, and samba, São Paulo is the business center of Brazil, the fifth largest country in the world. With the largest population in the Southern Hemisphere, Paulistas are quite proud of their culture. As such, they look to Rua Augusta as the heartbeat of their creative sensibilities.

Barely two miles in length, the journey along Augusta begins at Rua Estates Unidos in the tony residential section of Jardins. It then runs past the city's important financial hub, Avenida Paulista, and continues to the once magnificent but now forgotten and crumbling historic city center. Once rundown itself with empty or barely surviving shops, Augusta has been revitalized with a wide offering of bars, boutiques, bookstores, cafes, art galleries, and pricey restaurants. With a lively nightlife, music can be heard on every corner. Trendy clubs abound with musical preferences and genres revolving around alternative indie rock, hip-hop, and metal, as opposed to the expected Brazilian beats.

With São Paulo's standing as the 10th most expensive city in the world, the transformation of Augusta should not be confused with the proliferation of hipsters in Brooklyn's Williamsburg or the gentrification of South Boston. Augusta is also a magnet for the rich and famous. This bustling little street attracts creatives from all walks of life.

In 1969, the proprietor of one of the struggling shops on the corner of Rua Augusta and Avenida Paulista lamented low sales and slow-moving inventory in his store. Merchandise that languished on the selling floor for weeks was moved to a certain oblivion in the back stockroom, never to see the selling floor again. At the same time, an enterprising and visionary young businessman from Uberaba bought a fledgling mannequin company in São Paulo. Although new to the fashion and retail industries, Vilemondes Garcia de Andrade Filho, known simply as Garcia, recognized the capacity of mannequins to sell merchandise. He knew these fiberglass forms had the ability to attract attention and increase the hanger appeal of merchandise that was otherwise ignored. Garcia knew that mannequins were the most important tool a retailer could have to further their business. While he was a visionary, this ambitious young man's task would not be an easy one as old-world business philosophies were difficult to overcome. Undaunted, Garcia gathered a few mannequins and took them on the road. With business owners set in their ways, he knew he had to have an innovative approach. His first stop was that little boutique on the corner of Rua Augusta and Avenida Paulista.

The proud new owner of Expor Mannequins entered the shop with two of his best mannequins and asked to see the owner. "What is this?" proclaimed the owner. "I'm not interested in this silliness, no mannequins here in my shop. And besides, they're much too expensive."

Garcia replied,

> Expensive? No, they're not expensive at all. And you will see they will pay for themselves. In fact, I will let you borrow them for free for two weeks, and then you will see for yourself. What is your slowest-selling merchandise? We will dress these two mannequins with your slowest-selling merchandise and put them in the window. You will see, the merchandise will fly right out of your door, you will see.

After much protestation, the leery merchant brought out two pieces from the back stockroom and watched as Garcia trimmed the two mannequins with the slow-moving merchandise. Garcia then placed the mannequins in the window and promised to return in two weeks.

The two weeks passed quickly, and Garcia drove his old Simca Esplanada to Augusta to visit the shop owner and the two mannequins. As he drove past the store, he noticed that the mannequins were not wearing the same dresses that he had put on them. After parking his car, he hurried to the store, fearing that his experiment had failed. As soon as he entered the shop, he noticed a livelier atmosphere in the once-drab little store. "What happened here?" he asked the shop owner. "These are not the dresses I put on the mannequins. I told you to leave those dresses on the mannequins."

"Ha," proclaimed the proprietor with a smile. "I couldn't keep those same dresses on the mannequins."

"But why not?" came the troubled response from Mr. Garcia. The shopkeeper broke into an even bigger smile as he said, "Because all the dresses sold out. I emptied the stockroom of all those dresses. I want to buy those two mannequins in the window and two more for inside the store. Those mannequins are silent selling stars! I must have them." And so, Mr. Vilemondes Garcia de Andrade Filho, of Expor Mannequins had completed one of his first mannequin sales.

The selling power of mannequins is unmatched. They grace the windows and interiors of stores all over the world, from the Champs Élysées in Paris, Via Montenapoleone in Milan, and Fifth Avenue in New York to Rua Augusta in São Paulo. They are great tools of communication and engagement, delivering quality messages to all who encounter them. They bring merchandise to life and teach the customer how to accessorize and put an outfit together. They are standard bearers for the store brand and mirrors of culture and style. They show merchandise in lifestyle presentations and tell the customer what's trending and what's in vogue. They are the quintessential silent sales force compelling the customer to stop, look, and buy.

MANNEQUINS FOR BREAKFAST

The talk around the breakfast table in the Andrade household in São Paulo, Brazil was always lively and animated. The children of Vilemondes Garcia de Andrade Filho, the

Figure 16.1 The Expor Mannequin factory in São Paulo, Brazil. Photograph courtesy of Expor Mannequins.

founder of Expor Mannequins, would always listen intently to their father as they enjoyed their *Café da Manhã* which translates from Portuguese to "morning coffee." As Garcia's two young sons, Marcos and Guilherme voraciously attacked their *pão de queijo*, a small baked cheese-flavored roll and coffee, they excitedly asked questions and even offered their ideas.

"This happens a lot in young entrepreneurial families," said Marcos Andrade who went on to become the CEO of Expor Mannequins. "The business mixed with every aspect of family life, everyone is so involved with the business in one way or the other, wishing for things, hoping for things. To this day I tell people that growing up I had mannequins for breakfast."

Andrade explained his frustration at not being allowed to attend trade shows or client meetings when he was still a schoolboy. "I wanted to take orders, to get coffee, to entertain the customers, whatever I could do I wanted to do. Most of all, I wanted to try to sell." As soon as young Marcos was permitted to enter the shows with his father, he wanted to set up the mannequins and he wanted to talk to and interact with attendees of the show. "A lot of people said let's talk with this kid," recalled Andrade. "The breakfast table conversations and the first shows that I attended really illustrated the kind of involvement my brother and I had from an early age with the family business."

The Andrade breakfast table was the executive board room, conference room, and classroom. It was a point of connection and engagement with the business for Marcos and his younger brother Gui.

> We were totally connected with the business around the breakfast table. And if things were good, we had a good vacation, maybe we went to Disney World. And if we had a really good season Daddy would buy a new car. Everybody was so connected; it was really nice to be part of it. It was very exciting when we launched a new collection.

> There was so much chatter around the table every morning as we discussed whether the new mannequin or new concept will be one thing or the other. We would all discuss the latest idea and concept over bowls of steamed corn meal and cups of hot coffee. From the very early days, Gui and I started to learn what's important and why some things work, and some things don't work. It was like getting an MBA degree. We were so involved. It was an important part of our education. You learn by doing; seeing the result, seeing how things get started. You begin to understand that with some things you must take more time. You learn that there are things you need to plan for. It's nice when you're at the table and then there's an idea that you can become a part of. And you're involved with planning the execution, and seeing how it goes. And then there's another idea and you say oh yeah I remember that we did this, or we did that, and we should consider this or remember that.

The breakfast table lectures and discussions worked very well toward the development of two highly motivated young industry professionals, Marcos and Gui. Growing up in this environment, it was really difficult for the two brothers not to get involved as business plans were constantly being developed around the kitchen table. "It was amazing," said Andrade. "And then one year we had a really good season and Daddy bought a new car, and he gave me his old one. It was my first car, a Volkswagen, better than I ever could have imagined."

Even with their kitchen table education, there was little doubt that the two brothers would attend college. After high school, Marcos was off to study law at the University of São Paulo. The oldest university in the country, some liken it to the Harvard of Brazil. More Brazilian presidents have received their degrees from the University of São Paulo than any other college in the country.

After graduating, Marcos worked in a law office for a while with his uncle who was the president of the Bar Association of São Paulo. Soon after, he was drawn to the retail industry where he worked for many years in a small department store that sold everything from toys and stationery to apparel and electronics. They were a major resource for Paulistas shopping for toys and back-to-school items. A quick study and eager to learn and advance his career, Andrade soon became a buyer of electronics. And then he met the people from Hindsgaul Mannequins.

> I was still working in the department store when Hindsgaul sent a letter through the consulate looking for a partnership. My brother Gui was already working with my father at Expor. My father didn't speak English and Gui was too young with little experience so my father asked me if I would help with the business. I said yes and immediately got involved with the guys from Hindsgaul. Then in 1993, I went to work full-time for my father in the mannequin business. My years in the retail industry were a tremendous help to me as I began my career as a mannequin executive. It was extremely advantageous for me, knowing the needs of the retailer, being in their shoes, and knowing how they think. My time in retail proved to be extremely important as I took on a leadership role at Expor.

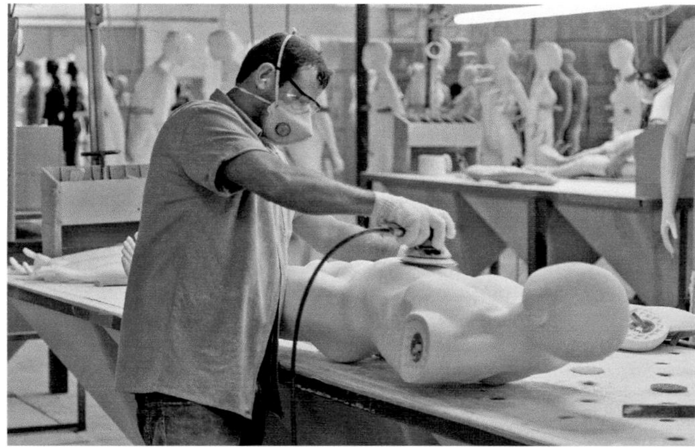

Figure 16.2 The Expor Mannequin factory in São Paulo, Brazil. Photograph courtesy of Expor Mannequins.

From the breakfast table while in grade school to the CEO of Latin America's largest mannequin supplier, Andrade witnessed the ongoing evolution of one of retail's most quintessential tools. Andrade recalled,

> When my father started Expor it was mostly realistic mannequins. People didn't like or didn't use abstract mannequins. It was amazing. Everybody wanted realistic back then in the '70s and '80s. Now visual merchandising has gained more prominence and importance. Visual merchandisers have assumed an influential role in the corporate structure as they now sit at the table in the executive boardroom."

It was a very natural evolution, one that Andrade had a front-row seat for.

> Today, people have a better understanding of the important function that the mannequin has assumed as an ambassador of the brand. Back when my father started the company people had more time to dedicate toward mannequins. Mannequins were something special in the '70s and '80s. In those days people took better care of the mannequins. The visual merchandisers were very protective of them, only they were permitted to handle them. They treated them in a special way. Maybe it was because they were so expensive or so fragile. Maybe they recognized that they were a bigger investment back then. And if there was any kind of a trend in mannequins it was very nice, but then everyone would have the same mannequin. You would see the same mannequin everywhere, it was amazing. It's very different today. Stores go to great lengths to ensure that the mannequins they select are in keeping with the brand image they want to project. They want mannequins that convey their values and their points of view. They want mannequins that are

> representative of who they are. They don't want the same mannequins as the store at the other end of the mall.

Andrade explained that just because Walmart is using a certain mannequin, it isn't necessarily right for you.

> If one retailer is successful and they use a particular mannequin, that does not mean that mannequin is for you. It doesn't mean you should use the same mannequin. You need to know the lifestyle and the values of your customer so the mannequin will reflect that. In all likelihood you're not appealing to the same demographic as Walmart, and your customers may have different needs.

Andrade believes that every retailer should use the tool that is most appropriate for them.

> The selection process is very exacting. You must select the vehicle that will provide the best return on your investment. You must choose the mannequin that will provide you with the fullest capacity to communicate and connect with your particular customer. It's like buying a Ferrari and living in the country, where you can't use the car properly. You really need a truck not a Ferrari. Analyze your market and determine what your ability is to deal with the tool. Do you need a truck, or do you need a Ferrari? Look carefully and analytically at the market to determine your needs.

While every culture has its own nuances and responses to changing technologies and changing times, Andrade recognizes that some trends are universal.

> Several years ago in Brazil and in many other places, there was a trend toward gold-colored mannequins. Every major retailer in Brazil was using hi-gloss golden mannequins. Before long, every retailer large and small, from São Paulo to Rio, wanted golden mannequins. Soon they were all clamoring for these gilded forms. After three months everyone had golden mannequins. It was like Christmas trees in all the windows. After a while, however, everyone began to respray their mannequins because they were tired of looking at the same mannequins in every store window.

One of the most important changes that Andrade witnessed and helped promote was customization.

> Years ago mannequins were much more static in their posses. They projected a stiff image. It took some time for mannequins to evolve into more dynamic and expressive forms that were more reflective of real people. It seems they went from

Figure 16.3 Graphic customization, Expor Mannequins. Photograph courtesy of Expor Mannequins.

> being statues to real representations of a lifestyle. It seems to me that mannequins are much more natural today.

As retail continues to evolve, there is a concerted effort to connect with the customer and to understand their needs, wants, and concerns. With retailers becoming more empathetic to the challenges facing everyday people, mannequins have also assumed a more compassionate pose. Andrade believes that mannequins can send supportive messages as though they were actors on the stage.

> It seems to me that the store is more empathetic to the customer than it used to be. Mannequins play an important role in creating a new level of empathy. Empathy is a very strong word. It creates a dialogue that leads to engagement. I believe mannequins are a key factor in establishing this engagement. This in large part is due to the materials that are now available to us. That and the technology that allows us to build mannequins that are much more natural. It's funny when I think back to the earlier mannequins that I remember when talking around the kitchen table. Those mannequins were like small dolls, like G.I. Joe. They were posing. Now mannequins are much more natural.

Mannequins are tools of communication. They interact with the customers who are looking for retailers that care about them. They also appeal to the customer's aspirations, their wants, and their needs. Andrade believes the smart retailer will use the mannequin as a point of engagement.

> Mannequins speak directly to the customer. They tell them what they want to hear, and the message can be very specific. If two people see the same mannequin in the

Figure 16.4 Multiple possibilities, Expor Mannequins. Photograph courtesy of Expor Mannequins.

> same window wearing a beautiful neatly pressed suit, the mannequin will say to one person that he will ace that job interview on Monday wearing this suit. You'll look professional, you'll look perfect. To the other person, it will say that you will look great on your date Friday night wearing that suit. The mannequin in the window is specific for your needs. The mannequin appeals to everyone differently based on their specific needs. That's why they work so well. They address your individual needs. The same mannequin will speak to people in different ways. This is amazing to me. I really love the ability of a mannequin to communicate on an individual basis to different people and its ultimate power as a tool for selling.

There are many participants in the business of designing and producing mannequins. As such, there are mannequins of varying degrees of quality and of course expense. The old adage is true, you get what you pay for. "The upper echelon of mannequin companies are quite complex," said Andrade.

> If a company is in the lower strata of manufacturers that just copy what is already out there, it's easy because the actual manufacturing process is an old process that uses fiberglass as the main substrate. It's easy to copy an existing form, create a mold, and pour the fiberglass. For example, suppose you have a mannequin that has a scratch. I come along and say I will paint it for you for $50. OK, you say and you give me the mannequin to repair. I get some resin and create a mold. Now I'm in business, I create a mannequin from the mold and then I sell it to another

retailer. This happens more often than you can imagine. This is a regular practice in mom-and-pop mannequin companies in many different countries.

For mannequin companies that design and produce original mannequins, the process is much more complex. Andrade explained,

> The old way of designing was an arduous and painstaking process of sculpture in clay. First, you would have to find a good professional, an artist, who could make a good prototype. This involves careful definition of the body and the face. It takes many years to develop a professional like this. When you find and develop a professional of the right caliber, the ensuing process takes a great deal of time. Usually, you would have a collection with 12 different positions and a few different heads. It could take up to a year for the sculptor to develop this collection. So before you even begin the process, you have to go to great lengths to determine what kind of collection you would want to invest your time and money in. If it's a female mannequin, who is she? What is her persona? What is she all about? Maybe she's an urban girl or maybe she has a romantic bent to her. Could she be a business leader or perhaps a free spirit? You ultimately have to decide if there is a market for this new collection. To whom would you sell it? If you have a good collection, that's great, Daddy will buy a new car. If the collection was not right then you wasted a full year.

While there are many designers, suppliers, and manufacturers in the mannequin business producing a great number of quality mannequins every year, the industry isn't a leading driver in the economies of the world's leading industrial nations. To succeed, it's the wise mannequin company that looks to other industries for the best practices, philosophies, and even technologies. Andrade advises,

> If you want to improve your manufacturing efficiency you have to take a look at the automotive industry or maybe the furniture industry that has a lot of customization and similarities to the mannequin business. It's important to reach out to other industries. An example that I believe is first and foremost, is "lean manufacturing." This is a process where you reduce staff that is non-useful for the production. So you establish stations where everything is around and conveniently located so you don't have to move and transport the product too far to another station. This movement doesn't add any value. You shorten the process by connecting stations. This involves strategic engineering of the logistics of the manufacturing process. This seems very obvious but still, a lot of companies don't do it. I believe this concept is something that Toyota started and then it spread around to other industries. You study the layout of your plant and then you re-organize, you make the layout suitable for your production system. It's a process, it's not a machine. It's a way of thinking that is very important. If there is some bottleneck you have to figure out what is hurting your production. Once discovered, the bottleneck must be eliminated.

There is a great deal of thinking and planning relative to the production process. Andrade explains,

> Once you have a well-defined and effective plan, you must work with your suppliers. A good example of this is when we moved from automotive paint to a special aeronautical industry paint. We made this move because we were sensitive to the needs and challenges of our customers. We understood that this aeronautical paint used for airplanes is nine times more resistant than the automotive paint we were using. So if a mannequin falls it won't scratch. And because of the volume that we were producing, we could use this paint without an increase in cost. This is something that we worked on with our suppliers.

Not only did Expor begin using a higher quality paint but they also redefined their approach to the colorways that they offered to their clients.

> We created a color lab. Instead of buying a color wheel where we ended up with many cans of yellow paint or red paint, we set up a very effective and efficient color lab where we would purchase the substrate or the main cans of white or neutral varnish and then just add the color. Then a customer would say, hey Marcos, I want Ferrari red or fire engine red or cherry red or their own customized red, and then we mix it and if you want one mannequin or a thousand, it doesn't matter because I can do it. The other way I would have to have thousands of cans of paint of many finished colors. Now I don't have that. I have the pigment and I can do any color you want. For us, it's clearly better and more efficient, and for the customer, it's better as well because we can quickly and nimbly respond to their needs, large or small. Now we don't have a lot of inventory that could stay there forever because nobody wants yellow for example.

One of Expor's global partners is Hindsgaul Mannequins. At the beginning of their business relationship, a Hindsgaul mannequin cost $700 to purchase in Europe. To import to Brazil was exorbitant due to the base price and the addition of import tax and freight. Because the mannequin costs were extremely high, most Brazilian retailers couldn't afford a Hindsgaul collection for their stores. The Denmark-based manufacturer suggested to Expor that they produce their mannequins in Brazil and just pay royalties for the design. In that way, they would make much more money because imported Hindsgauls just don't sell. "This made sense to us," recalled Andrade. "So we worked out the details with Hindsgaul and we started to do just that. As the program became successful, Hindsgaul said to us, 'Why don't you do this for all of South America?' So then we began selling to other countries such as Chile, Peru, and Colombia, among others."

While this program proved to be quite successful, Andrade quickly recognized some issues and challenges.

> The problem with mannequins is they're not simply a product to us. We see it as a relationship. We believe we are successful in the mannequin business because we have developed strong and lasting relationships with our customers. We want to understand their wants, needs, and challenges. We want to know how this mannequin will positively impact their business. Toward those ends, we want to help them choose the right mannequin to create sales.

Andrade believes the retailer is faced with a very complicated task. Yet in actuality, he claims that it's very simple,

> They want to create sales. At the end of the day, you want to sell merchandise. If you help me achieve this goal you are my friend. This is what we want to do. To achieve that it's complicated, although the final goal is very simple and measurable. It becomes more complicated because you must have the right mannequin. It must be well made, aesthetically pleasing, and do its job. For that, you cannot have a mannequin that is full of scars on its face, broken fingers, or a collage of masking tape holding the parts together. You would never want to put a mannequin on the selling floor or in your window if it looks like it just came from the war.

The mannequin maker realized the importance of continual service to the customer long after the sale is made.

> When we started thinking about exporting, we knew if we can't service the customer, soon he's going to have an army of broken mannequins. That will be a big problem because we can't serve him. He'll find a local guy who will repair the mannequins and this local guy will copy the mannequin from head to toe. We will sell this client just once and nevermore, or just when he needs new poses. So we went back to the drawing board to develop a way to fix this situation. The solution was a more resistant mannequin.

After an arduous period of research, design, and development, Andrade and his team came up with a new technology for durable plastic mannequins. "Our solution to the problem still wasn't right, it didn't represent the Expor brand. The plastic mannequins looked very cheap, and they looked ugly. They looked like plastic trays. This is not what we want to be." The Expor design team began working to find the perfect blend of materials to create a durable and beautiful mannequin.

> We had to work on the molds, which were very costly metal molds. Through trial and error, we found that the plastic reacted inconsistently in different conditions. If you had a head it would shrink. So different parts of the body would react differently. You could end up with an oversized backside and a tiny head. It looked ridiculous. We realized that we had to develop the technology. After many studied attempts we learned which parts would expand and which parts would contract. Finding the right plastic and using the right products was a painstaking process. It was finding the right

> recipe while always being aware of the art and science of mannequin design. So we put in a little bit of this and took away a little bit of that until we perfected the product.

This was a prime example of how technology proved to be a vital component of mannequin design as the industry moved forward. "We developed the well-made plastic mannequin so we could offer better value to our customer," recalled Andrade.

> If you want to invest in a good mannequin this is a mannequin that you should consider. We explained to our customers that their investment would be safe because this mannequin will not break. If you buy a mannequin in the traditional fiberglass composition, it might very well break on the first day because an employee may inadvertently drop it and then it is broken. And furthermore, if it has to be repaired it is even worse because it will be off the selling floor and you won't have the mannequin which is a super important selling tooling for your store. To repair the mannequin will take time and the logistics are extremely difficult.

This proved to be a great attraction for the Expor customer. It ensured they would have a guaranteed investment. Additionally, while the attraction was an unbreakable mannequin because it was made of plastic with some metal parts, it was also recyclable.

> At the time, sustainability wasn't that important to retailers. Their biggest concern was durability. They wanted a mannequin that did not break. Then there was an awakening. Sustainability became important. At Euroshop 2020 we showed the plastic mannequin at the Hindsgaul booth. We were delighted when the *Plex-T*

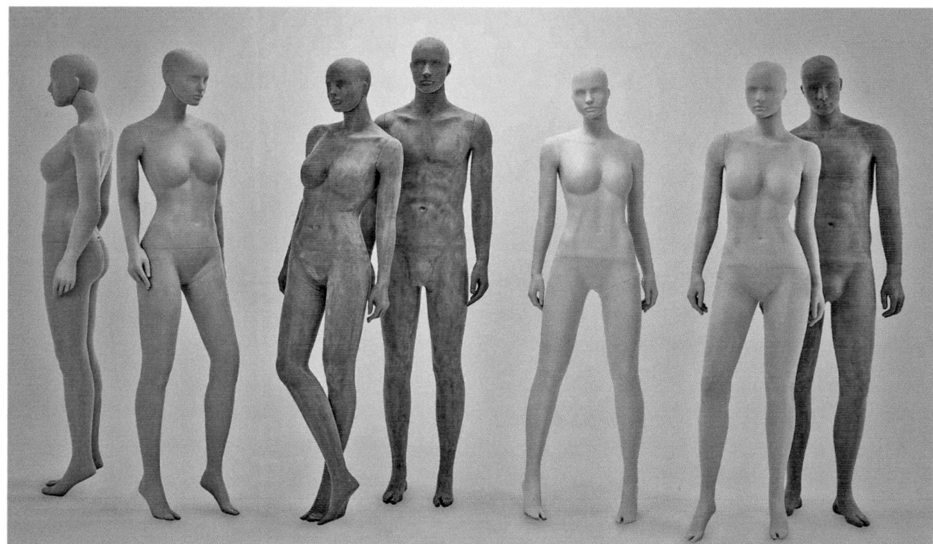

Figure 16.5 Mannequins manufactured with Expo's exclusive Plex-T resin. Photograph courtesy of Expor Mannequins.

> mannequin was selected as the most sustainable mannequin of all. Soon after, Lojas Renner, a major fashion retailer in the Brazilian market, once part of the JC Penney organization, launched the concept of the sustainable store. As covered in the newspapers this is a sustainable store from the mannequins that are recyclable to the furniture that uses only sustainably certified wood. So one feature that was a secondary became more important than its durability. The sustainable *Plex-T* mannequin was both practical and ethical. It connects with the customer on so many different levels. This is the power of technology.

Much of the movement, animation, and dynamics of mannequins developed in the early 21st century are the results of the technologies of the day. Expor was in front of the curve with the development and production of their *Plex-T* mannequin. Andrade notes that this technology even proceeded 3D printing. The first time Andrade worked with 3D mannequin printing was in 2008. His brother Gui had just returned to São Paulo from New York after a meeting with the visual merchandising team from Victoria's Secret. After showing the Expor line of mannequins, the design team told Gui they really liked what they saw but what they really prefer is to have mannequins in the likeness of the iconic Victoria's Secret angels. They asked Gui if Expor would be able to create the angel mannequins. Gui didn't hesitate with his answer. "If we do the angels, would we have the account?" They agreed. "Once we got the assignment, we started to talk to friends and colleagues," said the older Andrade brother.

> We knew this had great potential and the possibilities were endless. It was crazy. Then we met a guy who does scanning for cars. Since the industry was very slow in 2008, I was able to talk to him about mannequins. He was interested and eager to explore the possibilities. That was when we developed the first scanned collection of Expor Mannequins. We called this new line the *e-models*.

New technologies allowed Expor to better connect with and respond to the individual needs of customers from different countries and different cultures. Andrade recanted,

> I was showing a new collection of mannequins to a customer from Colombia. I was quite surprised at his response. He said they don't reflect the body of a Latin woman. They need more bust, more curves. They need to be more pronounced but a little bit smaller in stature. It was funny because the first time I went to Colombia for a show a guy looked at the mannequins and said, no no no, this mannequin needs more curves. She's so thin. No my friend, this mannequin is not Colombia. This was a feeling we already had from other countries. This included Brazil because as the market evolved we understood that the mannequin really needs to be connected to the public to create engagement and empathy. We needed to make the public see themselves in the mannequin. And to be absolutely honest, for the mannequin to do its job correctly, you don't see the mannequin. If you see the mannequin, something is wrong. The mannequin isn't to be seen, it's to be felt.

Like many of the other front-line mannequin designers, Andrade recognizes the importance of emotion.

> To create emotion and a connection you must understand how the customer wants to feel as they interact with others in a variety of circumstances. For example, how do they want to look on the weekend or how do they want to look in their office at the next company meeting? It's not about the mannequin, it's about you. When you don't see the mannequin, then it's doing its job. You see the story but not the mannequin. If you look at the mannequin and see that it has a broken finger, then the magic is gone because you're looking at a detail that has no importance at all. The mannequin should disappear. But the feeling and the story must emerge from the picture that you made. This is our main objective. 3D is great for that because it allows us to customize and offer greater variety that you could not achieve by hand.

Andrade not only spoke about the science of the mannequin but also about the art of the mannequin,

> Love is in the eye of the beholder. Maybe mannequins are just fancy clothes hangers for some and an art form for others. Although there is a definite science to it, I believe if you get emotionally involved, you see it as an art piece. While the impact mannequins have toward the ultimate goal of making a sale remains, I know how I feel when I see a beautiful store. I know someone really thought about it and executed

Figure 16.6 Sculpted heads providing a wide range of attitudes, Expor Mannequins. Photograph courtesy of Expor Mannequins.

> a beautiful plan that includes great visual merchandising. It doesn't only speak to my brain, but it also touches my heart. Connection is always about feelings. It must touch the heart of the customer. Then you will be building your brand. So you have to find the best ambassador for your brand to express the soul of your brand, and then connect. I always tell people that when you go to a fast food restaurant, and you drop your Coca-Cola on the floor you are embarrassed. Then it's a problem. And then some guy says hey don't worry my friend. I'll send another bottle of Coke for you. Go take your place, eat your meal. We're going to take care of this. This is your hero. You love this guy forever. Then you are a big fan of that restaurant. It's the really smart retailers who know that when we have a problem or a situation, this is a strong emotion, and if you deal with it with care and understanding you convert this to loyalty. This creates an emotion and then this will be remembered. Perhaps three days ago was not a very special day for you. If you're asked what you ate for lunch three days ago you say I don't know, I don't remember. But when you ask how was your first experience in this restaurant, you would remember because there were emotions connected to it. When you have the chance to create this connection in your store you can't miss the opportunity. This is what we try to do with the mannequins we make. To create these opportunities for our customers.

Andrade has seen many things during his long and rewarding career in the mannequin industry. One of his favorite stories goes back to his early days in the family business.

> I was really young, and we were a leader in the Brazilian mannequin industry. My father said that we needed some good public relations coverage that would reflect our position and point of view in the market. So for the first time, my father hired a public relations agency and a professional photographer to create a high-quality Expor Mannequin brochure. He was really keen to invest both money and time to get this just right. Because he was so intent on publishing an exciting and eye-catching marketing piece, he created a new series of lifestyle mannequins to be featured in the brochure. It was a line of mannequins that posed as real people with real style in real-life situations. We had a mannequin riding a horse, a mannequin in a sports car, and a mannequin on a yacht. It was really exciting. My father rented a yacht that launched from a beach near São Paulo. We set the mannequins up on the yacht as though they were enjoying a boat party on a beautiful sunny day. They were all wearing swimsuits, some with coverups and some holding a martini glass. From the shoreline, it appeared to be a group of very beautiful young women enjoying the day. The photographer rented a small boat and brought along a friend to assist him with the shoot. When the photographer was hired he was told to take pictures of the people partying on the boat.

The senior Andrade wanted it to look as life-like as possible. And it did, so much so that the photographer pulled his boat right alongside the yacht with the hope of asking the girls if they would join him for a ride on his nifty cigarette boat. "His friend was really excited about meeting these girls and having some fun," laughed Andrade as he retold the tale.

> When we arrived at the beach to watch the shoot we noticed that there was a bit of confusion. The photographer and his friend were really angry when they realized the beautiful women on the yacht were made of fiberglass. The photographer was so angry that he refused to take the pictures even though my father tried to convince him that it was all in fun. From time to time I run into that photographer, and he is still angry about that day on the beach near São Paulo.

As both retail and the world continue to turn and evolve, Andrade believes that while it is difficult to know the future role of mannequins, there will always be mannequins in the fashion store.

> I don't know what materials will be used, and maybe there will be a combination of different technologies. But I'm confident they will absolutely be needed and will continue to have an important role in creating engagement with the customer. The retailer must care more about the physical store than ever before. Store formats may change, perhaps they will be smaller and fewer, but they will continue to be an integral part of the brand. I think it must be understood that the store is not needed for the transaction, but it is fundamental to the customer-retailer relationship. When people go to a store they want to be in an environment that is very close to them, that talks to them. They want to be in an environment that makes them feel comfortable, that they really want to be in. They want to like the brand and to like the people that work in the store. They want to like the way they are treated; they want to like the colors and textures of the store and they want to like the feeling that they have. They even want to like the smell of the place. They want to like all of the points of contact that you have with them, and of course, this includes the mannequins. The more positive points of contact that the retailer has with the customer, the greater the connection they will have with the customer. There is a word that we hear a lot of today. The word is omni-channel. I don't particularly like that word. I much prefer omnipresence.

EPILOGUE

Mannequins are a true anthropological study. They're a reflection of who we are and a documentation of societal change and evolution. Over the course of the last hundred years, retail has been a theatrical backdrop for the latest fashions, cultural movements, and advancing technologies. As the curtains have been raised in the halls, windows, and aisles of stores across the retail spectrum, the mannequin has been the actor at center stage.

As the showplace for new concepts, new ideas, and the latest fashions, retail is the litmus for a changing market and a changing world. If we hold a mirror to the face of commercialism, the reflected image would be the visage of society. Mannequins, like any other art form, be it paint on canvas, or pen on parchment, move emotions while documenting the spirit of the day. Great art, architecture, and literature all blend and co-exist. All are reflective of their times and all have made an impact on retail design and the development of the mannequin. Historian Pierre Daix said, "The history of art is not just in sculpture. There is a whole cultural history behind it. You can't understand Cézanne without Stendhal, Manet without Baudelaire. In the period of modern art, the writers, painters, and the political revolution all came together."[1] Mannequin design and development stands firmly at the confluence of art, architecture, music, and technology. One art form influences another. The French neoclassical painter, Jean Auguste Dominique Ingres (August 29, 1780 – January 14, 1867) said to his painting students, "If I could make a musician out of you, you would profit as painters." Mannequin designers have profited greatly from their love and study of the great writers, painters, musicians, and even dancers of the past and present. Mannequins are truly an art form, responding to, reporting on, and participating in great cultural movements including art, architecture, literature, design, and technology. It would be difficult to understand the last 125 years of mannequin design without understanding a century of cultural, economic, and technological development. Today, we are crossing the threshold of a global community, facing great political change, fascinating new technologies, and difficult economic challenges. Moving forward, we look to the past with an eye on the future. We recall a period when varying forms of cultural expression "came together." Over the course of time, we have gone from the narrow cobblestone streets of the inner city to interstate super highways, and from intercontinental telegraph wires to internet connections across the far reaches of cyberspace. Analogously, mannequins have gone from wire, wax, and wood, to plaster, fiberglass, plastic, and beyond. While the 20th century brought us from the Model T Ford to the Chevrolet Corvette and the Ferrari Testarossa, it also brought us from wire and wood dress forms to mannequins being dressed and styled at the click of a mouse. A hundred years of advancing technology has equipped retailers with digital, virtual, and robotic mannequins that will support the industry until the next game-changing innovation is developed. However, it should be noted that the heart, soul, and artistic expression of the tactile, three-dimensional mannequin is irreplaceable.

Figure E.1 They captivate young and old alike. Photograph by Mikhael Anderson.

Reference

1. *Art News* (October 1996).

INDEX